Conversational Spanish Grammar for the Hospitality Classroom

Matt A. Casado

BICENTENNIAL

1807

WILEY

2007

BICENTENNIAL

JOHN WILEY & SONS, INC.

This book is printed on acid-free paper. ∞

Copyright © 2007 by John Wiley & Sons, Inc. All rights reserved

Published by John Wiley & Sons, Inc., Hoboken, New Jersey
Published simultaneously in Canada

For general information on our other products and services or for technical support, please
contact our Customer Care Department within the United States at (800) 762-2974, outside the
United States at (317) 572-3993 or fax (317) 572-4002.

Wiley also publishes its books in a variety of electronic formats. Some content that appears in
print may not be available in electronic books. For more information about Wiley products,
visit our web site at www.wiley.com.

Library of Congress Cataloging-in-Publication Data:
Casado, Matt A., 1937–
  Conversational Spanish grammar for the hospitality classroom / Matt Casado.
    p.   cm.
  Includes index.
  ISBN 13: 978-0-471-73009-5 (pbk.)
  ISBN 10: 0-471-73009-2 (pbk.)
  1. Spanish language—Conversation and phrase books (for restaurant and hotel personnel)
  I. Title.
  PC4120.R4C38   2006
  468.3'42102464795—dc22   2005036440

10 9 8 7 6 5 4 3 2 1

TO MARY PISTOLESI, A TEACHER

CONTENTS

PART TWO

KITCHEN OPERATIONS 51

CHAPTER 5

ADJECTIVES—COLORS 53

CHAPTER 6

STEM-CHANGING VERBS: "HAY QUE," "TENER QUE," "ANTES DE," "DESPUÉS DE" PLUS AN INFINITIVE 71

CHAPTER 7

COMMANDS—THE CALENDAR AND DATES 82

PART THREE

HOUSEKEEPING OPERATIONS 95

CHAPTER 8

REFLEXIVE VERBS—"HACE" WITH TIME AND WEATHER EXPRESSIONS—THE WEATHER 97

PART FIVE

HUMAN RESOURCES
(PERSONNEL DEPARTMENT) 183

CHAPTER 14

THE FUTURE TENSE—THE PRESENT SUBJUNCTIVE—
ADVERBS OF PLACE 185

CHAPTER 15

THE CONDITIONAL TENSE—THE IMPERFECT SUBJUNCTIVE TENSE—
ADVERBS OF INTENSITY 202

CHAPTER 16

GRAMMATICAL EXPRESSIONS—NONPROFESSIONAL VOCABULARY—
EXPRESSIONS OF EMOTION 212

GLOSSARY 223

INDEX 241

PREFACE

Most companies regard foreign language learning as a tool to remain competitive in an increasingly global environment. At the same time, new immigration patterns and birth trends in the United States are changing the composition of American society, particularly in large urban centers where the population of Hispanics is growing rapidly.

Many immigrant new arrivals initially join the hospitality industry in entry-level positions. The inability of these workers to speak and understand English creates a communication barrier between them and management that in some cases may hamper daily operations severely. Often, managers who don't speak their employees' language must rely on the effectiveness of bilingual supervisors or on outside interpreters to make themselves understood. This, in most cases, interferes with normal communication, breaking the chain of command between management and back-of-the-house workers. The need for better communication with line employees is so acute that when recruiting for entry-level management positions, hospitality companies prefer graduates who have at least a basic knowledge of a foreign language. Hospitality enterprises that hire employees who know Spanish will be more likely to meet the needs of their non-English-speaking workers and guests. For these reasons, hospitality academic programs are beginning to offer conversational language classes to prepare their students to work with non-English speakers.

The purpose of this book is to provide instructors and students of Hospitality Spanish with a textbook aimed at teaching conversational Spanish at the beginner and intermediate levels. It offers grammar concepts necessary for learning the fundamentals of the language, specialized vocabulary that applies to hospitality operations, and a large array of in-class exercises focused on improving student conversational skills. The book can be used in first- and/or second-semester hospitality college Spanish classes, by industry professionals, as well as in culinary and vocational programs. The pronunciation of words has been included to help students who are endeavoring to study conversational Spanish by themselves.

About the Author

Matt A. Casado, Ed.D., CHA, is professor in the School of Hotel and Restaurant Management at Northern Arizona University. He holds a bachelor of arts degree in Spanish, a master's degree in education, and a doctorate degree in educational leadership. A veteran of the hospitality industry, he trained in Switzerland and England before managing operations in Spain and the United States. A native Spanish speaker, he has taught conversational Hospitality Spanish at college level for seventeen years and has authored several articles on Hospitality Spanish in reference journals. He is the author of the book *Conversational Spanish for Hospitality Managers and Supervisors* published by John Wiley & Sons. Dr. Casado received a Fulbright senior specialists award as a visiting scholar to Burma (Myanmar) in 2005.

To the Instructor

The primary purpose of this book is to provide hospitality students with beginner and intermediate-Spanish skills that can be applied to their daily supervisory operations. The second intention is to provide college students with a basic framework of the Spanish language equivalent to one or two semester credits of the academic foreign language requirement. The content of each unit has been designed to cover around three and one-half hours of class time per week.

The book's grammar component is presented following a sequential inclusion of the nine form-classes, or parts of speech, that constitute the foundation of the Spanish language. The book also offers specialized vocabulary and pronunciation for five major hospitality operational departments—restaurant, kitchen, housekeeping, engineering, and human resources. Instructors should approach teaching the course from a conversational perspective by engaging students in intensive in-class oral interaction. At the same time, they should ensure that students obtain the corresponding fundamental knowledge of Spanish grammar. Samples of conversational interactions between a supervisor and an hourly employee are also presented. A large selection of in-class oral exercises has been incorporated in the text.

Because of the usually formal boss–worker relationship, the informal person **tú** (in singular and plural forms) has been omitted. Instead, the formal **usted/ustedes** forms are presented. Intended to be a beginner/intermediate-level textbook, compound tenses of the indicative, conditional, and subjunctive forms are not covered, except for the present perfect tense. Students wishing to learn how to conjugate and use compound tenses should enroll, following this course, in an advanced-Spanish class.

Finally, an *Instructor's Manual* (ISBN: 0-471-78195-9) is available to professors who have adopted the book. Instructors will be able to access it on a companion Website (www.wiley.com/college) with a password. The Instructor's Manual includes teaching notes for every unit, answers to in-class exercises, test questions and a sample course syllabus. In addition, the manual offers five sample guidelines for role-playing presentations and a sample guideline for interviewing a Spanish native speaker. Vocabulary words are provided with their masculine or feminine articles and with a key indicating if they are verb infinitives (*v.*) or adjectives (*adj.*). Articles, adverbs, conjunctions, pronouns, prepositions, and interjections are presented in separate sections.

To the Students

Tuition bills finally stop coming. Books have closed. There is no test left to take, no paper left to write. Cap and gown are thrown aside. The future is here. It's time to go to work. Who will get the most and best job offers in hospitality? Chances are the students who know some Spanish. In this age of frequent flying, many Spanish-speaking guests stay in American hotels and can be better accommodated by employees who speak their language. Even more important, many immigrants, with little knowledge of English, arriving from Latin America join the hospitality industry in entry-level positions. Managers who have no working knowledge of Spanish are at a great disadvantage in trying to communicate with their housekeeping, food and beverage, and maintenance personnel. American hotel and restaurant companies seek out graduates who know basic Spanish, and hospitality schools across the country have begun to provide courses in Hospitality Spanish.

This book is written for those classrooms. It offers vocabulary specialized for hospitality operations along with intermediate-grammar concepts necessary to understand the fundamentals of the language. A large selection of in-class exercises is also provided to improve your conversational skills.

PART ONE

RESTAURANT OPERATIONS

CHAPTER 1

PRELIMINARY LESSON

 OVERVIEW

Chapter 1 begins with Spanish pronunciation and provides basic, common conversational expressions. Subject pronouns and the present tense of **ser, estar,** and **tener** are introduced to build simple conversational and written sentences.

 UNIT CONTENT

The Sounds in Spanish • Stress in Spanish Words • Common Expressions
• Subject Pronouns • Present Tense of **ser, estar,** and **tener** •
Conversational Professional Interaction

The Sounds in Spanish

It takes months, if not years, for a nonnative speaker to pronounce a foreign language correctly. Usually, people who have not learned a second language while young never speak it without an accent. However, it is relatively easy to make oneself understood in Spanish because the language does not have as many sound inflections as English. On the other hand, consider the English words *no, not, now*—a student who begins to study English must learn to pronounce these words one at a time because there are few pronunciation rules. This is not the case in Spanish. For example, the letter **a,** pronounced by opening the mouth as with *father* in English, has, for all purposes, no other pronunciation in different words. Basically, the only sounds in Spanish that do not exist in English are those corresponding to the letters **g** (after e, i), **j, ñ, r,** and **rr.**

All letters in Spanish are always pronounced, except for **h, u** after **q,** and **u** in **gue, gui.** Because no other letters are silent, you would not see a Spanish word written with two t's or two d's, such as *letter* and *ladder* in English.

The Alphabet Sounds in Spanish

a	(ah)	like **a** in *father*	casa (*house*)
b	(beh)	like **b** in *boy*	bar (*bar*)
c	(seh)	like **c** in *car* before a, o, u	copa (*cup*)
		like **s** in *cent* before e, i	cena (*dinner*)

ch	(cheh)	like **ch** in *child*	chocolate (*chocolate*)
d	(deh)	like **d** in *done*	dedo (*finger*)
e	(eh)	like **e** in *bet*	enero (*January*)
f	(eh-feh)	like **f** in *far*	favor (*favor*)
g	(heh)	like **g** in *gate* before a, o, u	gustar (*to like*)
		like an exaggerated **h** in *ham* before e, i	ginebra (*gin*)
		When followed by **ue** or **ui**, the **u** is silent and the **g** sounds like the **g** in *gate*	guinda (*cherry*)
h	(ah-cheh)	always silent, unless preceded by **c**	hotel (*hotel*)
i	(ee)	like **ee** in *feet*	vino (*wine*)
j	(hoh-tah)	like an exaggerated **h** in *ham*	jamón (*ham*)
k	(kah)	like **k** in *kilogram*	kilo (*kilogram*)
l	(eh-leh)	like **l** in *let*	litro (*liter*)
ll	(eh-yeh)	like **y** in *yet*	llave (*key*)
m	(eh-meh)	like **m** in *man*	mano (*hand*)
n	(eh-neh)	like **n** in *no*	nabo (*turnip*)
ñ	(eh-nyeh)	like strong **ny** in *canyon*	piña (*pineapple*)
o	(oh)	like **o** in *organ*	ocho (*eight*)
p	(peh)	like **p** in *put*	pan (*bread*)
q	(koo)	like **k** in *kilogram*	queso (*cheese*)
r	(eh-reh)	like a trilled **r** in *rat* in the middle of a word	pero (*but*)
		like a strongly trilled **r** at the beginning of a word	roto (*broken*)
rr	(eh-rreh)	like a strongly trilled **r** in *rat*	carro (*car*)
s	(eh-seh)	like **s** in *see*	seta (*mushroom*)
t	(teh)	like **t** in *top*	tenedor (*fork*)
u	(oo)	like **oo** in *boot*	jugo (*juice*)
v	(oo-beh)	like **b** in *boy*	vino (*wine*)
x	(eh-kees)	like **s** in *sit* before a consonant	expreso (*express*)
		like **x** in *examine* before a vowel	exacto (*exact*)
y	(yeh)	like **ee** in *feet* when alone or at the end of a word	y (*and*)
		like a strong **y** in *yet* as a consonant	yema (*yolk*)
z	(seh-tah)	like **s** in *see*	zumo (*juice*)

Oral Practice

Repeat each word as you hear it from your instructor:

banquete (*banquet*)   ginebra (*gin*)   manguera (*hose*)   pera (*pear*)

sal (*salt*)   cena (*dinner*)   hotel (*hotel*)   nabo (*turnip*)   queso (*cheese*)

tabla (*board*)   dar (*to give*)   jamón (*ham*)   uña (*fingernail*)   rápido (*fast*) usted (*you*)   favor (*favor*)   kilo (*kilogram*)   vino (*wine*)   yo (*I*)

zumo (*juice*)   llama (*flame*)   goma (*rubber*)   zapato (*shoe*)

gelatina (*gelatine*)   Jorge (*George*)

EXERCISE 1.1

Find the pronunciation of the following words by referring to the alphabet sound list and be ready to speak them aloud at your instructor's request:

bebidas	taza	tenedor	secar	uñas
cerveza	loza	cafetera	silla	pan
carro	plato	cuenta	chicle	jarrita

Stress In Spanish Words

Words with an accent mark (é, for example) always receive the stress on the syllable that carries the accent mark: **café** (cah-féh).

Words without accent marks are governed by the following two rules:

1. In words that end in a vowel, **n** or **s,** the stress falls on the next to the last syllable: **mesero** (meh-séh-roh), **lavan** (láh-vahn), **carros**(cáh-rrohs).

2. In words that end in consonants (except **n** or **s**), the stress falls on the last syllable: **hotel** (oh-téhl), **usted** (oos-téhd), **secar** (seh-cáhr).

EXERCISE 1.2

Pronounce the following words stressing the correct syllable:

copa	cristalería	trapear	jalea
menú	canapé	número	servilleta
pimiento	plaqué	turno	almacén

Common Expressions

All languages have a number of expressions that are used often in everyday life. Anyone attempting to speak and understand Spanish needs to be familiar with simple expressions, ranging from greetings and introductions to farewells. The following is a list of idiomatic expressions classified into different categories.

Greetings

Bienvenido. (bee-ehn-beh-née-doh)	*Welcome.*
Buenos días. (boo-éh-nohs dée-ahs)	*Good morning.*
Buenas tardes. (boo-éh-nahs táhr-dehs) (*until sunset*)	*Good afternoon.*
Buenas noches. (boo-éh-nahs nóh-chehs) (*after sunset*)	*Good evening.*
¡Hóla! (óh-lah!) (*informal greeting*)	*Hi!*
¿Qué tal? (keh tahl?) (*informal greeting*)	*How is it going?*
¿Qué pasa? (keh páh-sah?) (*informal greeting*)	*What is going on?*

EXERCISE 1.3

Greet another student in Spanish using these phrases and wait for his or her response:

1. ¡Buenas noches!   2. ¡Hóla!   3. ¡Buenas tardes!   4. ¿Qué tal?
5. ¡Bienvenido!

EXERCISE 1.4

Translate the following greeting phrases and be ready to pronounce them in Spanish:

1. *Good morning!*   2. *How is it going?*   3. *Welcome!*
4. *Good afternoon! (3 P.M.)*   5. *Hi!*   6. *Good evening! (11 P.M.)*

EXERCISE 1.5

With a partner, respond to the following greetings in Spanish:

1. ¡Hóla, buenos días!   2. ¡Buenas tardes!   3. ¡Hóla!   4. ¡Buenas noches!
5. ¿Qué tal?

Introductions

Me llamo . . . (meh yáh-moh . . .)	*My name is . . .*
¿Cómo se llama usted? (cóh-moh seh yáh-mah oos-téhd?)	*What is your name?*
Me alegro de conocerle(a). (meh ah-léh-groh deh coh-noh-séhr-leh(ah))	*I am glad to know you.*

Me alegro de verle(a). (meh ah-léh-groh deh béhr-leh(ah)	*I am glad to see you.*
Tanto gusto. (táhn-toh góos-toh)	*Glad to meet you.*
Mucho gusto. (móo-choh góos-toh)	*Nice to meet you.*
Igualmente. (ee-goo-ahl-méhn-teh)	*Same to you.*
Encantado(a). (ehn-cahn-táh-doh(ah)	*Pleased to meet you.*
¿Cómo está usted? (cóh-moh ehs-tá oos-téhd?)	*How are you?*
Bien, gracias, ¿y usted? (bee-éhn gráh-see-ahs ee oos-téhd?)	*Very well, thank you, and you?*
Bien, gracias. (bee-éhn gráh-see-ahs)	*Very well, thank you.*

EXERCISE 1.6

Introduce yourself to another student in Spanish using the following phrases and wait for his or her response:

1. Me alegro de verle. 2. El gusto es mío. 3. Igualmente. 4. Hóla, me llamo Carlos. 5. Encantado. 6. El gusto es mío.

EXERCISE 1.7

Translate the following phrases and be ready to pronounce them in Spanish:

1. *Hi, what is your name?* 2. *My name is Carlos.* 3. *Glad to know you.* 4. *How are you?* 5. *Very well, thank you, and you?* 6. *Very well, thank you.*

EXERCISE 1.8

With a partner, respond to the following introductions addressed to you:

1. Me alegro de verle(a). 2. ¿Cómo está usted? 3. Mucho gusto. 4. Me alegro de conocerle(a). 5. Tanto gusto. 6. ¿Cómo se llama usted? 7. Me llamo Carlos, ¿y usted? 8. Soy Lupita. 9. Encantado. 10. El gusto es mío.

Communication and Courtesy

¿Sabe usted inglés? (sáh-beh oos-téhd een-gléhs)	*Do you know English?*

Sí, sé inglés. (see, seh een-gléhs)	*Yes, I know English.*
No sé inglés. (noh seh een-gléhs)	*I don't know English.*
¿Sabe usted español? (sáh-beh oos-téhd ehs-pah-nyóhl)	*Do you know Spanish?*
Hablo español un poco. (áh-bloh ehs-pah-nyóhl oon póh-coh)	*I speak Spanish a little.*
¿Habla usted inglés? (áh-blah oos-tehd een-gléhs?)	*Do you speak English?*
Sí, hablo inglés. (see áh-bloh een-gléhs)	*Yes, I speak English.*
¡Gracias! (gráh-see-ahs)	*Thank you!*
De nada. (deh náh-dah)	*You're welcome.*
Por nada. (pohr náh-dah)	*You're welcome.*
Por favor. (pohr fah-bóhr)	*Please.*
¿Comprende? (cohm-préhn-deh?)	*Do you understand?*
No comprendo. (noh cohm-préhn-doh)	*I don't understand.*
No comprendo bien el español (noh cohm-préhn-doh bee-éhn ehl ehs-pah-nyóhl)	*I don't understand Spanish well.*
¿Cómo se dice . . . en español? (cóh-moh seh dée-seh . . . ehn ehs-pah-nyóhl?)	*How do you say . . . in Spanish?*
Se dice . . . . (seh dée-seh . . .)	*You say . . .*
Repita, por favor. (reh-pée-tah, pohr fah-bóhr)	*Repeat, please.*
Hable más despacio. (áh-bleh mahs dehs-páh-see-oh)	*Speak more slowly.*
Hable más alto. (áh-bleh mahs áhl-toh)	*Speak louder.*
No entiendo lo que dice. (noh ehn-tee-éhn-doh loh keh dée-seh)	*I don't understand what you are saying.*
¡Con permiso! (kohn pehr-mée-soh)	*Excuse me!*
¡Perdón! (pehr-dóhn)	*Pardon me!*
Lo siento. (loh see-éhn-toh)	*I am sorry.*

EXERCISE 1.9

In pairs, ask and answer the following phrases:

Estudiante uno:	¿Cómo se dice "por favor" en inglés?
Estudiante dos:	Se dice *please.*
Estudiante uno:	¿Sabe usted español?
Estudiante dos:	Sé español un poco.
Estudiante uno:	¿Habla usted inglés?
Estudiante dos:	Sí, hablo inglés.
Estudiante uno:	¿Comprende usted inglés?
Estudiante dos:	No comprendo inglés, hablo español.

Estudiante uno:　　　¿Entiende usted?
Estudiante dos:　　　No entiendo lo que dice.

EXERCISE 1.10

Translate the following sentences and pronounce them in Spanish:

1. *Speak louder, please.* _____
2. *I don't know Spanish well.* _____
3. *I speak Spanish a little.* _____
4. *Speak more slowly.* _____
5. *Excuse me.* _____
6. *Yes, I speak English.* _____
7. *I don't understand!* _____
8. *How do you say "morning" in Spanish?* _____
9. *You say* mañana. _____
10. *Thank you!* _____

EXERCISE 1.11

With a partner, find the answers to the following questions and respond when you are asked:

1. ¿Cómo se dice *ashtray* en español?
2. ¿Cómo se dice cubeta en inglés?
3. ¿Habla usted inglés?
4. ¿Sabe usted español?
5. ¿Comprende usted?
6. ¿Habla usted español?
7. ¿Sabe usted inglés?
8. ¿Cómo se dice *pardon me* en español?
9. ¿Cómo se dice "con permiso" en inglés?
10. ¿Comprende español?

Farewells

Hasta luego. (áhs-tah loo-éh-goh)	*See you later.*
Adiós. (ah-dee-óhs)	*Good-bye.*
Hasta mañana. (áhs-tah mah-nyáh-nah)	*See you tomorrow.*
Hasta el lunes. (áhs-tah ehl lóo-nehs)	*See you Monday.*
Hasta la vista. (áhs-tah lah vées-tah)	*See you again.*
Que lo pase bien. (keh loh páh-seh bee-éhn)	*Have a good time.*

Que tenga un buen día. (keh téhn-gah oon
   boo-éhn dée-ah)   *Have a good day.*
Nos vemos. (nohs véh-mohs) (*informal*)   *See you.*

EXERCISE 1.12

Say farewell to another student in Spanish using these phrases and wait for
his or her response:

1. Que tenga un buen día.   2. Hasta el lunes.   3. Adiós.   4. Hasta luego.
5. Que lo pase bien.

EXERCISE 1.13

Say farewell to another student in Spanish using these phrases and wait for
his/her response:

1. *See you Monday.*   2. *Have a good day.*   3. *Good-bye.*   4. *See you later.*
5. *Have a good time.*

EXERCISE 1.14

Answer the following phrases in Spanish:

1. ¡Hasta mañana!   2. ¡Adiós!   3. ¡Nos vemos!   4. ¡Hasta la vista!
5. ¡Hasta el lunes!

Subject Pronouns

(The subject pronoun **tú** is used for friends, family, and children. Here we will be
using only the more formal **usted** because of the required formal boss–worker,
manager-guest relationship.)

Subject pronouns are not always required in Spanish since the verb ending often
indicates the subject. The subject *it,* for all practical purposes, is not used in Spanish. The pronouns **usted, ustedes** are often abbreviated **Ud., Uds.** or **Vd., Vds.**
Nosotros and **ellos** are used to refer to a mixed group.

I	yo (yoh)
he	él (ehl)
she	ella (éh-yah)
you (sing.)	usted (oos-téhd)
we (m.)	nosotros (noh-sóh-trohs)

we (f.)	nosotras (noh-sóh-trahs)
they (m.)	ellos (éh-yohs)
they (f.)	ellas (éh-yahs)
you (pl.)	ustedes (oos-téh-dehs)

EXERCISE 1.15

Pronounce slowly and carefully the following subject pronouns:

1. nosotros   2. ustedes   3. él   4. ellas   5. ella

EXERCISE 1.16

Translate the following pronouns and be ready to pronounce them in Spanish:

1. *He* _____
2. *You (one subject)* _____
3. *You (two or more subjects)* _____
4. *She* _____
5. *We (mixed group, males and females)* _____
6. *They (all females)* _____
7. *We (all females)* _____
8. *I* _____
9. *He* _____
10. *We (all males)* _____

EXERCISE 1.17

Assign Spanish object pronouns to the following subjects:

1. *Jorge*   2. *Lupita*   3. *Jorge and Lupita*   4. *Lupita and Juanita*
5. *Lupita and I (I is a male)*   6. *Lupita and I (both female)*   7. *Lupita, Juanita, and Jorge*   8. *Lupita, Juanita, and Dolores*   9. *Lupita, Miguel, and I*   10. *Miguel, Juan, and I (I is a male)*

Present Tense of **ser, estar,** and **tener**

Although these verbs are irregular, students should be acquainted with them cause they are used often in Spanish conversation. The verbs **ser** and **estar** pre a problem to English-speaking students because both are translated *to be*. The of these verbs (when to use one or the other) will be discussed in a later ch

	ser (sehr)	**estar** (ehs-táhr)	**tener** (teh-néhr)
yo	soy (sóh-ee)	estoy (ehs-tóh-ee)	tengo (téhn-goh)
él, ella, usted	es (ehs)	está (ehs-táh)	tiene (tee-éh-neh)
nosotros, nosotras	somos	estamos	tenemos
	(sóh-mohs)	(ehs-táh-mohs)	(teh-néh-mohs)
ellos, ellas, ustedes	son (sohn)	están (ehs-táhn)	tienen (tee-éh-ehn)

EXERCISE 1.18

Pronounce the following statements in Spanish:

1. él tiene   2. nosotros somos   3. ellas están   4. nosotras tenemos
5. yo soy   6. yo estoy   7. ustedes tienen   8. ella es   9. usted está
10. yo tengo

EXERCISE 1.19

Translate the following phrases using both pronouns and verb forms and be ready to pronounce them in Spanish:

1. *They have (two options)* _____

2. *He is (two options)* _____

3. *I am (two options)* _____

4. *You are (four options)* _____

5. *She has* _____

6. *We are (four options)* _____

7. *I have* _____

8. *She is (two options)* _____

9. *He has* _____

10. *They are (four options)* _____

EXERCISE 1.20

In pairs, translate the following phrases into English including the corresponding subject pronouns:

1. soy   2. tienen (*three options*)   3. está (*three options*)   4. somos (*two options*)   5. tengo   6. están (*three options*)   7. tiene (*three options*)
8. tenemos (*two options*)   9. Jorge tiene   10. Lupita *and* Dolores tienen

Conversational Professional Interaction

In groups of two, translate, practice, and be ready to role-play the following dialogue between a restaurant supervisor and an hourly employee:

Estudiante uno (supervisor):   ¡Buenos días! Me alegro de conocerle(a).

Estudiante dos (hourly worker):   ¡Buenos días! Igualmente.

Estudiante uno: ¿Quién es usted?

Estudiante dos: Soy Lupita. ¿Y usted?

Estudiante uno: Soy el supervisor.

Estudiante uno: ¿Cómo está usted?

Estudiante dos: Bien, ¿y usted?

Estudiante uno: Bien, gracias.

Estudiante dos: ¿Habla usted español?

Estudiante uno: Hablo español un poco.

Estudiante dos: ¿Comprende usted inglés?

Estudiante uno: Sí, comprendo inglés.

Estudiante dos: ¿Cómo se dice "de nada" en inglés?

Estudiante uno: Se dice "you are welcome."

Estudiante dos: ¿Cómo se llama?

Estudiante uno: Me llamo Carlos.

Estudiante dos: Encantado(a).

Estudiante uno: El gusto es mío.

📋 QUESTIONS TO THE CLASS 📋

Answer the following questions asked by your instructor (or by another student) without looking at your textbook or any class notes:

1. ¿Qué tal?
2. ¿Cómo se llama usted?
3. ¿Cómo está usted?
4. ¿Sabe usted inglés?
5. ¿Sabe usted español?
6. ¿Habla usted inglés?
7. ¿Habla usted español?
8. ¿Comprende?
9. ¿Cómo se dice "qué tal" en inglés?
10. ¿Cómo se dice "you're welcome" en español?

CHAPTER 2

THE PRESENT INDICATIVE TENSE OF REGULAR VERBS

QUESTIONS

NEGATIONS

 **OVERVIEW**

This chapter presents our first list of technical restaurant vocabulary and introduces the present tense of regular verbs. Students will also learn how to form questions and negations in Spanish.

 **UNIT CONTENT**

Technical Restaurant Vocabulary (I) • The Present Tense of Regular Verbs • How to Make Questions in Spanish • Most Common Interrogative Words in Spanish • Negations • Conversational Professional Interaction • Cultural Vignette

Technical Restaurant Vocabulary (I)

a la carte	a la carta (*adj.*) (ah lah cáhr-tah)
appetizer	el aperitivo (ah-peh-ree-tée-voh)
ashtray	el cenicero (seh-nee-séh-roh)
au jus	en su jugo (*adj.*) (ehn soo hóo-goh)
au lait	con leche (*adj.*) (cohn léh-cheh)
banquet	el banquete (bahn-kéh-teh)
bar	el bar (bahr)

base plate	el plato base (pláh-toh báh-seh)
beer	la cerveza (sehr-véh-sah)
beverages	las bebidas (beh-bée-dahs)
bill	la cuenta (coo-énh-tah)
bowl	el tazón (tah-sóhn)
bow tie	la palomita (pah-loh-mée-tah)
bread	el pan (pahn)
bread basket	la cesta para pan (séhs-tah páh-rah pahn)
bread plate	el plato para pan (pláh-toh páh-rah pahn)
bread warmer	el calentador de pan (cah-lehn-tah-dóhr deh pahn)
buffet	el buffet (boo-féh)
bus tub	la cubeta (coo-béh-tah)
bus person	el/la ayudante de mesero (ah-yoo-dáhn-teh deh meh-séh-roh)
butter	la mantequilla (mahn-teh-kée-yah)
butter knife	el cuchillo para mantequilla (coo-chée-yoh páh-rah mahn-teh-kée-yah)
canape	el canapé (cah-nah-péh)
cashier	el cajero (cah-héh-roh)
	la cajera (cah-héh-rah)
chair	la silla (sée-yah)
cheese	el queso (kéh-soh)
chewing gum	el chicle (chée-cleh)
china	la loza (lóh-sah)
(to) clear the table	limpiar la mesa (*v.*) (leem-pee-áhr lah méh-sah)
coffee	el café (cah-féh)
coffee break	el coffe break (cóh-fee bréh-eek)
coffee grinder	el molino de café (moh-lée-noh deh cah-féh)
coffee maker	la cafetera (cah-feh-téh-rah)
coffeepot	la jarra para café (háh-rrah páh-rah cah-féh)
condiments	los aderezos (ah-deh-réh-sohs)
cookies	las galletas dulces (gah-yéh-tahs dóol-sehs)
cork	el tapón (tah-póhn)
corkscrew	el sacatapón (sah-cah-tah-póhn)
	el sacacorchos (sah-cah-cóhr-chohs)
crackers	las galletas (gah-yéh-tahs)
creamer	la jarrita para leche (hah-rrée-tah páh-rah léh-cheh)
crumbs	las migajas (mee-gáh-hahs)
cup	la taza (táh-sah)
customer	el/la cliente (clee-éhn-teh)
decaffeinated coffee	el café descafeinado (cah-féh dehs-cah-feh-ee-náh-d
department	el departamento (deh-pahr-tah-méhn-toh)
dessert	el postre (póhs-treh)
dessert cart	el carro de postres (cáh-rroh deh póhs-trehs
dessert plate	el plato de postre (pláh-toh deh póhs-treh
dining room	el comedor (coh-meh-dóhr)
dinner	la cena (séh-nah)

dishwasher (machine)	el lavaplatos (lah-vah-pláh-tohs)
dishwasher (person)	el/la lavaplatos (lah-vah-pláh-tohs)
(to) dry	secar (*v.*) (seh-cáhr)
(to) dust	sacudir (*v.*) (sah-coo-déer)
finger	el dedo (déh-doh)
fingernail	la uña (óo-nyah)
first course	el primer plato (pree-méhr pláh-toh)
food and beverage	los alimentos y bebidas (ah-lee-méhn-tohs ee beh-bée-dahs)
food order	la comanda (coh-máhn-dah)
fork	el tenedor (teh-neh-dóhr)
garnish (food)	la guarnición (goo-ahr-nee-see-óhn)
glass	el vaso (váh-soh)
glassware	la cristalería (crees-tah-leh-rée-ah)

Auxiliary Vocabulary Words

a (ah)	*to*
ahora (ah-óh-rah)/ahorita (ah-oh-rée-tah)	*now*
aquí (ah-kée)	*here*
con (cohn)	*with*
de (deh)	*of, from*
de acuerdo (deh ah-coo-éhr-doh)	*okay*
el (ehl) (*m.*)	*the*
en (ehn)	*in, at*
este (éhs-teh)	*this*
la (lah) (*f.*)	*the*
las (lahs) (*f. pl.*)	*the*
los (lohs) (*m. pl.*)	*the*
muy (móo-ee)	*very*
para (páh-rah)	*for, to*
por (pohr)	*for*
sí (see)	*yes*
también (tahm-bee-éhn)	*also*
un (oon) (*m.*)	*a*
una (óo-nah) (*f.*)	*a*
y (ee)	*and*

EXERCISE 2.1

Match the following list of restaurant vocabulary words, practice their pronunciation, and be ready to speak them aloud:

1. *beer*	_____	a. molino de café
2. *cheese*	_____	b. cajero
3. *creamer*	_____	c. cristalería
4. *crackers*	_____	d. cubeta
5. *food order*	_____	e. pan
6. *china*	_____	f. comanda
7. *glassware*	_____	g. queso
8. *bread warmer*	_____	h. cerveza
9. *bill*	_____	i. galletas
10. *condiments*	_____	j. plato para pan
11. *coffee maker*	_____	k. loza
12. *bus tub*	_____	l. tazón
13. *butter*	_____	m. plato caliente
14. *appetizer*	_____	n. cuenta
15. *coffee grinder*	_____	o. cafetera
16. *bread plate*	_____	p. aderezos
17. *bowl*	_____	q. aperitivo
18. *bread*	_____	r. mantequilla
19. *cashier*	_____	s. calentador de pan
20. *coffee warmer*	_____	t. jarrita para leche

The Present Tense of Regular Verbs

In English, verbs are rather simple. Few endings are added, and these are relatively uniform (*I speak, he speaks*). In Spanish more endings are used, and these tell you the person and number of the subject. Most verbs in Spanish are regular, meaning that they have similar endings when they are conjugated. However, there are some irregular verbs that are very commonly used—for example, **ser, estar,** and **tener.** (The present tense of these verbs has already been covered in Chapter 1.) Knowing the present tense of frequently used regular verbs will be sufficient to help you get by in most situations in the workplace. Regular verbs are divided into three categories depending on whether the infinitive of the verb ends in **ar, er,** or **ir.** The infinitive of verbs is always stressed on the last syllable. The present tense is formed by dropping the ending of the infinitive and adding the endings that follow. Memorize the following table:

Conjugation of the Present Tense of Regular Verbs

	ar verbs	**er** verbs	**ir** verbs
yo	o	o	o
él, ella, usted	a	e	e
nosotros, nosotras	amos	emos	imos
ellos, ellas, ustedes	an	en	en

Observe that the first person singular ending for all regular verbs is **o**. The third person plural forms are formed by adding **n** to the third person singular forms.

Common Hospitality Regular Verbs

abrir (ah-bréer) (*to open*)

arreglar (ah-rreh-gláhr) (*to fix, to repair*)

asar (ah-sáhr) (*to roast, to bake*)

bailar (bah-ee-láhr) (*to dance*)

barrer (bah-rréhr) (*to sweep*)

beber (beh-béhr) (*to drink*)

comer (coh-méhr) (*to eat*)

comprar (cohm-práhr) (*to buy*)

comprender (cohm-prehn-déhr) (*to understand*)

contestar (cohn-tehs-táhr) (*to answer*)

contratar (cohn-trah-táhr) (*to hire*)

enviar (ehn-vee-áhr) (*to send*)

escribir (ehs-cree-béer) (*to write*)

estudiar (ehs-too-dee-áhr) (*to study*)

hablar (ah-bláhr) (*to speak*)

limpiar (leem-pee-áhr) (*to clean*)

llevar (yeh-váhr) (*to carry/bring*)

preguntar (preh-goon-táhr) (*to ask*)

preparar (preh-pah-ráhr) (*to prepare*)

reparar (reh-pah-ráhr) (*to repair*)

sacudir (sah-coo-déer) (*to dust*)

subir (soo-béer) (*to go up, to bring up*)

surtir (soor-téer) (*to stock*)

terminar (tehr-mee-náhr) (*to finish*)

tomar (toh-máhr) (*to take, to drink*)

trabajar (trah-bah-háhr) (*to work*)

EXERCISE 2.2

Translate the following words or phrases after providing the appropriate subject pronoun:

1. abrimos (two options) _____

2. bebe café (three options)_____

3. comprenden español (three options) _____

4. escribo inglés _____

5. trabajan (three options) _____

6. beben coca-cola (three options) _____

7. habla español _____

8. preparo pan _____

9. comemos canapés (two options) _____

10. barro _____

EXERCISE 2.3

Translate the following phrases and pronounce them in Spanish:

1. Nosotros estamos aquí. _____

2. Yo tengo el café con leche. _____

3. Jorge y Lupita barren aquí. _____

4. Yo barro aquí también. _____

5. Él come el postre con un tenedor. _____

6. De acuerdo, yo preparo los postres en el comedor. _____

7. Nosotras hablamos con el lavaplatos también. _____

8. Ella sube ahora. _____

9. Ellos trabajan en el departamento de alimentos y bebidas. _____

10. El primer plato está aquí. _____

EXERCISE 2.4

With a partner, pronounce the following sentences in Spanish and find out their meaning in English:

1. Juan tiene el molino de café.

2. Los tazones están en la cubeta.

3. El cajero es de México.

4. Jorge come queso y yo bebo cerveza.

5. Antonio y Lupita limpian la loza.

6. El lavaplatos barre el comedor.

7. Nosotros hablamos con los clientes.

8. Las sillas son para el banquete.

9. El ayudante de mesero tiene el queso.

10. Yo tengo la jarra para café.

EXERCISE 2.5

Translate the following sentences and pronounce them in Spanish:

1. *Lupita is from Mexico.*
2. *Jorge and Lupita mop the floor now.*
3. *The dishwasher dries the glassware.*
4. *Jorge and Lupita are in the dining room* (use **estar**).
5. *I eat with a fork.*
6. *The dessert plate is in the dishwasher.*
7. *She has the fork.*
8. *Lupita and I clean the coffee grinder.*
9. *The china and the glassware are in the dining room.*
10. *I speak with the dishwasher.*

EXERCISE 2.6

Take five different subjects from the following list, five different verbs from the above list and/or **ser, estar, tener,** and five different words from the restaurant technical vocabulary (I) and compose five creative sentences in the present tense. Be ready to pronounce them at your instructor's request.

nosotros—el comedor—Lupita—Lupita y Jorge—Lupita y yo—nosotras—Jorge—yo—el tazón—ustedes—el ayudante de mesero—el lavaplatos

Example: **Nosotros tenemos las galletas.**

How to Form Questions in Spanish

The most convenient way to form questions in Spanish is to place an interrogative word before the verb or to put the corresponding form of the verb first in a sentence. For example: **¿Quién tiene el plato? ¿Tiene usted el plato?**

The English interrogative words *do* and *does* are never expressed in Spanish. In Spanish questions, a subject pronoun is usually placed immediately after the verb. Interrogative words always have a written accent. An inverted question mark is placed before the question.

Most Common Interrogative Words in Spanish

¿cómo? (cóh-moh)	*how?*	¿de quién? (deh kee-éhn)	*whose?*
¿cuál? (coo-áhl)	*which?*	¿dónde? (dóhn-deh)	*where?*

¿cuándo? (coo-áhn-doh)	*when?*	¿por qué? (pohr kéh)	*why?*
¿cuánto? (coo-áhn-toh)	*how much?*	¿qué? (keh)	*what?*
¿cuántos? (coo-áhn-tohs)	*how many?*	¿quién? (kee-éhn)	*who?*

Examples:

¿Cuándo trabaja usted?   *When do you work?*

¿Cuántos platos de postre tenemos?   *How many dessert plates do we have?*

¿Trabaja usted en el comedor?   *Do you work in the dining room?*

¿Tenemos nosotros los platos de postre?   *Do we have the dessert plates?*

EXERCISE 2.7

With a partner, answer the following questions posed to you:

1. ¿Tiene usted la jarrita para leche?
2. ¿Dónde está la comanda?
3. ¿Quién prepara las bebidas?
4. ¿Cuándo es el banquete?
5. ¿Limpia el lavaplatos los tazones?
6. ¿Barre el ayudante de mesero las migajas?
7. ¿Sacude Jorge las sillas?
8. ¿Prepara el cajero los condimentos?
9. ¿Habla español el cajero?
10. ¿Quién tiene el sacatapón?

EXERCISE 2.8

Form questions with the following statements:

1. Juan trabaja en Chili's.
2. El pan es para el banquete.
3. El banquete es en el comedor.
4. Tenemos los platos de postre.
5. Yo no barro las migajas.
6. Juan barre las sillas.
7. Usted no habla inglés.
8. El sacacorchos está aquí.
9. El cajero tiene las bebidas.
10. Pedro es el ayudante de mesero.

EXERCISE 2.9

For each of the following verbs, give the corresponding forms of the present tense; then, with a partner, answer the questions posed to you:

1. ¿(hablar) usted español? _____

2. ¿(hablar) Lupita español? _____

3. ¿(asar) yo el pan? _____

4. ¿(limpiar) los ayudantes de mesero el comedor? _____

5. ¿(comer) usted postres?_____

6. ¿(barrer) Jorge las migajas? _____

7. ¿(tener) usted los aderezos? _____

8. ¿(beber) ellos café? _____

9. ¿quién (sacudir) las sillas? _____

10. ¿(trabajar) usted en Boston? _____

11. ¿(abrir) Lupita el comedor? _____

12. ¿(ser) usted el lavaplatos? _____

13. ¿(escribir) usted inglés? _____

14. ¿(tener) usted los platos base? _____

15. ¿dónde (estar) usted? _____

16. ¿(ser) Jorge un cajero? _____

Negations

🧳

To make a sentence negative in Spanish, place the word **no** immediately before the verb. For example: **Jorge no tiene los tenedores,** *Jorge doesn't have the forks.* Other negative words, such as **nunca** (*never*), can also be used. For example: **Yo nunca tengo los vasos,** *I never have the glasses.* The English words *don't* and *doesn't* are never expressed in a negative sentence in Spanish.

Examples: Yo no trabajo aquí.   *I don't work here.*

Jorge no tiene el queso.   *Jorge doesn't have the cheese.*

EXERCISE 2.10

Convert the following positive sentences into negative sentences:

1. Lupita es de México.   _____

2. Ella trabaja aquí.   _____

3. Nosotros comemos en el comedor.   _____

4. El ayudante de mesero habla con la cajera. _____

5. El lavaplatos limpia los tenedores. _____

6. Soy cajero. _____

7. Yo tengo los platos. _____

8. Jorge trabaja. _____

9. Lupita tiene los ceniceros. _____

10. Lupita y Jorge beben cerveza. _____

EXERCISE 2.11

Translate the following sentences and pronounce them in Spanish:

1. *I don't clean the ashtrays; Jorge cleans the ashtrays.* 2. *Lupita doesn't bake the bread.* 3. *Jorge is not here* (use **estar**). 4. *Lupita is not the dishwasher; she is the cashier.* 5. *Jorge and I don't have forks.* 6. *I never drink beer.* 7. *She doesn't eat bread and butter.* 8. *The coffee grinder is not in the dining room* (use **estar**). 9. *Jorge never clears the tables.* 10. *I don't have a bow tie.*

EXERCISE 2.12

Change the following affirmative sentences into negative sentences, making sure that you understand the meaning of each sentence:

1. Juan trabaja en el comedor. 2. Las bebidas están en el bar. 3. El cajero tiene la cuenta. 4. Yo tengo el destapador. 5. Los vasos están en el lavaplatos. 6. Los clientes comen en el comedor. 7. Yo surto la loza. 8. Lupita prepara los canapés. 9. El ayudante de mesero sacude las sillas en el comedor. 10. Jorge prepara el banquete.

Conversational Professional Interaction

In groups of two, translate, practice, and be ready to role-play the following dialogue between a restaurant supervisor and an hourly employee:

Estudiante uno (supervisor):   ¡Buenos días! ¿Quién es usted?

Estudiante dos (empleado por hora):   ¡Buenos días! Soy la ayudante de mesero.

Estudiante uno: Bienvenida.

Estudiante dos: Encantada de conocerle.

Estudiante uno: ¿De dónde es usted?

Estudiante dos: Soy de Tucson. ¿Cómo se llama usted?

Estudiante uno: Me llamo Carlos. Usted trabaja en el comedor.

Estudiante dos: ¿Quién sacude las sillas?

Estudiante uno: Usted sacude las sillas y surte la loza.

Estudiante dos: ¿Barro yo el comedor?

Estudiante uno: Sí, y limpia los ceniceros también.

Estudiante dos: ¿Dónde como?

Estudiante uno: Usted come aquí, en el comedor.

Estudiante dos: De acuerdo.

📧 QUESTIONS TO THE CLASS 📧

Answer the following questions asked by your instructor (or by another student) without looking at your textbook or any class notes:

1. ¿Quién barre el comedor?
2. ¿Dónde está Jorge?
3. ¿Es Lupita de México?
4. ¿Tiene Jorge el molino de café?
5. ¿Qué come Antonio?
6. ¿Cómo está usted?
7. ¿Cuándo es el banquete?
8. ¿Por qué no está Juan en el comedor?
9. ¿Limpian los ayudantes de mesero las migajas?
10. ¿Es usted ayudante de mesero?

CULTURAL VIGNETTE

Communication in Spanish can be either formal and respectful, as in the case of manager/employee or manager/guest relationships, or friendly, as in the case of people who know each other well. This difference is signaled by the pronouns **usted** and **tú.** To avoid misunderstandings, a hospitality manager should communicate with workers and guests using **usted.** Shaking hands is nearly always done when meeting or when leaving; a mere nod of the head, common in other cultures, is not enough. Spanish women often exchange kisses, and it is common for adult men to kiss adult women after they have been introduced. Male friends often pat each other on the back when they see each other. Hispanic people often stand closer to each other when speaking than people in some other cultures do.

CHAPTER 3

ARTICLES

NOUNS

THE VERB "GUSTAR"

 ## OVERVIEW

Chapter 3 deals with Spanish articles and presents nouns useful to hospitality industry professionals. The verb **gustar** is covered separately from other verbs because it is particularly difficult for nonnatives. The Spanish language has no verb meaning *to like*. Instead, the verb **gustar,** meaning *to be pleasing (to),* is used.

 ## UNIT CONTENT

Technical Restaurant Vocabulary (II) • Definite Articles •
Indefinite Articles • Spanish Nouns • The Spanish Verb **Gustar** •
Conversational Professional Interaction • Cultural Vignette

Technical Restaurant Vocabulary (II)

goblet	la copa (cóh-pah)
(to) greet	saludar (*v.*) (sah-loo-dáhr)
grooming	el aseo personal (ah-séh-oh pehr-soh-náhl)
guest	el/la cliente (clee-éhn-teh)
	el/la huésped (oo-éhs-pehd)
high chair	la silla de niños (sée-yah deh née-nyohs)
honey	la miel (mee-éhl)
host	el recepcionista (reh-sehp-see-oh-nées-tah)
hostess	la recepcionista (reh-sehp-see-oh-nées-tah)
hot plate	el plato caliente (pláh-toh cah-lee-éhn-teh)

hot water	el agua caliente (áh-goo-ah cah-lee-éhn-teh)
hygiene	la higiene (ee-hee-éh-neh)
ice	el hielo (ee-éh-loh)
ice bucket	la hielera (ee-eh-léh-rah)
ice cream	el helado (eh-láh-doh)
ice cubes	los cubitos de hielo (coo-bée-tohs deh ee-éh-loh)
iced tea	el té frío (teh frée-oh)
jam	la mermelada (mehr-meh-láh-dah)
jam holder	la mermeladera (mehr-meh-lah-déh-rah)
jelly	la jalea (hah-léh-ah)
juice	el jugo (hóo-goh)
	el zumo (sóo-moh)
ketchup	el ketchup (kéht-choop)
kitchen	la cocina (coh-sée-nah)
knife	el cuchillo (coo-chée-yoh)
lemonade	la limonada (lee-moh-náh-dah)
lid	la tapadera (tah-pah-déh-rah)
lunch	el almuerzo (ahl-moo-éhr-soh)
matches	los cerillos (seh-rée-yohs)
meal	la comida (coh-mée-dah)
meal course	el plato (pláh-toh)
menu	el menú (meh-nóo)
menu item	el platillo (plah-tée-yoh)
microwave oven	el microondas (mee-croh-óhn-dahs)
milk	la leche (léh-cheh)
(to) mop	trapear (v.) (trah-peh-áhr)
mop wringer	el escurridor (ehs-coo-rree-dóhr)
mustard	la mostaza (mohs-táh-sah)
name tag	la placa con su nombre (pláh-cah cohn soo nóhm-breh)
napery	la mantelería (mahn-teh-leh-rée-ah)
napkin	la servilleta (sehr-vee-yéh-tah)
oil and vinegar	el aceite y vinagre (ah-seh-ée-teh ee vee-náh-greh)
orange marmalade	la mermelada de naranja (mehr-meh-láh-dah deh nah-ráhn-hah)
paper towel	la toalla de papel (toh-áh-yah deh pah-péhl)
paper work	la papelería (pah-peh-leh-rée-ah)
peach jam	la mermelada de durazno (mehr-meh-láh-dah deh doo-ráhs-noh)
pepper (seasoning)	la pimienta (pee-mee-éhn-tah)
pepper shaker	el pimentero (pee-mehn-téh-roh)
pitcher	la jarra (háh-rrah)
place setting	el plaqué (plah-kéh)
plate	el plato (pláh-toh)

(to) refill	rellenar (*v.*) (reh-yeh-náhr)
requisition	el pedido (peh-dée-doh)
rim	el borde (bóhr-deh)
(to) rinse	enjuagar (*v.*) (ehn-hoo-ah-gáhr)
roll	el panecillo (pah-neh-sée-yoh)
room number	el número de habitación (nóo-meh-roh deh ah-bee-tah-see-óhn)
room service	el servicio a cuartos (sehr-vée-see-oh ah coo-áhr-tohs)
room setup	la preparación del salón (preh-pah-rah-see-óhn dehl sah-lóhn)
salad	la ensalada (ehn-sah-láh-dah)
salad dressing	el aderezo para ensaladas (ah-deh-réh-soh páh-rah ehn-sah-láh-dah)
salad fork	el tenedor de ensalada (teh-neh-dóhr deh ehn-sah-láh-dah)
salad plate	el plato de ensalada (pláh-toh deh ehn-sah-láh-dah)
salt	la sal (sahl)
salt shaker	el salero (sah-léh-roh)

Auxiliary Vocabulary Words

because	porque (póhr-keh)
(to) bring	traer (*v.*) (trah-éhr)
day	el día (dée-ah)
floor	el piso (pée-soh)
	el suelo (soo-éh-loh)
hand	la mano (máh-noh)
many	muchos/as (móo-chohs/ahs)
miss	la señorita (seh-nyoh-rée-tah)
mister	el señor (seh-nyóhr)
Mrs.	la señora (seh-nyóh-rah)
much	mucho/a (móo-choh/ah)
once	una vez (óo-nah vehs)
people	la gente (héhn-teh)
	las personas (pehr-sóh-nahs)
restaurant	el restaurante (rehs-tah-oo-ráhn-teh)
there is, there are	hay (áh-ee)
to the left	a la izquierda (ah lah ees-kee-éhr-dah)
to the right	a la derecha (ah lah deh-réh-chah)
twice	dos veces (dohs véh-ses)

EXERCISE 3.1

Match the following list of restaurant vocabulary words, practice their pronunciation, and be ready to speak them aloud:

1. *paper towel*	_____	a.	salero
2. *roll*	_____	b.	pimentero
3. *lid*	_____	c.	rellenar
4. *oil and vinegar*	_____	d.	copa
5. *kitchen*	_____	e.	té frío
6. *mop wringer*	_____	f.	higiene
7. *peach jam*	_____	g.	jugo
8. *(to) mop*	_____	h.	hielera
9. *to the right*	_____	i.	huésped
10. *(to) greet*	_____	j.	miel
11. *(to) refill*	_____	k.	panecillo
12. *salt shaker*	_____	l.	aceite y vinagre
13. *pepper shaker*	_____	m.	toalla de papel
14. *hygiene*	_____	n.	mermelada de durazno
15. *goblet*	_____	o.	tapadera
16. *ice bucket*	_____	p.	cocina
17. *juice*	_____	q.	escurridor
18. *iced tea*	_____	r.	trapear
19. *honey*	_____	s.	saludar
20. *guest*	_____	t.	a la derecha

Definite Articles

All nouns in Spanish are either masculine or feminine. The masculine singular form is **el,** and the masculine plural is **los;** the feminine singular is **la,** and the feminine plural is **las.** Whereas in English there is just one definite article (*the*), in Spanish there are four possible options: **el, la, los,** and **las.** Almost all nouns ending in **o** are masculine, while those ending in **a, d,** or **ción** are usually feminine. (Two important exceptions are **la mano,** *the hand,* and **el día,** *the day.*) In general, the article is used whenever *the* is used in English. With **señor, señora,** and **señorita** the corresponding article is used when you speak about a person, not when you are speaking to the person. For example, **El señor Smith es de Tucson** but **señor Smith, ¿de dónde es usted?**

Nouns beginning with **a** take the article **el** even if they are feminine—for example, **el agua.**

    el used before masculine singular nouns, as in **el plato**

    la used before feminine singular nouns, as in **la sal**

    los used before masculine plural nouns, as in **los saleros**

    las used before feminine plural nouns, as in **las cubetas**

There are two article/preposition contractions in Spanish: **a el** becomes **al** (ahl), meaning *to the,* and **de el** becomes **del** (dehl), meaning *from the/of the.* Examples: **al restaurante,** meaning *to the restaurant;* **del restaurante,** meaning *from the restaurant.*

EXERCISE 3.2

Provide the appropriate definite article for each of the following words:

1. servicio a cuartos _____
2. mostaza _____
3. pimienta _____
4. borde _____
5. pimienta _____
6. pan _____

7. día _____
8. agua _____
9. señor _____
10. mano _____
11. higiene _____

EXERCISE 3.3

Change to plural, making sure that you understand the meaning of each noun:

1. el aseo personal _____
2. el plato de postre _____
3. los cerillos _____
4. el platillo _____
5. el trapeador _____

6. el cubito de hielo _____
7. el agua _____
8. el día _____
9. el plato caliente _____
10. la jalea _____

EXERCISE 3.4

Translate the following words and pronounce them in Spanish.

1. *the crackers* _____
2. *the hand* _____
3. *the coffeepot* _____
4. *the bus person* _____
5. *the day* _____

6. *the creamer* _____
7. *the high chair* _____
8. *the hygiene* _____
9. *the dining rooms* _____
10. *the water* _____

Indefinite Articles

The word for *a* or *an* is **un** before a masculine singular noun and **una** before a feminine singular noun. These words also mean *one.* Examples: **un cocinero** (*a male cook*), **una cocinera** (*a female cook*), **tengo uno,** *I have one (masculine object),* **tengo una,** *I have one (feminine object).* The plural of **un** is **unos;** the plural of **una** is **unas.**

EXERCISE 3.5

Identify the indefinite articles in the following sentences and pronounce the sentences in Spanish:

1. Yo aso un pollo. _____

2. Jorge bebe una coca-cola. _____

3. Lupita y Antonio trabajan en un hotel. _____

4. ¿Quién tiene las ensaladas? Yo tengo una. _____

5. ¿Cuántos saleros tiene Lupita? Lupita tiene uno. _____

6. Jorge es un mesero. _____

7. Lupita es una cajera. _____

8. Él bebe una cerveza. _____

9. Ella come una galleta. _____

10. Ellos tienen un aparador. _____

EXERCISE 3.6

Find the meaning of the following sentences and pronounce them in Spanish:

1. *Jorge prepares a table with a chair.* _____

2. *Antonio roasts a chicken.* _____

3. *How many forks do we have? I have one.* _____

4. *Who has the napkins? Pedro has one.* _____

5. *Jorge and Lupita have an ashtray.* _____

6. *He has an orange.* _____

7. *They have a table.* _____

8. *She has a chair.* _____

9. *They eat ice cream.* _____

10. *I roast a chicken.* _____

Spanish Nouns

All nouns in Spanish are either masculine or feminine. (For practical purposes, the neuter **lo** will not be dealt with in this book.) Most nouns ending in **o** are masculine, whereas those ending in **a** are feminine. In general, the plural of nouns is formed by adding an **s** to words ending in a vowel and **es** to words ending in a consonant.

Some Names of Countries Common to the Hospitality Industry in the United States

In Spanish, some names of countries are masculine and others are feminine.

Argentina	Argentina (*f.*) (ahr-hehn-tée-nah)
Canada	Canadá (*m.*) (cah-nah-dáh)
Chile	Chile (*m.*) (chée-leh)
Costa Rica	Costa Rica (*f.*) (cóhs-tah rée-cah)
Cuba	Cuba (*f.*) (cóo-bah)
Guatemala	Guatemala (*f.*) (goo-ah-teh-máh-lah)
Mexico	México (*m.*) (méh-hee-coh)
Panama	Panamá (*m.*) (pah-nah-máh)
Puerto Rico	Puerto Rico (*m.*) (poo-érh-toh rée-coh)
Spain	España (*f.*) (ehs-páh-nyah)
United States	Estados Unidos (*m.*) (ehs-táh-dohs oo-née-dohs)

EXERCISE 3.7

Pronounce the names of the following countries clearly, remembering to put the stress on the syllable with an accent:

1. Cuba   2. Panamá   3. Estados Unidos   4. Guatemala   5. Puerto Rico
6. España   7. Canadá   8. México   9. Chile   10. Argentina

EXERCISE 3.8

Change the following words into their plural form:

1. la tapadera _____

2. el jugo _____

3. la sal _____

4. el borde _____

5. el molino de café _____

6. el menú _____

7. el ayudante de mesero _____

8. el lavaplatos _____

9. el tenedor _____

10. el pan _____

EXERCISE 3.9

Change the following words into their singular form:

1. las sillas de niño _____
2. los escurridores _____
3. los tenedores de ensalada _____
4. los números de habitación _____
5. las servilletas _____
6. los lavaplatos _____
7. las mermeladas _____
8. los plaqués _____
9. los saleros _____
10. los cubitos de hielo _____

EXERCISE 3.10

In pairs, ask and answer the following phrases, making sure that you understand what you are asking or answering:

Estudiante uno: ¿Es la mermelada de México?

Estudiante dos: No, la mermelada es de Canadá.

Estudiante uno: ¿Están las copas con la mantelería?

Estudiante dos: Sí, las copas están con la mantelería.

Estudiante uno: ¿De dónde es la señorita Pérez?

Estudiante dos: La señorita Pérez es de Cuba.

Estudiante uno: ¿Dónde están los tenedores?

Estudiante dos: Los tenedores están en el lavaplatos.

Estudiante uno: ¿Es la mantequilla de los Estados Unidos?

Estudiante dos: No, la mantequilla es de Argentina.

Estudiante uno: ¿Tenemos ensalada en el menú?

Estudiante dos: No entiendo lo que dice.

EXERCISE 3.11

Translate the following sentences and pronounce them in Spanish:

1. *The paper towels are in the kitchen* (use **estar**). _____
2. *The host prepares the ice for the guests.* _____
3. *The bus persons dust the chairs in the restaurant.* _____
4. *Miss Gomez prepares the hot water for the tea.* _____
5. *The ice bucket and the lid are here* (use **estar**). _____
6. *We have the honey.* _____
7. *Lupita bakes the bread.* _____

8. *Jorge is from Puerto Rico* (use **ser**). _____
9. *The hot plate is in the dining room.* _____
10. *I have two ice buckets.* _____

The Spanish Verb **Gustar**

💼

An English sentence using the verb *to like* should be changed into one using *to be pleasing (to)* before it can be translated into Spanish. For example: instead of *I like this coffee,* think *this coffee is pleasing to me.* With this structure *coffee,* not *I,* becomes the subject. The subject generally comes at the end of the sentence in this construction. For example: **Me gusta el queso** (literally, *cheese pleases me*).

Only two forms of **gustar** are regularly used in the present tense: **gusta,** if one thing or an action is pleasing, and **gustan,** if more than one thing is pleasing. For example, **Me gusta el café** *(I like coffee),* **Me gusta cocinar** *(I like to cook),* **Me gustan los postres** *(I like desserts).*

To make a question with **gustar,** place the indirect pronoun before the verb; for example: **¿Le gusta el café? ¿A usted le gustan los zumos?**

To make a negative statement, place the negative **no** before the indirect pronoun; for example: **No me gusta el café, No le gustan los zumos.**

me gusta(n) (meh góos-tah)(n)	*I like*
le gusta(n) (leh góos-tah)(n)	*he/she likes—you like*
nos gusta(n) (nohs góos-tah)(n)	*we like*
les gusta(n) (lehs góos-tah)(n)	*they/you like*

To emphasize or to clarify the indirect object pronoun, an emphatic phrase **(a mí, a él,** etc.) may be used before it. Examples:

(a mí) me gusta el café.	*I like coffee.*
(a mí) me gusta trabajar.	*I like to work.*
(a mí) me gustan las galletas.	*I like crackers.*
(a él) le gusta el café.	*He likes coffee.*
(a él) le gusta trabajar.	*He likes to work.*
(a él) le gustan las galletas.	*He likes crackers.*
(a ella) le gusta el café.	*She likes coffee.*
(a ella) le gusta trabajar.	*She likes to work.*
(a ella) le gustan las galletas.	*She likes crackers.*
(a usted) le gusta el café.	*You like coffee.*
(a usted) le gusta trabajar.	*You like to work.*
(a usted) le gustan las galletas.	*You like crackers.*
(a nosotros/as) nos gusta el café.	*We like coffee.*
(a nosotros/as) nos gusta trabajar.	*We like to work.*
(a nosotros/as) nos gustan las galletas.	*We like crackers.*
(a ellos/as) les gusta el café.	*They like coffee.*

(a ellos/as) les gusta trabajar.	*They like to work.*
(a ellos/as) les gustan las galletas.	*They like crackers.*
(a ustedes) les gusta el café.	*You (plural) like coffee.*
(a ustedes) les gusta trabajar.	*You (plural) like to work.*
(a ustedes) les gustan las galletas.	*You (plural) like crackers.*
A Jorge le gusta Lupita.	*Jorge likes Lupita.*
A Lupita le gusta Jorge.	*Lupita likes Jorge.*
(a mí) no me gusta la miel.	*I don't like honey.*
¿(a usted) le gusta la miel?	*Do you like honey?*

EXERCISE 3.12

Translate the following sentences into English:

1. A nosotros no nos gusta sacudir las sillas en el restaurante.
   _____

2. ¿Le gusta la mermelada de naranja?
   _____

3. Me gusta trabajar en la cocina. _____
4. No me gusta la miel. _____
5. ¿Les gusta el helado?
   _____

6. A ellos les gusta beber té. _____
7. A mí me gustan las galletas, pero no me gusta la ensalada.
   _____

8. A Jorge le gusta Lupita, pero a ella no le gusta Jorge.
   _____

9. ¿Le gusta a usted secar platos? _____
10. Me gusta el aceite y vinagre con la ensalada.
    _____

11. ¿Le gusta el café?
    _____

EXERCISE 3.13

Write a sentence expressing an activity that you like to do and a thing or object that you especially like. For example: **Me gusta trabajar; Me gusta el queso.** Then, make the two sentences negative.

EXERCISE 3.14

Write a sentence expressing the idea that you like (or dislike) the following things or activities:

beer—appetizers—cheese—to dust—to sweep—honey—kitchen—to mop— iced tea

EXERCISE 3.15

Translate the following sentences and pronounce them in Spanish:

1. *I like desserts.*
2. *Tomás likes Lupita.*
3. *We like the plates, but we don't like the forks.*
4. *They like to dance salsa.*
5. *The cooks don't like to work in the dining room.*
6. *Jorge doesn't like to drink milk.*
7. *He likes beer.*
8. *The waiters don't like to sweep the kitchen.*
9. *I don't like to mop.*
10. *The guest doesn't like the menu.*

EXERCISE 3.16

Ask one imaginary person, and then a group of people, whether or not they like the following activities and things—for example, **¿Le gusta beber limonada? ¿Le gusta el helado? ¿Le gustan los helados?:**

1. secar platos
2. el helado
3. el café con leche
4. trapear la cocina
5. Tom Cruise
6. limpiar el restaurante
7. trabajar en Taco Bell
8. el pan con mantequilla
9. trapear el restaurante
10. Lupita y Jorge

CONVERSATIONAL PROFESSIONAL INTERACTION

In groups of two, translate, practice, and be ready to role-play the following dialogue between a restaurant supervisor and an hourly employee:

Estudiante uno (supervisor): Buenos días, Lupita. ¿Trabaja usted en el comedor?

Estudiante dos (empleado por hora): Sí, trabajo en el comedor. ¿Dónde está el almacén?

Estudiante uno: El almacén está a la derecha de la cocina.

Estudiante dos: Carlos, ¿tenemos un banquete?

Estudiante uno: Sí, tenemos un banquete.

Estudiante dos: ¿Qué platillos tenemos?

Estudiante uno:	Tenemos dos platillos, queso con galletas, postre, pan y mantequilla y café.
Estudiante dos:	¿Quién es el ayudante de mesero?
Estudiante uno:	El ayudante de mesero es Jorge.
Estudiante dos:	¿Barre Jorge el comedor?
Estudiante uno:	No, el lavaplatos barre el comedor; el ayudante de mesero limpia la mesa.
Estudiante dos:	¿Cuándo comemos nosotros?
Estudiante uno:	Ustedes no comen porque tenemos muchos clientes.
Estudiante dos:	De acuerdo, señor Pérez.

▥ QUESTIONS TO THE CLASS ▥

Answer the following questions asked by your instructor (or by another student) without looking at your textbook or any class notes:

1. ¿Tiene usted los saleros?
2. ¿Es Lupita de Cuba?
3. ¿Le gustan los postres a usted?
4. ¿Le gusta cocinar a Juan?
5. A mi no me gusta lavar los platos ¿y a usted?
6. ¿Dónde está el escurridor?
7. ¿De dónde es el señor Navarro?
8. ¿Tienen los saleros sal?
9. ¿Le gusta a usted hablar español?
10. ¿Le gustan a usted las ensaladas?

CULTURAL VIGNETTE

The concept of family in Hispanic countries is different from that of North America. Two, sometimes three, generations often live under the same roof, participating actively in all family endeavors. Unmarried children might live in the family home until they are in their thirties, and the rest of the family usually encourages them to do so. Hospitality managers should be aware that on occasion different members of the family of a Hispanic employee may accompany him or her to the place of work when off duty—for example, to collect the paycheck on payday.

CHAPTER 4

Irregular Verbs

"ir a + an Infinitive"

Numbers

Time

 ## OVERVIEW

Chapter 4 presents a selection of verbs whose endings don't follow the pattern of regular verbs. The irregular verbs selected in this chapter are frequently used in everyday hospitality situations. The chapter explains the construction **ir a + an infinitive** that can be used to indicate future plans or actions. Sections on how to express numbers and tell time in Spanish are also included.

UNIT CONTENT

Technical Restaurant Vocabulary (III)   •   The Present Tense of Irregular Verbs
•   The Verb **Ir** Followed by the Word **a** and an Infinitive   •   Cardinal
Numbers   •   Ordinal Numbers   •   Telling the Time of Day in Spanish   •
Conversational Professional Interaction   •   Cultural Vignette

Technical Restaurant Vocabulary (III)

sanitation	el saneamiento (sah-neh-ah-mee-éhn-toh)
saucer	el plato de café (pláh-toh deh cah-féh)
seafood	los mariscos (mah-rées-cohs)

second course	el segundo plato (seh-góon-doh pláh-toh)
(to) see	ver (*v.*) (vehr)
self-service	el autoservicio (áh-oo-toh-serh-vée-see-oh)
(to) serve	servir (e→i) (*v.*) (sehr-véer)
service napkin	la servilleta de servicio (sehr-vee-yéh-tah deh sehr-vée-see-oh)
service station	la estación de servicio (ehs-tah-see-óhn deh sehr-vée-see-oh)
service table	la mesa de servicio (méh-sah deh sehr-vée-see-oh)
(to) set the table	poner la mesa (*v.*) (poh-néhr lah méh-sah)
shake	el batido (bah-tée-doh)
sheet pan	la bandeja (bahn-déh-hah)
shelf	la repisa (reh-pée-sah)
	el estante (ehs-táhn-teh)
shift	el turno (tóor-noh)
side stand	el aparador (ah-pah-rah-dóhr)
silverware	la cubertería (coo-behr-teh-rée-ah)
sink (kitchen)	el fregadero (freh-gah-déh-roh)
soda dispenser	la máquina de refrescos (máh-kee-nah deh reh-fréhs-cohs)
soft drink	el refresco (reh-fréhs-coh)
(to) sort	separar (*v.*) (seh-pah-ráhr)
soup	la sopa (sóh-pah)
soup plate	el plato para sopa (pláh-toh páh-rah sóh-pah)
soup spoon	la cuchara para sopa (coo-cháh-rah páh-rah sóh-pah)
spoon	la cuchara (coo-cháh-rah)
station	la estación (ehs-tah-see-óhn)
(to) stock	surtir (*v.*) (soor-téer)
storeroom	el almacén (ahl-mah-séhn)
strawberries	las fresas (fréh-sahs)
strawberry jam	la mermelada de fresa (mehr-meh-láh-dah deh fréh-sah)
sugar	el/la azúcar (ah-sóo-cahr)
sugar bowl	el azucarero (ah-soo-cah-réh-roh)
(to) sweep	barrer (*v.*) (bah-rréhr)
syrup	el jarabe (hah-ráh-beh)
table	la mesa (méh-sah)
tablecloth	el mantel (mahn-téhl)
table linens	la mantelería (mahn-teh-leh-rée-ah)
(to) take the order	tomar la comanda (*v.*) (toh-máhr lah coh-máhn-dah)
tea	el té (teh)
teapot	la tetera (teh-téh-rah)
teaspoon	la cucharilla (coo-chah-rée-yah)
tip	la propina (proh-pée-nah)
(piece of) toast	la tostada (tohs-táh-dah)
(to) toast	asar (*v.*) (ah-sáhr)

toaster	el tostador (tohs-tah-dóhr)
to-go box	la caja para llevar (cáh-hah páh-rah yeh-váhr)
to-go cup	el vaso para llevar (váh-soh páh-rah yeh-váhr)
tongs	las pinzas (péen-sahs)
tray	la bandeja (bahn-déh-hah)
	la charola (*f.*) (chah-róh-lah)
tray stand, scissors	las tijeras (tee-héh-rahs)
uniform	el uniforme (oo-nee-fóhr-meh)
waiter	el mesero (meh-séh-roh)
	el camarero (cah-mah-réh-roh)
	el mozo (móh-soh)
waitress	la mesera (meh-séh-rah)
	la camarera (cah-mah-réh-rah)
	la moza (móh-sah)
water	el agua (áh-goo-ah)
water glass	el vaso para agua (váh-soh páh-rah áh-goo-ah)
water pitcher	la jarra para agua (háh-rrah páh-rah áh-goo-ah)
wine	el vino (vée-noh)
wine glass	el vaso para vino (váh-soh páh-rah vée-noh)
wine list	la carta de vinos (cáhr-tah deh vée-nohs)
(to) wrap up	envolver (o→ue) (*v.*) (ehn-vohl-véhr)

Auxiliary Vocabulary Words

💼

also	también (tahm-bee-éhn)
always	siempre (see-éhm-preh)
but	pero (péh-roh)
dollar	dólar (dóh-lahr)
today	hoy (óh-ee)
tomorrow	mañana (mah-nyáh-nah)
yesterday	Ayer

EXERCISE 4.1

Match the following list of restaurant vocabulary words, practice their pronunciation, and be ready to speak them aloud:

1. *tongs*   _____ a. mantel

2. *(to) serve*   _____ b. mermelada de fresa

3. *tray stand*   _____ c. cucharilla

4. *sugar bowl*   _____ d. envolver

5. *seafood*   _____ e. lista de vinos

6. *side stand*   _____ f. vaso para agua

7. *tablecloth*	_____	g. plato para sopa
8. *shelf*	_____	h. mesero
9. *(to) wrap up*	_____	i. autoservicio
10. *wine list*	_____	j. poner la mesa
11. *water glass*	_____	k. mariscos
12. *waiter*	_____	l. azucarero
13. *teaspoon*	_____	m. servir
14. *self-service*	_____	n. aparador
15. *soda dispenser*	_____	o. estante
16. *soup plate*	_____	p. pinzas
17. *(to) take the order*	_____	q. tijeras
18. *(to) set the table*	_____	r. cubertería
19. *strawberry jam*	_____	s. máquina de refrescos
20. *silverware*	_____	t. tomar la comanda

The Present Tense of Irregular Verbs

There are a few irregular verbs in Spanish that are frequently used. For classification sake, the selected irregular Spanish verbs that follow have been categorized into two arbitrary groups. The first group contains irregular verbs whose present tense first person **(yo)** ends in **go,** and the second group includes those whose present tense first person ends in **oy.**

"go" verbs

decir (deh-séer)	*to tell*	yo digo
		él/ella/usted dice
		nosotros/as decimos
		ellos/ellas/ustedes dicen
hacer (ah-séhr)	*to do/make*	hago—hace—hacemos—hacen
poner (poh-néhr)	*to put*	pongo—pone—ponemos—ponen
salir (sah-léer)	*to leave*	salgo—sale—salimos—salen
tener (teh-néhr)	*to have*	tengo—tiene—tenemos—tienen
traer (trah-éhr)	*to bring*	traigo—trae—traemos—traen
venir (veh-néer)	*to come*	vengo—viene—venimos—vienen

EXERCISE 4.2

Understand the meaning of the following sentences and pronounce them in Spanish:

1. María tiene los platos de café.
2. Vengo del restaurante.

3. El mesero trae los platos.

4. Yo salgo de la cocina.

5. La mesera hace el café.

6. El ayudante de mesero pone la cubertería en el lavaplatos.

7. Yo tengo las bandejas.

8. Antonio sale del almacén.

9. Nosotros servimos a los clientes.

10. El cajero no hace la sopa.

"oy" verbs

dar (dahr)	*to give*	yo doy él/ella/usted da nosotros/as damos ellos/ellas/ustedes dan
estar (ehs-táhr)	*to be*	estoy—está—estamos—están
ir (eer)	*to go*	voy—va—vamos—van
ser (sehr)	*to be*	soy—es—somos—son

EXERCISE 4.3

Understand the meaning of the following sentences and pronounce them in Spanish:

1. Yo doy el jarabe al cliente.

2. Las mesas están en el comedor.

3. Jorge va al restaurante ahora.

4. Yo no soy de México; soy de España.

5. Nosotros vamos a surtir la estación de servicio con cucharillas.

6. Yo no voy a Canadá; Carlos va a Canadá.

7. Lupita y yo somos de Costa Rica.

8. Ellos dan los vasos para agua al mesero.

9. Él está en el almacén.

10. Yo estoy en la cocina.

EXERCISE 4.4

Give the corresponding forms or the present tense of the following irregular verbs:

1. El cajero (dar) una silla al cliente. _____

2. Yo siempre (decir) la verdad (lah vehr-dád, *the truth*). _____

3. Las meseras (ir) al comedor. _____

4. Yo (poner) la cubertería en las mesas. _____

5. Yo (saber) español. _____

6. Nosotros (venir) al restaurante. _____

7. Jorge y Lupita (ir) a la cocina. _____

8. Ellos (salir) del almacén. _____

9. Yo no (ir) a México. _____

10. Ella (traer) la cubertería. _____

EXERCISE 4.5

With a partner, ask and answer the following phrases, making sure that you understand what you are asking or answering:

Estudiante uno:	¿Quién hace el té frío?
Estudiante dos:	Yo hago el té frío para el banquete.
Estudiante uno:	¿Va usted al comedor?
Estudiante dos:	Sí, voy al comedor.
Estudiante uno:	¿Quién trae las bandejas a la cocina?
Estudiante dos:	Lupita y Jorge traen las bandejas.
Estudiante uno:	¿Es usted de San Diego?
Estudiante dos:	Sí, soy de San Diego.
Estudiante uno:	¿Está Antonio en la cocina?
Estudiante dos:	No, Antonio está en el comedor.
Estudiante uno:	¿Quién da el uniforme al ayudante de mesero?
Estudiante dos:	Yo doy el uniforme al ayudante de mesero.

EXERCISE 4.6

Translate the following sentences and pronounce them in Spanish:

1. *The waiter sets the table in the dining room* (use **poner la mesa**).

   _____

2. *Jorge and Lupita bring the trays to the kitchen.*

   _____

3. *Lupita leaves now.* _____

4. *The bus person gives the plates to the waitress.* _____

5. *I make the coffee.* _____

6. *Jorge comes from the storeroom.* _____

7. *I go to the kitchen.* _____

8. *Lupita goes to the dining room.* _____

9. *Lupita and I are from San Diego* (use **ser**). _____

10. *I am in the kitchen* (use **estar**). _____

The Verb **Ir** Followed by the Word **a** and an Infinitive

The expression **ir a,** followed by the infinitive of a verb, is used very often in Spanish to indicate future plans or actions. It is equivalent to the English expression *"going to,"* as in *Tomorrow I am going to sweep the restaurant.* For example, **Mañana voy a barrer el suelo.**

EXERCISE 4.7

Understand the meaning of the following sentences and pronounce them in Spanish:

1. Los meseros van a poner las mesas.
2. El ayudante de mesero va a hacer café.
3. Lupita va a ir a Nueva York.
4. El cajero no va a sacudir las sillas.
5. ¿Va a servir Jorge el pan y mantequilla?
6. Sí, Jorge va a servir el pan y mantequilla.
7. El camarero va a poner las mesas.
8. Nosotros vamos a preparar las ensaladas para el almuerzo.
9. Pedro va a secar los platos.
10. Jorge y Antonio van a trabajar el turno de mañana.

EXERCISE 4.8

In pairs, ask and answer the following phrases, making sure that you understand what you are asking or answering:

Estudiante uno:	¿Quién va a limpiar la mesa?
Estudiante dos:	Pepe va a limpiar la mesa.
Estudiante uno:	¿Va la mesera a servir el postre?
Estudiante dos:	Sí, ella va a servir el postre.
Estudiante uno:	¿Van Jorge y Lupita a limpiar las cubetas?
Estudiante dos:	No, el lavaplatos va a limpiar las cubetas.
Estudiante uno:	¿Va usted a hablar con Lupita?
Estudiante dos:	No, Lupita no trabaja.
Estudiante uno:	¿Quiénes van a sacudir las sillas?
Estudiante dos:	Miguel y Joaquín van a sacudir las sillas.
Estudiante uno:	¿Va ella a barrer el comedor?
Estudiante dos:	Sí, Lupita va a barrer el comedor.

Cardinal Numbers

Cardinal numbers do not change their form to agree with the noun, except **uno** and numbers ending in **uno** that drop the **o** before a masculine noun—for example, **veinte y un platos.** The form **una** is used before a feminine noun—for example, **veinte y una cucharas.**

The numbers from 16 to 19 and 21 to 29 are often written as they are pronounced—for example, **veintinueve.**

0	cero (séh-roh)	50	cincuenta (seen-coo-éhn-tah)
1	uno, una (óo-noh)	51	cincuenta y uno (see-coo-éhn-tah ee óo-noh)
2	dos (dohs)	60	sesenta (seh-séhn-tah)
3	tres (trehs)	61	sesenta y uno (seh-séhn-tah ee óo-noh)
4	cuatro (coo-áh-troh)	70	setenta (seh-téhn-tah)
5	cinco (séen-coh)	71	setenta y uno (seh-téhn-tah ee óo-noh)
6	seis (séh-ees)	80	ochenta (oh-chéhn-tah)
7	siete (see-éh-teh)	81	ochenta y uno (oh-chéhn-tah ee óo-noh)
8	ocho (óh-choh)	90	noventa (noh-véhn-tah)
9	nueve (noo-éh-veh)	91	noventa y uno (noh-véhn-tah ee óo-noh)
10	diez (dee-éhs)	100	cien (see-éhn)
11	once (óhn-seh)	101	ciento uno (see-éhn-toh óo-noh)
12	doce (dóh-seh)	200	doscientos (dohs-see-éhn-tohs)
13	trece (tréh-seh)	300	trescientos (trehs-see-éhn-tohs)
14	catorce (cah-tóhr-seh)	400	cuatrocientos (coo-ah-troh-see-éhn-tohs)
15	quince (kéen-seh)	500	quinientos (kee-nee-éhn-tohs)
16	diez y seis (dee-éhs ee séh-ees)	600	seiscientos (seh-ees-see-éhn-tohs)
17	diez y siete (dee-éhs ee see-éh-teh)	700	setecientos (seh-teh-see-éhn-tohs)
18	diez y ocho (dee-éhs ee óh-choh)	800	ochocientos (oh-choh-see-éhn-tohs)
19	diez y nueve (dee-éhs ee noo-éh-veh)	900	novecientos (noh-veh-see-éhn-tohs)
20	veinte (véh-een-teh)	1000	mil (meel)
21	veinte y uno (véh-een-teh ee óo-noh)	1001	mil uno (meel óo-noh)
30	treinta (tréh-een-tah)	1101	mil ciento uno (meel see-éhn-toh óo-noh)
31	treinta y uno (tréh-een-tah ee óo-noh)	2000	dos mil (dohs meel)
40	cuarenta (coo-ah-réhn-tah)	2005	dos mil cinco (dohs meel séen-coh)
41	cuarenta y uno (coo-ah-réhn-tah ee óo-noh)		

EXERCISE 4.9

Pronounce clearly the following numbers in Spanish, making sure that you know their equivalent in English:

1. diez y nueve
2. cincuenta y cinco
3. setecientos
4. quinientos cinco
5. dos mil cinco
6. setenta
7. diez mil cuatrocientos sesenta y seis
8. trescientos dos
9. once
10. novecientos noventa y nueve

EXERCISE 4.10

Pronounce the following sentences in Spanish, making sure that you know their meaning in English:

1. Hay veinte y cinco platos aquí.
2. Jorge hace sopa para cuarenta clientes.
3. El ayudante de mesero trae trece platos al comedor.
4. Lupita da siete cuchillos al mesero.
5. Lupita pone treinta platos en la estación de servicio.
6. Yo aso seis pollos.
7. Carlos tiene cuarenta y cinco mil dólares.
8. Los meseros preparan veinte y dos mesas.
9. Hay siete sillas de niño en el almacén.

EXERCISE 4.11

Write the following numbers in Spanish:

6 _____	88 _____
9 _____	91 _____
11 _____	105 _____
15 _____	144 _____
18 _____	555 _____
22 _____	702 _____
35 _____	991 _____
46 _____	1002 _____

58 _____	1543 _____
69 _____	2005 _____
73 _____	2112 _____

EXERCISE 4.12

In pairs, ask and answer the following sentences in Spanish using the present tense:

1. ¿Da el ayudante de mesero cuarenta y cuatro tenedores al mesero?
2. ¿Cuántas tazas hay en el almacén?
3. ¿Es la mesa siete para seis o para siete clientes?
4. ¿Cuántas servilletas doy a la mesera?
5. ¿Cuántos azucareros hay en la cocina?
6. ¿Tenemos cincuenta platos para el banquete?
7. ¿Son los tazones para Jorge?
8. ¿Dónde están los veinte y un cuchillos?
9. ¿Cuántas cucharas pongo en la mesa?
10. ¿Hago cuarenta tostadas?

Ordinal Numbers

Ordinal numbers in Spanish agree in gender and number with the nouns they modify, as do adjectives (see Chapter 5). The words **primero** and **tercero** drop the final **o** before a masculine singular noun. For example, *the third glass* is written and pronounced **el tercer vaso.**

primero, -a (pree-méh-roh, ah)	1st	sexto, -a (séhs-toh, ah)	6th
segundo, -a (seh-góon-doh, ah)	2nd	séptimo, -a (séhp-tee-moh, ah)	7th
tercero, -a (tehr-séh-roh, ah)	3rd	octavo, -a (ohc-táh-voh, ah)	8th
cuarto, -a (coo-áhr-toh, ah)	4th	noveno, -a (noh-véh-noh, ah)	9th
quinto, -a (kéen-toh, ah)	5th	décimo, -a (déh-see-moh, ah)	10th

EXERCISE 4.13

Pronounce the following sentences in Spanish, making sure you understand their meaning in English:

1. El cuarto uno cero dos está en el segundo piso.
2. El primer vaso es para vino; el tercero es para cerveza.
3. El tercer tenedor es para pescado.
4. La primera silla es para la señora canadiense.
5. El primer plato es sopa.

EXERCISE 4.14

Translate the following phrases and pronounce them in Spanish:

1. *The first glass* _____
2. *The first spoon* _____
3. *The fourth roll (bread)* _____
4. *The tenth chair* _____
5. *The fifth uniform* _____
6. *The seventh sugar bowl* _____
7. *The eighth teaspoon* _____
8. *The tenth sheet pan* _____
9. *The first bottle of wine* _____
10. *The second cup of tea* _____

Telling the Time of Day in Spanish

The word **hora** (óh-rah) means *hour.* To ask the time of day, the question **¿Qué hora es?** is used. The expression *o'clock* is not translated in Spanish. Example: *It is one o'clock* is translated as **Es la una.**

The feminine article **la** or **las** is used with the cardinal number corresponding to the hour; **es** is used only when followed by **la una,** and in all other cases **son** is used. Examples: *It is one o'clock,* **Es la una** (ehs lah óo-nah). *It is two o'clock,* **Son las dos** (sohn lahs dohs).

A.M. is translated approximately as follows:

From 12:00 A.M. until sunrise, the expression **de la madrugada** (deh lah mah-droo-gáh-dah) is used. Example: **Son las dos de la madrugada,** *It is 2 A.M.*

From sunrise until 12:00 P.M., the expression **de la mañana** (deh lah mah-nyáh-nah) is used. Example: **Son las nueve de la mañana,** *It is 9 A.M.*

P.M. is translated approximately as follows:

From 12 P.M. until sunset, the expression **de la tarde** (deh lah táhr-deh) is used. Example: **"Son las cinco de la tarde,"** *It is 5 P.M.*

From sunset until 12:00 A.M., the expression **de la noche** (deh lah nóh-cheh) is used. Example: **Son las once de la noche,** *It is 11 P.M.*

Generally, up to and including the half hour, minutes are added to the hour after **y.** Example: **Son las doce y veinte,** *It is twenty after twelve.* Between the half hour and the next hour the minutes are subtracted from the next hour by using **menos.** Example: **Son las doce menos veinte,"** *It is twenty to twelve.*

The noun **cuarto** is often used for a quarter of an hour, and the adjective **media** for a half hour. For example:

"Es la una y cuarto." *It is a quarter after one.*

"Son las diez y media." *It is half past ten.*

"Son las nueve menos cuarto." *It is a quarter to nine.*

What is the time? is translated by **¿Qué hora es?**

At what time? is translated by **¿A qué hora?**

En punto means *on the dot.*

EXERCISE 4.15

Pronounce the following sentences in Spanish, making sure that you understand their meaning:

1. Son las doce y cuarto.
2. Es la una y media.
3. Usted trabaja a las tres hoy.
4. ¿A qué hora trabajan Lupita y Jorge?
5. Lupita y Jorge trabajan a las once y media.
6. Yo aso los pollos a la una y media.
7. El mesero prepara el té frío a las nueve.
8. Los lavaplatos trabajan de las once y media a las seis y cuarto.
9. El ayudante de mesero trae los ceniceros a la una.
10. Ella hace la limonada a las seis en punto.

EXERCISE 4.16

Draw a clock on the board (or on a piece of paper) and mark on it the following times:

1. 1:15 P.M. 2. 12:25 P.M. 3. 11:00 P.M. 4. 2:30 A.M. 5. 1:05 P.M.
6. 12:35 A.M. 7. 1:55 P.M. 8. 8:50 P.M. 9. 12:00 P.M. 10. 12:00 A.M.

EXERCISE 4.17

With a partner, ask and answer the following phrases, making sure that you understand what you are asking or answering:

Estudiante uno:	¿A qué hora trabaja Pedro?
Estudiante dos:	Pedro trabaja a las ocho.
Estudiante uno:	¿Es el banquete a las seis o a las siete?
Estudiante dos:	El banquete es a las seis y media.
Estudiante uno:	¿Hago el té a las cuatro o a las cinco?
Estudiante dos:	A las cuatro, por favor.
Estudiante uno:	¿Qué hora es?
Estudiante dos:	Son las cinco menos veinticinco.
Estudiante uno:	¿Hace Lupita el café a las doce o a la una?
Estudiante dos:	Lupita hace el café a la una.
Estudiante uno:	¿Es el banquete a las once o a las once y media?
Estudiante dos:	El banquete es a las once y cuarto.

CONVERSATIONAL PROFESSIONAL INTERACTION

In groups of two, translate, practice, and be ready to role-play the following dialogue between a restaurant supervisor and an hourly employee:

Estudiante uno (supervisor):   Hóla, Lupita. ¿a qué hora trabaja usted?
Estudiante dos (empleado por hora):   Trabajo en el comedor a las ocho.
Estudiante uno: ¿Va usted a servir mesas hoy?
Estudiante dos: Sí, pero primero voy a poner las mesas.
Estudiante uno: ¿Tenemos servilletas y manteles?
Estudiante dos: Sí, tenemos veinte y cinco manteles y ochenta servilletas.
Estudiante uno: ¿Quién limpia los azucareros?
Estudiante dos: El ayudante de mesero va a limpiar los azucareros.
Estudiante uno: Lupita, ¿hace usted el té frío hoy?
Estudiante dos: No, yo hago el café y surto los aparadores con vasos.
Estudiante uno: ¡De acuerdo! Yo voy a hablar con el cajero.

🧳 QUESTIONS TO THE CLASS 🧳

Answer the following questions asked by your instructor (or by another student) without looking at your textbook or any class notes:

1. ¿A qué hora sale usted?
2. ¿Viene usted a trabajar a la una o a las dos?
3. ¿Da usted las bandejas a la mesera o al lavaplatos?
4. ¿Es usted de los Estados Unidos?
5. ¿Quién va a poner las mesas en el comedor?
6. ¿Vamos a lavar la máquina de refrescos?
7. ¿Cuántas cucharas tenemos para el banquete?
8. ¿Está el señor Rodríguez en la primera o en la segunda mesa?
9. ¿Trabaja Pedro a las tres o a las cuatro?
10. ¿Viene usted de Phoenix o de Tucson?

CULTURAL VIGNETTE

The manager–employee relationship is usually more formal in the workplace for Hispanic people than it is for non-Latin workers in businesses in the United States. Hourly employees avoid eye contact with their bosses as a sign of respect for them. As a manager, it is wise to maintain a sense of personal distance, both physical and emotional, when dealing with employees and guests of other cultures.

PART TWO

KITCHEN OPERATIONS

ADJECTIVES

COLORS

OVERVIEW

Chapter 5 introduces adjectives in four categories: descriptive, possessive, and demonstrative, and adjectives of nationality. The adjectives selected in this chapter are directly related to hospitality operations. Colors, divided into categories by word ending, are also presented.

UNIT CONTENT

Technical Kitchen Vocabulary (I) • Descriptive Adjectives •
Possessive Adjectives • Demonstrative Adjectives • Adjectives of
Nationality • Colors • Adjectives as Nouns • Conversational
Professional Interaction • Cultural Vignette

Technical Kitchen Vocabulary (I)

apple	la manzana (manh-sáh-nah)
apron	el delantal (deh-lahn-táhl)
asparagus	los espárragos (ehs-páh-rrah-gohs)
avocado	el aguacate (ah-goo-ah-cáh-teh)
bacon	el tocino (toh-sée-noh)
bacteria	la bacteria (bahk-téh-ree-ah)
banana	la banana (bah-náh-nah)
	el plátano (pláh-tah-noh)
basket	la cesta (séhs-tah)
beans	los frijoles (free-hóh-lehs)
beef	la carne de res (cáhr-neh deh rehs)
beefsteak	el bistec (bees-téhc)
(to) boil	hervir (e→ie) (*v.*) (ehr-véer)
bone	el hueso (oo-éh-soh)

bread	el pan (pahn)
(to) bread	empanar (v.) (ehm-pah-náhr)
breaded	empanado (adj.) (ehm-pah-náh-doh)
breakfast	el desayuno (deh-sah-yóo-noh)
(to have) breakfast	desayunar (v.) (deh-sah-yoo-náhr)
broccoli	el brécol (bréh-cohl)
(to) broil	asar a la parrilla (v.) (ah-sáhr ah lah pah-rrée-yah)
broiler	la parrilla (pah-rrée-yah)
bus tub	la cubeta (coo-béh-tah)
butter	la mantequilla (mahn-teh-kée-yah)
cake	el pastel (pahs-téhl)
can	el bote (bóh-teh)
	la lata (láh-tah)
can, to be able	poder (o→ue) (v.) (poh-déhr)
can opener	el abrelatas (ah-breh-láh-tahs)
carrots	las zanahorias (sah-nah-óh-ree-ahs)
cauliflower	la coliflor (coh-lee-flóhr)
celery	el apio (áh-pee-oh)
cent	el centavo (sehn-táh-voh)
chef	el jefe de cocina (héh-feh deh coh-sée-nah)
cheese	el queso (kéh-soh)
cherry	la cereza (seh-réh-sah)
chicken	el pollo (póh-yoh)
chipped	desportillado (adj.) (dehs-pohr-tee-yáh-doh)
chocolate	el chocolate (choh-coh-láh-teh)
chop (such as pork or lamb)	la chuleta (choo-léh-tah)
(to) chop	cortar (v.) (cohr-táhr)
clams	las almejas (ahl-méh-hahs)
cloth	el trapo (tráh-poh)
coffee	el café (cah-féh)
coffee cup	la taza para café (táh-sah páh-rah cah-féh)
coffee maker	la cafetera (cah-feh-téh-rah)
colander	el colador (coh-lah-dóhr)
cold	el frío (frée-oh)
	frío (adj.) (freé-oh)
cook	el/la cocinero/a (coh-see-néh-roh, ah)
(to) cook	cocinar (v.) (coh-see-náhr)
corn	el maíz (mah-ées)
cover	la tapadera (tah-pah-déh-rah)
(to) cover	cubrir (v.) (coo-bréer)
crab	el cangrejo (cahn-gréh-hoh)
cucumber	el pepino (peh-pée-noh)
cup	la taza (táh-sah)
(to) cut	cortar (v.) (cohr-táhr)
cutting board	la tabla para cortar (táh-blah pah-rah cohr-táhr)

decaffeinated	descafeinado (*adj.*) (dehs-cah-feh-ee-náh-doh)
decaffeinated coffee	el café descafeinado (cah-féh dehs-cah-feh-ee-náh-doh)
deep fryer	la freidora (freh-ee-dóh-rah)
(to) defrost	descongelar (*v.*) (dehs-cohn-heh-láhr)
degrees	los grados (gráh-dohs)
dessert	el postre (póhs-treh)
detergent	el detergente (deh-tehr-héhn-teh)
dinner	la cena (séh-nah)
(to have) dinner	cenar (*v.*) (seh-náhr)
dish	el plato (pláh-toh)
dishwasher	el lavaplatos (lah-vah-pláh-tohs)
dishwasher rack	la rejilla (reh-hée-yah)
dishwashing machine	la máquina lavaplatos (máh-kee-nah lah-vah-pláh-tohs)
dollar	el dólar (dóh-lahr)
dough	la masa (máh-sah)
drain	el desagüe (deh-sáh-goo-eh)
(to) drain	vaciar (*v.*) (vah-see-áhr)
dry	seco (*adj.*) (séh-coh)
(to) dry	secar (*v.*) (seh-cáhr)
dumpster	el vertedero (vehr-teh-déh-roh)
egg	el huevo (oo-éh-voh)
egg holder	la huevera (oo-eh-véh-rah)
fat	la grasa (gráh-sah)
	graso (*adj.*) (gráh-soh)
filter	el filtro (féel-troh)
(to) filter	filtrar (*v.*) (feel-tráhr)
fish	el pescado (pehs-cáh-doh)
flour	la harina (ah-rée-nah)
food	la comida (coh-mée-dah)
food scraps	los desperdicios (dehs-pehr-dée-see-ohs)
(to) freeze	congelar (*v.*) (cohn-heh-láhr)
freezer	el congelador (cohn-heh-lah-dóhr)
French fries	las papas fritas (páh-pahs frée-tahs)
fried	frito (*adj.*) (frée-toh)
friend	el/la amigo/a (ah-mée-goh/ah)
frozen	congelado (*adj.*) (cohn-heh-láh-doh)
fruit	la fruta (fróo-tah)
(to) fry	freir (e→i) (*v.*) (freh-éer)
frying pan	la sartén (sahr-téhn)
garbage	la basura (bah-sóo-rah)
garbage can	el cubo de basura (cóo-boh deh bah-sóo-rah)
garbage disposal	el triturador (tree-too-rah-dóhr)
garlic	el ajo (áh-hoh)
garnish	la guarnición (goo-ahr-nee-see-óhn)

gloves	los guantes (goo-áhn-tehs)
grapefruit	el pomelo (poh-méh-loh)
	la toronja (toh-róhn-hah)
grapes	las uvas (óo-vahs)
grease trap	la trampa de grasa (tráhm-pah deh gráh-sah)
greasy	grasiento (*adj.*) (grah-see-éhn-toh)
griddle	la plancha (pláhn-chah)
grill	la parrilla (pah-rrée-yah)
(to) grill	asar a la parrilla (*v.*) (ah-sáhr ah lah pah-rrée-yah)
(to) grind	moler (*v.*) (moh-léhr)
ground meat	la carne molida (cáhr-neh moh-lée-dah)
hair net	la redecilla (reh-deh-sée-yah)

EXERCISE 5.1

Match the following list of restaurant vocabulary words, practice their pronunciation, and be ready to speak them aloud:

1. *(to) grind*	_____	a.	parrilla
2. *frying pan*	_____	b.	colador
3. *garbage disposal*	_____	c.	delantal
4. *flour*	_____	d.	desagüe
5. *freezer*	_____	e.	moler
6. *dinner*	_____	f.	freidora
7. *drain*	_____	g.	hervir
8. *egg*	_____	h.	abrelatas
9. *dry*	_____	i.	triturador
10. *cucumber*	_____	j.	cesta
11. *deep fryer*	_____	k.	pepino
12. *detergent*	_____	l.	harina
13. *chef*	_____	m.	sartén
14. *cloth*	_____	n.	congelador
15. *broiler*	_____	o.	jefe de cocina
16. *(to) boil*	_____	p.	cena
17. *can opener*	_____	q.	seco
18. *colander*	_____	r.	detergente
19. *basket*	_____	s.	huevo
20. *apron*	_____	t.	trapo

Descriptive Adjectives

Descriptive adjectives are usually those that tell something about the nature of the noun they describe. Unlike in English, descriptive adjectives typically follow the noun they qualify. For example: **el mesero mexicano,** *the Mexican waiter.* However, descriptive adjectives that <u>enhance quality</u> normally precede the noun. For example: **Pedro es un gran cocinero,** *Pedro is a great cook.*

Descriptive adjectives agree in gender and number with the nouns they describe. In most cases, if the masculine singular of the adjective ends in **o,** the adjective will have the four endings **o, a, os, as.**

For example, *fried* takes the following four forms:

el pescado frito

la carne frita

los frijoles fritos

las papas fritas

Adjectives whose masculine singular does not end in **o** are the same in the masculine and feminine, singular and plural.

For example,

El plato está caliente. *The plate is hot.*

La sartén está caliente. *The frying pan is hot.*

Los platos están calientes. *The plates are hot.*

Las sartenes están calientes. *The frying pans are hot.*

Adjectives of nationality whose masculine ends in a consonant add an **a** for the feminine.

For example,

Juan es español.

Juanita es española.

Adjectives form their plurals the same way that nouns form theirs.
For example,

el té bueno; los tés buenos; el té verde; los tés verdes

Selected Descriptive Adjectives Useful to the Hospitality Manager

(Only the masculine singular form of each adjective has been provided.)

afilado (ah-fee-láh-doh)	*sharp*
alto (áhl-toh)	*tall*
amable (ah-máh-bleh)	*kind*
asado (ah-sáh-doh)	*roasted*
bajo (báh-hoh)	*short*
barato (bah-ráh-toh)	*inexpensive*
bien hecho (bee-éhn éh-choh)	*well done*
bueno (boo-éh-noh)	*good*
caliente (cah-lee-éhn-teh)	*warm*
cansado (cahn-sáh-doh)	*tired*

caro (cáh-roh)	*expensive*
chico (chée-coh)	*tiny*
congelado (cohn-heh-láh-doh)	*frozen*
descongelado (dehs-cohn-heh-láh-doh)	*thawed*
desportillado (dehs-pohr-tee-yáh-doh)	*chipped*
dulce (dóol-seh)	*sweet*
elegante (eh-leh-gáhn-teh)	*elegant*
empanado (ehm-pah-náh-doh)	*breaded*
enfermo (ehn-féhr-moh)	*sick*
estropeado (ehs-troh-peh-áh-doh)	*damaged*
feliz (feh-lées)	*happy*
fresco (fréhs-coh)	*fresh*
frío (frée-oh)	*cold*
frito (frée-toh)	*fried*
fuera de servicio (foo-éh-rah deh sehr-vée-see-oh)	*out of order*
grande (gráhn-deh)	*large*
grasiento (grah-see-éhn-toh)	*greasy*
hecho (éh-choh)	*done, made*
limpio (léem-pee-oh)	*clean*
listo (lées-toh)	*ready*
maduro (mah-dóo-roh)	*ripe*
malo (máh-loh)	*bad*
molido (moh-lée-doh)	*ground*
moreno (moh-réh-noh)	*dark-haired*
nuevo (noo-éh-voh)	*new*
pelado (peh-láh-doh)	*peeled*
pequeño (peh-kéh-nyoh)	*small*
picado (pee-cáh-doh)	*minced*
picante (pee-cáhn-teh)	*hot (to taste)*
planchado (plahn-cháh-doh)	*ironed*
poco hecho (póh-coh éh-choh)	*medium rare*
preparado (preh-pah-ráh-doh)	*prepared*
rápido (ráh-pee-doh)	*fast*
roto (róh-toh)	*broken*
rubio (róo-bee-oh)	*blond*
salado (sah-láh-doh)	*salty*
sangrante (sahn-gráhn-teh)	*rare (meats)*
sucio (sóo-see-oh)	*dirty*
tostado (tohs-táh-doh)	*toasted*
viejo (vee-éh-hoh)	*old*

EXERCISE 5.2

Match the following list of restaurant vocabulary words, practice their pronunciation, and be ready to speak them aloud:

1. *dirty*	_____	a. bueno
2. *minced*	_____	b. malo
3. *fast*	_____	c. enfermo
4. *good*	_____	d. picado
5. *sick*	_____	e. sucio
6. *fried*	_____	f. limpio
7. *clean*	_____	g. rápido
8. *bad*	_____	h. frito
9. *tired*	_____	i. poco hecho
10. *medium rare*	_____	j. cansado

EXERCISE 5.3

Understand the meaning of the following sentences and pronounce them in Spanish:

1. El pescado frito está en la cocina.
2. La carne de res está poco hecha.
3. El tazón pequeño está desportillado.
4. El pollo descongelado está en la bandeja.
5. Dos meseros están enfermos hoy.
6. El lavaplatos moreno es argentino.
7. La sopa está dulce.
8. Las galletas saladas son para el almuerzo, la carne picada es para la cena.
9. Los vasos para el té frío están limpios.
10. Los manteles y las servilletas están planchados.

EXERCISE 5.4

Match up the following adjectives and nouns using each word only once:

1. rotas	_____	a. las papas
2. picada	_____	b. el té
3. buenos	_____	c. los platos
4. fritas	_____	d. la carne
5. nuevos	_____	e. los meseros

6. planchada   _____ f. la mesera
7. sucios   _____ g. la servilleta
8. elegante   _____ h. los cocineros
9. desportillados   _____ i. las tazas
10. listo   _____ j. los tenedores

EXERCISE 5.5

Fill the blanks with matching descriptive adjectives:

1. El delantal de Lupita está _____.
2. El pan para los clientes está _____.
3. El bistec no está _____.
4. Las papas fritas están _____.
5. Los cuchillos del jefe de cocina son muy _____.
6. Las tablas de cortar no están _____.
7. La mesera _____ no trabaja hoy.
8. Me gustan las zanahorias _____.
9. El cocinero español es _____.
10. El pollo para el almuerzo está _____.

EXERCISE 5.6

Describe the following nouns using two different adjectives for each one:

1. Batman
2. El español
3. Tom Cruise
4. The Rolling Stones
5. Roseanne

EXERCISE 5.7

In pairs, ask and answer the following phrases, making sure that you
understand what you are asking or answering:

Estudiante uno: ¿Están los delantales sucios en la cocina?
Estudiante dos: No, los delantales sucios están en el almacén.
Estudiante uno: ¿Para cuál mesa es el pan tostado?
Estudiante dos: El pan tostado es para la mesa cinco.
Estudiante uno: ¿Están los manteles planchados?

Estudiante dos:	Sí, los manteles y las servilletas están planchados.
Estudiante uno:	¿Está rota la máquina lavaplatos?
Estudiante dos:	La máquina lavaplatos no está rota.
Estudiante uno:	¿Para dónde es el bistec medio hecho?
Estudiante dos:	El bistec medio hecho es para la mesa diez.
Estudiante uno:	¿Es el pollo asado para el banquete?
Estudiante dos:	Sí, el pollo asado es para el banquete.

Possessive Adjectives

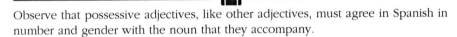

Observe that possessive adjectives, like other adjectives, must agree in Spanish in number and gender with the noun that they accompany.

Possessive before Nouns

Singular Object	Plural Object
mi (mee) *my*	mis (mees) *my*
su (soo) *your, his, her, its, their*	sus (soos) *your, his, her, its, their*
nuestro (*m.*) (noo-éhs-troh) *our*	nuestros (*m.*) (noo-éhs-trohs) *our*
nuestra (*f.*) (noo-éhs-trah) *our*	nuestras (*f.*) (noo-éhs-trahs) *our*

Examples: **Mi cuchillo está afilado,** *My knife is sharp.* **Mis cuchillos están afilados,** *My knives are sharp.* **Su delantal está sucio,** *Your apron is dirty.* **Sus delantales están sucios,** *Your aprons are dirty.*

Possessive after Nouns

mío (mée-oh), mía, míos, mías	*mine*
suyo (sóo-yoh), suya, suyos, suyas	*yours, his, hers, theirs*
nuestro, nuestra, nuestros, nuestras	*ours*

Examples: **El postre es mío, Los postres son míos. La zanahoria es nuestra, Las zanahorias son nuestras.**

Possession with de

Possession in Spanish can also be expressed with **de** (*of*). The English way of expressing possession by apostrophe *s, Pedro's knives,* is not used in Spanish. Examples: *the cook's uniform,* **el uniforme del cocinero;** *the waitresses' trays,* **las bandejas de las meseras.**

EXERCISE 5.8

Pronounce the following sentences in Spanish, making sure that you understand their meaning in English:

1. Los platos limpios son nuestros.
2. Nuestros platos limpios están en la estación de servicio.
3. El abrelatas es suyo (four options).
4. Su cocinero es de Chile (four options).
5. Sus cocineros son muy buenos (four options).
6. El bistec bien hecho es mío.
7. Mi bistec está bien hecho.
8. Nuestra bandeja es grande.
9. Sus postres están preparados en la cocina (four options).
10. El cuchillo de Pedro está muy afilado.

EXERCISE 5.9

Match the following sentences:

1. *Lupita's bus tub is chipped.* _____ a. Las mesas del banquete están listas.

2. *The cook's knives are good.* _____ b. La cubeta de Lupita está desportillada.

3. *Jorge's napkins.* _____ c. Los cuchillos de los cocineros son afilados.

4. *The banquet tables are ready.* _____ d. Los cuchillos del cocinero son buenos.

5. *The cooks' knives are sharp.* _____ e. Las servilletas de Jorge.

EXERCISE 5.10

Translate the following sentences using the correct possessive adjectives before the noun. Make sure that you understand the meaning of each sentence.

1. *His frying pan is clean* (use **estar**). _____

2. *Your hands are dirty* (use **estar**). _____

3. *Our plates are chipped* (use **estar**). _____

4. *Your coffee is decaffeinated* (use **ser**).

   _____

5. *Their dessert is on the service station* (use **estar**).

   _____

6. *His uniform is ready* (use **estar**). _____

7. *Your clean trays are in the kitchen* (use **estar**).

   _____

8. *Our restaurant is very good* (use **ser**). _____

9. *Your fingernails are dirty* (use **estar**). _____

10. *My chocolate is from Canada* (use **ser**).

   _____

EXERCISE 5.11

Translate the following sentences using the correct possessive adjectives after the noun. Make sure that you understand the meaning of each sentence.

1. *The knife is mine* (use **ser**). _____

2. *The dough is his* (use **ser**). _____

3. *The dry plates are ours* (use **ser**). _____

4. *The ground meat is theirs* (use **ser**). _____

5. *The fried fish is hers* (use **ser**). _____

6. *The cutting board is yours* (use **ser**). _____

7. *Are the clean bowls yours?* (use **ser**). _____

8. *Is the ironed tablecloth his?* (use **ser**). _____

9. *No, it is Lupita's* (use **ser**). _____

10. *Are the carrots theirs?* (use **ser**). _____

EXERCISE 5.12

With a partner, ask and answer the following phrases, making sure that you understand what you are asking or answering:

Estudiante uno:	¿Son sus cuchillos afilados?
Estudiante dos:	Sí, los cuchillos del cocinero son muy afilados.
Estudiante uno:	¿Está el uniforme de Pedro limpio?
Estudiante dos:	No, el uniforme de Pedro está sucio.
Estudiante uno:	¿Es bueno el menú del restaurante?
Estudiante dos:	Sí, el menú del restaurante es bueno.
Estudiante uno:	¿Dónde está el pastel del jefe de cocina?
Estudiante dos:	El pastel del jefe de cocina está en la mesa.
Estudiante uno:	¿Es el restaurante barato?
Estudiante dos:	No, el restaurante es muy caro.
Estudiante uno:	¿Está usted cansado(a)?
Estudiante dos:	Sí, estoy muy cansado(a).

Demonstrative Adjectives

Demonstrative adjectives are used to single out and express the location of the nouns they modify.

For objects closer to the speaker than to the listener:

este (éhs-teh) (followed by *m. s.* noun)	*this*
esta (éhs-tah) (followed by *f. s.* noun)	*this*
esto (éhs-toh) (neut. *s.*)	*this* (unidentified object)
estos (éhs-tohs) (followed by *m. pl.* noun)	*these*
estas (éhs-tahs) (followed by *f. pl.* noun)	*these*

For objects closer to the listener than to the speaker:

ese (éh-seh) (followed by *m. s.* noun)	*that*
esa (éh-sah) (followed by *f. s.* noun)	*that*
eso (éh-soh) (neut. *s.*)	*that* (unidentified object)
esos (éh-sohs) (followed by *m. pl.* noun)	*those*
esas (éh-sas) (followed by *f. pl.* noun)	*those*

For objects far away from both listener and speaker:

aquel (ah-kéhl) (followed by *m. s.* noun)	*that*
aquella (ah-kéh-yah) (followed by *f. s.* noun)	*that*
aquello (ah-kéh-yoh) (neut. *s.*)	*that* (unidentified object)
aquellos (ah-kéh-yohs) (followed by *m. pl.* noun)	*those*
aquellas (ah-kéh-yahs) (followed by *f. pl.* noun)	*those*

EXERCISE 5.13

Pronounce the following sentences in Spanish, making sure you understand their meaning in English:

1. Estas chuletas son para la mesa seis.
2. Aquel mesero es de México.
3. Esas almejas son frescas.
4. Aquellas tazas están desportilladas.
5. Ese pollo está empanado.
6. Aquel pollo frito es para la cena.
7. Estos pasteles están muy buenos.
8. Aquel cocinero está enfermo.
9. ¿De quién son estas manzanas?
10. ¿Son estas almejas para el almuerzo?

EXERCISE 5.14

In pairs, ask and answer the following phrases, making sure that you understand what you are asking or answering:

Estudiante uno:	¿Están estos vasos sucios?
Estudiante dos:	Sí, esos vasos están sucios.
Estudiante uno:	¿Es aquella bandeja suya?
Estudiante dos:	No, aquella bandeja no es mía; es de Pedro.
Estudiante uno:	¿Es este apio fresco?
Estudiante dos:	Sí, ese apio es muy fresco.
Estudiante uno:	¿Es ese uniforme para Jorge?
Estudiante dos:	Sí, este uniforme es para Jorge.
Estudiante uno:	¿Son buenos esos panecillos?
Estudiante dos:	Esos panecillos no son buenos.
Estudiante uno:	¿Son estas tazas y aquellos tazones suyos?
Estudiante dos:	Sí, son míos.

EXERCISE 5.15

Insert the appropriate demonstrative adjective (three options in all cases):

1. _____ carne es para la mesa cinco.
2. _____ lavaplatos está roto.
3. _____ cuchillo y _____ platos están sucios.
4. ¡ _____ es un desastre!
5. _____ mesera habla español.
6. _____ cocineros son rápidos.
7. _____ té está frío.
8. _____ cocineros son de México.
9. ¿Son _____ delantales suyos?
10. ¿Es _____ jarra para agua o para vino?

EXERCISE 5.16

Answer the following questions making sure that you understand what you are saying:

1. ¿Es éste su tenedor?
2. ¿Son éstas sus cucharas?
3. ¿De quién es la tabla de cortar?

4. ¿Quién es ese cocinero?

5. ¿Están listas aquellas bandejas?

6. ¿Quiénes son aquellos meseros?

7. ¿Está limpio el comedor?

8. ¿Es aquel cocinero de Perú o de Cuba?

9. ¿Cuántos platos hay en aquella cubeta?

10. ¿De quién es ese vaso?

Adjectives of Nationality

Unlike in English, adjectives of nationality are not capitalized in Spanish.

Masc. sing.	Masc. pl.	Fem. sing.	Fem. pl.
argentino	argentinos	argentina	argentinas
canadiense	canadienses	canadiense	canadienses
chileno	chilenos	chilena	chilenas
costarriqueño	costarriqueños	costarriqueña	costarriqueñas
cubano	cubanos	cubana	cubanas
guatemalteco	guatemaltecos	guatemalteca	guatemaltecas
mexicano	mexicanos	mexicana	mexicanas
panameño	panameños	panameña	panameñas
puertorriqueño	puertorriqueños	puertorriqueña	puertorriqueñas
español	españoles	española	españolas
norteamericano	norteamericanos	norteamericana	norteamericanas

EXERCISE 5.17

Pronounce the following sentences in Spanish making sure that you understand their meaning in English:

1. El mesero costarriqueño se llama Jorge.

2. Los clientes de la mesa once son españoles.

3. ¿Es la mesera puertorriqueña?

4. No es puertorriqueña; es panameña.

5. El jefe de cocina es argentino; es de Argentina.

6. Los cocineros mexicanos son muy elegantes.

7. El menú es de comida norteamericana, pero hay dos platillos chilenos.

8. A la cajera guatemalteca le gusta Jorge.

9. La comida española no es picante.

10. La comida mexicana es picante.

EXERCISE 5.18

With a partner, ask and answer the following phrases, making sure that you understand what you are asking or answering:

Estudiante uno:	¿Es Pedro de Puerto Rico?
Estudiante dos:	Sí, es puertorriqueño.
Estudiante uno:	¿De dónde es el cajero nuevo?
Estudiante dos:	El cajero nuevo es de México; es mexicano.
Estudiante uno:	¿Es español este vino?
Estudiante dos:	No, es francés.
Estudiante uno:	¿Son las meseras cubanas o argentinas?
Estudiante dos:	No son cubanas ni argentinas; son de Costa Rica.
Estudiante uno:	¿Es el restaurante venezolano bueno?
Estudiante dos:	Sí, es muy bueno y barato.
Estudiante uno:	¿Es usted chileno(a)?
Estudiante dos:	No soy chileno(a); soy norteamericano(a).

Colors

As with descriptive adjectives, the endings of colors whose last letter is **o** are: **o, a, os, as.** Examples: **blanco—blanca—blancos—blancas,**   *white.*

amarillo (ah-mah-rée-yoh)	*yellow*
anaranjado (ah-nah-rahn-háh-doh)	*orange*
blanco (bláhn-coh)	*white*
dorado (doh-ráh-doh)	*golden*
morado (moh-ráh-doh)	*purple*
moreno (moh-réh-noh)	*brown (hair)*
negro (néh-groh)	*black*
rojo (róh-hoh)	*red*
rosado (roh-sáh-doh)	*pink*
rubio (róo-bee-oh)	*blond*
tinto (téen-toh)	*red (for wines)*

Colors not ending in **o** do not have a feminine form; they only have a plural form. Examples: **azul—azules** and **verde—verdes.**

azul (ah-sóol)	*blue*
gris (grees)	*gray*
marrón (mah-rróhn)	*brown*
verde (véhr-deh)	*green*

The following colors only have one form when used to describe masculine, feminine, and plural nouns:

café (cah-féh)	*coffee*
naranja (nah-ráhn-hah)	*orange*
rosa (róh-sah)	*pink*

In most cases, colors follow the nouns they qualify. The usual expression for asking about colors is: **¿de qué color es . . . .?** (deh keh coh-lóhr ehs . . . .)

EXERCISE 5.19

Pronounce the following sentences in Spanish, making sure that you understand their meaning in English:

1. Los manteles marrones son para el banquete.
2. Las servilletas amarillas y rosas son para el restaurante.
3. ¿De qué color son los delantales de los lavaplatos?
4. Los delantales de los lavaplatos son blancos.
5. La cajera morena es mexicana.
6. El mesero rubio es chileno.
7. El vino blanco está en el aparador.
8. El vino rosado es para la mesa veinte.
9. Las tazas azules están sucias.
10. Estos plátanos están verdes.

EXERCISE 5.20

In pairs, ask and answer the following phrases, making sure that you understand what you are asking or answering:

Estudiante uno:	¿De qué color es su pelo (péh-loh) (*hair*)?
Estudiante dos:	El pelo de Lupita es rubio.
Estudiante uno:	¿Dónde están las manzanas rojas?
Estudiante dos:	Las manzanas rojas están en la cocina.
Estudiante uno:	¿Quién es ese chico moreno?
Estudiante dos:	Es Pedro; es de Francia.
Estudiante uno:	¿Quieren vino tinto o blanco?
Estudiante dos:	Queremos vino tinto, por favor.
Estudiante uno:	¿Para qué mesa es el pan blanco?
Estudiante dos:	El pan blanco es para la mesa doce.
Estudiante uno:	¿De qué color es el uniforme de Jorge?
Estudiante dos:	El uniforme de Jorge es marrón y verde.

Adjectives as Nouns

Adjectives may function as nouns when combined with articles. *I like the red one* translates in Spanish as **Me gusta el rojo** (or **la roja**), and *The blonde one is the cook* can be translated as **La rubia es la cocinera.**

EXERCISE 5.21

Pronounce the following sentences with adjectives as nouns in Spanish, making sure that you understand their meaning in English:

1. El pescado está en la cocina; el congelado es mío, el fresco es de Jorge.
2. Las servilletas están en el almacén; las rojas son para el banquete.
3. Los pimientos son para el almuerzo; los rojos van con el pescado, los verdes van con la carne.
4. Los nuevos son del cocinero mexicano (*referring to new knives*).
5. El rubio es panameño (*referring to a blond employee from Panama*).

EXERCISE 5.22

Translate the following sentences into Spanish:

1. *The green one (referring to a pepper) is for the cook* (use **ser**).

   _____

2. *The thawed ones (referring to more than one fish) are for lunch* (use **ser**).

   _____

3. *The frozen one (referring to a chicken) is for dinner* (use **ser**).

   _____

4. *The Mexican ones (referring to two cooks) are very elegant* (use **ser**).

   _____

5. *The brunette one (referring to a woman at the cash register) is from Colombia* (use **ser**). _____

   _____

Conversational Professional Interaction

In groups of two, translate, practice, and be ready to role-play the following dialogue between a restaurant supervisor and an hourly employee:

Estudiante uno (supervisor):   Buenos días, Miguel, ¿está listo para trabajar?

Estudiante dos (empleado por hora):	Sí, señora Dolores.
Estudiante uno:	¿Es este uniforme suyo?
Estudiante dos:	Sí, ese uniforme es mío.
Estudiante uno:	Me gusta su uniforme; está muy limpio.
Estudiante dos:	¿Qué hago hoy?
Estudiante uno:	Hoy usted trabaja con el cocinero mexicano.
Estudiante dos:	¿Con Jorge? ¿Dónde está Jorge?
Estudiante uno:	Está en la cocina.
Estudiante dos:	De acuerdo. Voy a preparar las legumbres.
Estudiante uno:	Las cubetas para las legumbres están limpias.
Estudiante dos:	¿Trabaja hoy el lavaplatos cubano?
Estudiante uno:	El lavaplatos cubano no trabaja hoy.
Estudiante dos:	De acuerdo. Yo voy a lavar la cubertería también.
Estudiante uno:	Gracias Jorge. ¡Usted es un buen cocinero!

📖 QUESTIONS TO THE CLASS 📖

Answer the following questions asked by your instructor (or by another student) without looking at your textbook or any class notes:

1. ¿De quién es el uniforme blanco?
2. ¿Es el jefe de cocina amable?
3. ¿Está el bistec bien hecho o poco hecho?
4. ¿Son estos pepinos suyos?
5. ¿Son suyas estas manzanas?
6. ¿Para quién son aquellas bandejas?
7. ¿Es el cocinero rubio nicaragüense o guatemalteco?
8. ¿Cómo se llama la cajera norteamericana?
9. ¿Le gustan las manzanas verdes o las rojas?
10. ¿Es este cuchillo el mío o el suyo?

CULTURAL VIGNETTE

Hispanic people are often given more than one name, such as **José María** or **María Isabel.** All people have two last names; the first is the father's last name, and the second is the mother's. Thus, the name **Luís Díaz Martínez** indicates that Luis's father is **el señor Díaz** and that Luis's mother is **la señora Martínez.** When spoken to, Luis should be addressed as **señor Díaz** and not as **señor Martínez.** Married women often keep their maiden names, so Luis's mother would be addressed as **señora Martínez,** and his father as **señor Díaz.**

CHAPTER 6

STEM-CHANGING VERBS

"HAY QUE," "TENER QUE," "ANTES DE," "DESPUÉS DE" PLUS AN INFINITIVE

OVERVIEW

This chapter covers stem-changing verbs in Spanish. The expressions **hay que, tener que, antes de,** and **después de** followed by an infinitive are also discussed.

UNIT CONTENT

Technical Kitchen Vocabulary (II) • The Present Tense of Stem-changing Verbs • The Expression **Hay que** Plus an Infinitive • The Expression **Tener que** Plus an Infinitive • The Expressions **Antes de** and **Después de** Plus an Infinitive • Conversational Professional Interaction • Cultural Vignette

Technical Kitchen Vocabulary (II)

ham	el jamón (hah-móhn)
hamburger	la hamburguesa (ahm-boor-guéh-sah)
handle	el asa (áh-sah)
hard-boiled egg	el huevo duro (oo-éh-voh dóo-roh)
hood (kitchen)	la campana (cahm-páh-nah)
hors d'oeuvres	los hors d'oeuvres (ohrs déhvres)
ice	el hielo (ee-éh-loh)
ice cream	el helado (eh-láh-doh)
juice	el jugo (hóo-goh)
	el zumo (sóo-moh)
kettle	la marmita (mahr-mée-tah)
ladle	el cazo (cáh-soh)

lamb	el cordero (cohr-déh-roh)
lemon	el limón (lee-móhn)
lettuce	la lechuga (leh-chóo-gah)
lime	la lima (lée-mah)
liter	el litro (lée-troh)
lobster	la langosta (lahn-góhs-tah)
mayonnaise	la mayonesa (mah-yoh-néh-sah)
meat	la carne (cáhr-neh)
meatball	la albóndiga (ahl-bóhn-dee-gah)
medium done	medio hecho (*adj.*) (méh-dee-oh éh-choh)
melon	el melón (meh-lóhn)
microwave (oven)	el microondas (mee-croh-óhn-dahs)
milk	la leche (léh-cheh)
milk dispenser	el surtidor de leche (soor-tee-dóhr deh léh-cheh)
(to) mince	picar (*v.*) (pee-cáhr)
(to) mix	mezclar (*v.*) (mehs-cláhr)
mixer	la mezcladora (mehs-clah-dóh-rah)
mop	el trapeador (trah-peh-ah-dóhr)
	la fregona (freh-góh-nah)
(to) mop	trapear (*v.*) (trah-peh-áhr)
mushroom	la seta (séh-tah)
mustard	la mostaza (mohs-táh-sah)
napkin	la servilleta (sehr-vee-yéh-tah)
napkin holder	el servilletero (sehr-vee-yeh-téh-roh)
oil	el aceite (ah-séh-ee-teh)
omelet	la tortilla de huevos (tohr-tée-yah deh oo-éh-vohs)
onion	la cebolla (seh-bóh-yah)
orange	la naranja (nah-ráhn-hah)
ounce	la onza (óhn-sah)
oven	el horno (óhr-noh)
over-easy	vuelto poco hecho (*adj.*) (voo-éhl-toh póh-coh éh-choh)
oyster	la ostra (óhs-trah)
pan	la cazuela (cah-soo-éh-lah)
pancake	el panqueque (pahn-kéh-keh)
pantry	la despensa (dehs-péhn-sah)
parsley	el perejil (peh-reh-héel)
pastry	el pan dulce (pahn dóol-seh)
pastry shop	la pastelería (pahs-teh-leh-rée-ah)
pear	la pera (péh-rah)
(to) peel	pelar (*v.*) (peh-láhr)
pepper (green)	el chile verde (chée-leh véhr-deh)
pepper (red)	el chile rojo (chée-leh róh-hoh)
pepper (spice)	la pimienta (pee-mee-éhn-tah)
pepper (vegetable)	el pimiento (pee-mee-éhn-toh)
	el chile (chée-leh)

pie	el pastel (pahs-téhl)
pineapple	la piña (pée-nyah)
(to) plate	emplatar (*v.*) (ehm-plah-táhr)
(to) poach	hervir (e→ie) a fuego lento (*v*) (her-véer ah foo-éh-goh léhn-toh)
pork	el puerco (poo-éhr-coh)
	el cerdo (séhr-doh)
pot	la olla (óh-yah)
potato	la papa (páh-pah)
	la patata (pah-táh-tah)
poultry	la carne de ave (cáhr-neh deh áh-veh)
pound	la libra (lée-brah)
rag	el trapo (tráh-poh)
refrigerator	el refrigerador (reh-free-heh-rah-dóhr)
rice	el arroz (ah-rróhs)
(to) rinse	enjuagar (ehn-hoo-ah-gáhr)
roasted meat	la carne asada (cáhr-neh ah-sáh-dah)
roll	el panecillo (pah-neh-sée-yoh)
rolling pin	el rodillo (roh-dée-yoh)
rubber mat	la estera de goma (ehs-téh-rah deh góh-mah)
salad	la ensalada (ehn-sah-láh-dah)
salmon	el salmón (sahl-móhn)
salt	la sal (sahl)
sandwich	el sandwich (sáhn-oo-eech)
(to) sanitize	sanear (*v.*) (sah-neh-áhr)
sauce	la salsa (sáhl-sah)
saucer	el plato de café (pláh-toh deh cah-féh)
sausage	la salchicha (sahl-chée-chah)
(to) sauté	saltear (*v.*) (sahl-teh-áhr)
sautéed	salteado (*adj.*) (sahl-teh-áh-do)
scrambled eggs	los huevos revueltos (oo-éh-vohs reh-voo-éhl-tohs)
(to) scrub	restregar (e→ie) (*v.*) (rehs-treh-gáhr)
scrub pad	el estropajo (ehs-troh-páh-hoh)
shellfish	los mariscos (mah-rées-kohs)

EXERCISE 6.1

Match the following list of restaurant vocabulary words, practice their pronunciation, and be ready to speak them aloud:

1. *salt* _____ a. puerco

2. *(to) rinse* _____ b. setas

3. *oven* _____ c. aceite

4. *pineapple* _____ d. perejil

5. *ice cream*	_____	e. picar
6. *meatball*	_____	f. asa
7. *milk dispenser*	_____	g. cordero
8. *napkin*	_____	h. ostra
9. *onion*	_____	i. pastelería
10. *pork*	_____	j. servilleta
11. *mushrooms*	_____	k. surtidor de leche
12. *handle*	_____	l. helado
13. *oyster*	_____	m. cebolla
14. *oil*	_____	n. salchicha
15. *parsley*	_____	o. arroz
16. *pastry shop*	_____	p. enjuagar
17. *rice*	_____	q. sal
18. *(to) mince*	_____	r. piña
19. *lamb*	_____	s. albóndiga
20. *sausage*	_____	t. horno

EXERCISE 6.2

Write a sentence with each one of the following kitchen vocabulary words using the present tense:

estera de goma _____

saneador _____

carne de ave _____

arroz _____

rodillo _____

mezclar _____

naranja _____

pelar _____

servilletero _____

picado _____

EXERCISE 6.3

Translate the following English words into Spanish and learn how to pronounce them correctly:

ham _____

kitchen _____

mayonnaise _____

milk _____

mop _____

over-easy _____

pie _____

to plate _____

pot _____

roll _____

The Present Tense of Stem-Changing Verbs

🧳

Some Spanish verbs change their stems in the present tense of all persons except the first plural (**nosotros, nosotras**). After dropping the infinitive endings **ar, er, ir,** the **e** of the last syllable changes to **ie,** and **o** in the last syllable changes to **ue.** Some verbs of the third conjugation only, **ir,** may change from **e** to **i.**

- The **e** of the last syllable of the stem may change to either **ie** or **i.** For example, the verb **hervir** (*to boil*) is conjugated in the present tense as follows:

yo	hiervo
él, ella, usted	hierve
nosotros, nosotras	hervimos
ellos, ellas, ustedes	hierven

The verb **servir** (*to serve*) is conjugated in the present tense as follows:

yo	sirvo
él, ella, usted	sirve
nosotros, nosotras	servimos
ellos, ellas, ustedes	sirven

- The **o** of the last syllable of the stem changes to **ue.** For example, the verb **almorzar** (*to have lunch*) is conjugated in the present tense as follows:

yo	almuerzo
él, ella, usted	almuerza
nosotros, nosotras	almorzamos
ellos, ellas, ustedes	almuerzan

Here is a list, in alphabetical order, of some common stem-changing verbs used in hospitality activities:

almorzar	o→ue	(ahl-mohr-sáhr)	*to have lunch*
cerrar	e→ie	(seh-rráhr)	*to close*
comenzar	e→ie	(coh-mehn-sáhr)	*to begin*
contar	o→ue	(cohn-táhr)	*to count*
costar	o→ue	(cohs-táhr)	*to cost*
dormir	o→ue	(dohr-méer)	*to sleep*
empezar	e→ie	(ehm-peh-sáhr)	*to begin*
encender	e→ie	(ehn-sehn-déhr)	*to light*
encontrar	o→ue	(ehn-cohn-tráhr)	*to find*
entender	e→ie	(ehn-tehn-déhr)	*to understand*
fregar	e→ie	(freh-gáhr)	*to scrub*
hervir	e→ie	(ehr-véer)	*to boil*
mover	o→ue	(moh-véhr)	*to move*
pedir	e→i	(peh-déer)	*to ask for*
perder	e→ie	(pehr-déhr)	*to lose*
poder	o→ue	(poh-déhr)	*can*

preferir	e→ie	(preh-feh-réer)	*to prefer*
probar	o→ue	(proh-báhr)	*to taste*
querer	e→ie	(keh-réhr)	*to want*
recordar	o→ue	(reh-cohr-dáhr)	*to remember*
sentar	e→ie	(sehn-táhr)	*to seat*
servir	e→i	(sehr-véer)	*to serve*
vestir	e→i	(vehs-téer)	*to dress*
volver	o→ue	(vohl-véhr)	*to come back*

EXERCISE 6.4

Understand the meaning of the following sentences that contain stem changes and pronounce them in Spanish:

1. Jorge prefiere la comida italiana.
2. El turno de noche comienza a las diez.
3. El menú cuesta catorce dólares.
4. Nosotros cerramos el restaurante esta tarde a las seis.
5. Ese mesero no quiere trabajar el turno de mañana.
6. No recuerdo donde está Lupita ahora.
7. El cocinero vuelve à las tres.
8. Ella siempre empieza a pelar las papas a las nueve de la mañana.
9. El lavaplatos de Honduras no entiende inglés bien.

EXERCISE 6.5

Conjugate the infinitive form of the verbs given, making sure that you understand the meaning of each sentence:

1. Jorge (volver) de Costa Rica mañana. _____
2. Antonia (hervir) las papas para la cena. _____
3. Yo siempre (encontrar) los cuchillos en el almacén. _____
4. Miguel y yo no (querer) trabajar el turno de tarde. _____
5. ¿Quién (encender) el horno en la cocina? _____
6. Los cocineros no (servir) los platillos a los clientes. _____
7. Antonio siempre (perder) sus cuchillos. _____
8. Lupita (preferir) bailar salsa. _____
9. Yo no (recordar) quien trabaja mañana. _____
10. ¿Quién (querer) una cerveza? _____

EXERCISE 6.6

With a partner, ask and answer the following phrases, making sure that you understand what you are asking or answering:

Estudiante uno:	¿Quién sirve a los clientes?
Estudiante dos:	Nosotros servimos a los clientes.
Estudiante uno:	¿Cuentan los meseros las servilletas después de la cena?
Estudiante dos:	Sí, los meseros siempre cuentan las servilletas.
Estudiante uno:	¿Prueba Pedro la sopa?
Estudiante dos:	No, Jorge prueba la sopa.
Estudiante uno:	¿Encienden los meseros el horno?
Estudiante dos:	No, los cocineros encienden el horno.
Estudiante uno:	¿Entienden ustedes español?
Estudiante dos:	Sí, entendemos español e inglés bien.
Estudiante uno:	¿Cuándo cierra el restaurante?
Estudiante dos:	El restaurante cierra a las once de la noche

The Expression **Hay que** Plus an Infinitive

In Chapter 3, we learned that *there is, there are* translate into Spanish as **hay.** When this expression is followed by **que** plus an infinitive, it means *it is necessary to* or *one (we, you) must.* For example, **Hay que asar dos pollos** means *We must roast two chickens;* **Hay dos pollos en el refrigerador** means *There are two chickens in the refrigerator.*

EXERCISE 6.7

Understand the meaning of the following sentences containing the expression **hay** and **hay que** and pronounce them in Spanish:

1. Hay que trabajar mucho esta noche porque tenemos un banquete para doscientos clientes.
2. ¿Qué hay que hacer?
3. Hay que pelar papas.
4. Hay dos clientes en el restaurante.
5. No hay que limpiar la cocina esta tarde.
6. Jorge, hay que hervir treinta zanahorias.
7. No hay manteles en el almacén.
8. ¿Hay que fregar el piso en el comedor?
9. Hay que estudiar español.
10. No hay huevos en el refrigerador.

EXERCISE 6.8

In pairs, ask and answer the following phrases, making sure that you understand what you are asking or answering:

Estudiante uno:	¿Hay que hervir las legumbres ahora?
Estudiante dos:	Sí, hay que hervir las legumbres.
Estudiante uno:	¿Hay panecillos para el almuerzo?
Estudiante dos:	Sí, hay cincuenta panecillos para el almuerzo.
Estudiante uno:	¿Qué hay que hacer ahora?
Estudiante dos:	Ahora hay que limpiar la campana en la cocina.
Estudiante uno:	¿Hay huevos duros para la ensalada?
Estudiante dos:	No hay huevos duros para la ensalada.
Estudiante uno:	¿Hay limones en el almacén?
Estudiante dos:	Sí, hay muchos limones en el almacén.
Estudiante uno:	¿Hay que preparar ostras para la cena?
Estudiante dos:	Sí, hay que abrir treinta ostras.

The Expression **Tener que**
Plus an Infinitive

The idiomatic expression **tener que** plus an infinitive means *to have to* or *must*. For example, **Usted tiene que emplatar el primer plato ahora** means *You have to plate the first course now.*

EXERCISE 6.9

Understand the meaning of the following sentences that contain the expression **tener que** and pronounce them in Spanish:

1. Juan tiene que lavar los platos ahora.
2. ¿Tengo que trabajar mañana?
3. Nosotros tenemos que preparar una mesa para siete personas.
4. Lupita y Jorge tienen que lavar los vasos para el banquete.
5. ¿Quién tiene que trapear el suelo en el restaurante?
6. Miguel tiene que trapear el suelo.
7. ¿Tenemos que hervir las zanahorias a las cinco o a las seis?
8. Usted tiene que hervir el salmón a fuego lento.
9. Pedro tiene que freir el cordero con poco aceite.
10. ¿Tiene usted los cuchillos?

EXERCISE 6.10

Translate the following sentences and pronounce them in Spanish:

1. *Must we boil the celery now?* _____

2. *Do I have to come to work tomorrow?* _____

3. *Does Jorge have to serve table six?* _____

4. *Must they plate the fish on the yellow plates or on the brown plates?*
   _____

5. *Do we have to serve the water now?* _____

6. *Must Dolores clean the kitchen hood?*
   _____

7. *Who must wash the cucumbers?* _____

8. *Who has to serve the banquet?* _____

9. *Must we cut the ham now or at three o'clock?*
   _____

10. *Must I go?* _____

The Expressions **Antes de** and **Después de** Plus an Infinitive

When followed by a verb, the expressions **antes de** (*before*) and **después de** (after) require that the verb be in infinitive form. Examples: **antes de cenar** (*before having dinner*) or **después de desayunar** (*after having breakfast*).

EXERCISE 6.11

Understand the meaning of the following sentences that contain the expressions **antes de** and **después de** and pronounce them in Spanish:

1. ¿Preparo las mesas antes de trapear el piso?
2. No, después de trapear el piso.
3. Antes de cocinar, el cocinero corta las legumbres.
4. Después de cocinar, el cocinero limpia la cocina.
5. ¿Hiervo el pescado antes o después de hervir la carne de ave?
6. ¿Tenemos que freir las papas antes del almuerzo?
7. Usted tiene que freir las papas para el banquete antes de las seis.
8. Después del banquete, los cocineros limpian la cocina.
9. Después de servir el banquete, los meseros sacuden las sillas en el restaurante.
10. Antes de comenzar a trabajar, los meseros surten los aparadores.

EXERCISE 6.12

With a partner, ask and answer the following phrases, making sure that you understand what you are asking or answering:

Estudiante uno: ¿Hay que lavar los platos antes de lavar la loza?

Estudiante dos: Sí, hay que lavar los platos antes de lavar la loza.

Estudiante uno: ¿Surto los aparadores antes o después de sacudir las sillas?

Estudiante dos: Después de sacudir las sillas, por favor.

Estudiante uno: ¿Trabaja Jorge antes de ir a Nueva York?

Estudiante dos: No, Jorge trabaja después de venir de Nueva York.

Estudiante uno: ¿Debo limpiar los ceniceros después del banquete?

Estudiante dos: Sí, usted debe limpiar los ceniceros después del banquete.

Estudiante uno: ¿Cierra el restaurante antes de las ocho?

Estudiante dos: No, el restaurante cierra después de las doce.

Estudiante uno: ¿Corto las legumbres antes de cortar la carne?

Estudiante dos: No corte las legumbres antes de cortar la carne.

CONVERSATIONAL PROFESSIONAL INTERACTION

In groups of two, translate, practice, and be ready to role-play the following dialogue between a kitchen supervisor and an hourly employee:

Estudiante uno (supervisor):   ¿Quién cierra el restaurante hoy?

Estudiante dos (empleado por hora): Lupita cierra el restaurante después de trapear la cocina.

Estudiante uno: ¿Qué hace Lupita?

Estudiante dos: Lupita cuenta las servilletas y los manteles.

Estudiante uno: ¿Y Jorge, qué hace?

Estudiante dos: Jorge tiene que hervir las papas para la cena.

Estudiante uno: ¿Cuántas personas tenemos para el banquete?

Estudiante dos: Hoy tenemos cincuenta personas en el banquete.

Estudiante uno: ¿Prefieren los clientes ensalada o sopa?

Estudiante dos: Prefieren sopa antes de comer el pescado.

Estudiante uno: ¿Cuánto cuesta el banquete por persona?

Estudiante dos: El banquete cuesta diez dólares y cincuenta centavos.

Estudiante uno: ¿Quién sirve el banquete?

Estudiante dos:	Antonio y yo tenemos que servir el banquete.
Estudiante uno:	Miguel, hay que probar la sopa antes de comenzar el servicio.
Estudiante dos:	Yo siempre pruebo la sopa antes del servicio, jefe.
Estudiante uno:	Yo sé, Miguel. ¡Usted es un buen cocinero!

CULTURAL VIGNETTE

It is customary for Hispanic people to invite anyone who shows up just before or during meal times to join them at the table. This formal invitation should be rejected. If the person (or persons) really wants the caller to sit down to eat, he/she will repeat the invitation several times. It is only then when the offer should be accepted. While most Americans cut their food, put the knife down, and eat the portions holding the fork on the right hand, Spaniards and Latin Americans usually eat holding the fork in the left hand and the knife in the right hand. To indicate that one has finished eating, the silverware is placed together in the center of the plate. While eating, the host (or hostess) will insist throughout the meal that guests have extra portions of food. If they don't persistently refuse, they will automatically be served another helping.

CHAPTER 7

COMMANDS

THE CALENDAR AND DATES

OVERVIEW

Chapter 7 covers the imperative tense (commands), an important language component for hospitality managers and supervisors. This section also deals with dates in Spanish, including the days of the week and the months of the year.

UNIT CONTENT

Technical Kitchen Vocabulary (III) • Commands (Giving Orders or Advice)
• The Calendar • Days of the Week • Months of the Year •
Conversational Professional Interaction • Cultural Vignette

Technical Kitchen Vocabulary (III)

shrimp	los camarones (cah-mah-róh-nehs)
silverware	la cubertería (coo-behr-teh-rée-ah)
sink	el fregadero (freh-gah-déh-roh)
skimmer	la espumadera (ehs-poo-mah-déh-rah)
slice	la rebanada (reh-bah-náh-dah)
(to) slice	rebanar (*v.*) (reh-bah-náhr)
smoke	el humo (óo-moh)
(to) smoke	fumar (*v.*) (foo-máhr)
soap	el jabón (hah-bóhn)
soap dispenser	el distribuidor de jabón (dees-tree-boo-ee-dóhr deh hah-bóhn)
soapy water	el agua jabonosa (áh-goo-ah hah-boh-nóh-sah)
soft-boiled egg	el huevo pasado por agua (oo-éh-voh pah-sáh-doh pohr áh-goo-ah)
(to) sort	separar (*v.*) (seh-pah-ráhr)

soup	la sopa (sóh-pah)
soup plate	el plato sopero (pláh-toh soh-péh-roh)
spatula	la espátula (ehs-páh-too-lah)
(to) spill	derramar (*v.*) (deh-rrah-máhr)
spinach	las espinacas (ehs-pee-náh-cahs)
spoon	la cuchara (coo-cháh-rah)
sprayer	el rociador (roh-see-ah-dóhr)
steamer	la marmita al vapor (mahr-mée-tah ahl vah-póhr)
stew	el estofado (ehs-toh-fáh-doh)
storeroom	el almacén (ahl-mah-séhn)
strawberries	las fresas (fréh-sahs)
sugar	el azúcar (ah-sóo-cahr)
sugar packet	la bolsita de azúcar (bohlsée-tah deh ah-sóo-cahr
sunny side up	yema no hecha (*adj.*) (yéh-mah noh éh-chah)
(to) sweep	barrer (*v.*) (bah-rréhr)
tea	el té (teh)
tea bag	la bolsita de té (bohl-sée-tah deh teh)
teaspoon	la cucharilla (coo-chah-rée-yah)
temperature	la temperatura (tehm-peh-rah-tóo-rah)
(to) thaw	descongelar (*v.*) (dehs-cohn-heh-láhr)
toast	la tostada (tohs-táh-dah)
(to) toast	tostar (o→ue) (*v.*) (tohs-táhr)
toasted	tostado (*adj.*) (tohs-táh-doh)
toaster	la tostadora (tohs-tah-dóh-rah)
tomato	el tomate (toh-máh-teh)
tomato sauce	la salsa de tomate (sáhl-sah deh toh-máh-teh)
tongs	las pinzas (péen-sahs)
trash	la basura (bah-sóo-rah)
tuna fish	el atún (ah-tóon)
turkey	el pavo (páh-voh)
veal	la ternera (tehr-néh-rah)
vegetables	las legumbres (leh-góom-brehs)
	las verduras (vehr-dóo-rahs)
vinegar	el vinagre (vee-náh-greh)
walk-in freezer	la cámara congeladora (cáh-mah-rah cohn-heh-lah-dóh-rah)
walk-in refrigerator	la cámara fría (cáh-mah-rah frée-ah)
warm	caliente (*adj.*) (cah-lee-éhn-teh)
(to) wash	lavar (*v.*) (lah-váhr)
watermelon	la sandía (sahn-dée-ah)
well done	bien hecho (*adj.*) (bee-éhn éh-choh)
(to) whip	batir (*v.*) (bah-téer)
white wine	el vino blanco (vée-noh bláhn-coh)
wire whip	el batidor (bah-tée-dohr)
(to) wrap	envolver (o→ue) (*v.*) (ehn-vohl-véhr)
wringer	el escurridor (ehs-coo-rree-dóhr)

EXERCISE 7.1

Match the following list of restaurant vocabulary words, practice their pronunciation, and be ready to speak them aloud:

1. *wire whip* _____ a. descongelar
2. *soup plate* _____ b. fregadero
3. *sugar packet* _____ c. escurridor
4. *soft-boiled egg* _____ d. almacén
5. *warm* _____ e. ternera
6. *turkey* _____ f. cámara congeladora
7. *well done* _____ g. atún
8. *shrimp* _____ h. separar
9. *(to) spill* _____ i. distribuidor de jabón
10. *strawberries* _____ j. sopa
11. *storeroom* _____ k. bolsita de azúcar
12. *(to) thaw* _____ l. caliente
13. *tuna fish* _____ m. bien hecho
14. *wringer* _____ n. pavo
15. *sink* _____ o. camarones
16. *soap dispenser* _____ p. plato sopero
17. *(to) sort* _____ q. derramar
18. *soup* _____ r. batidor
19. *veal* _____ s. fresas
20. *walk-in freezer* _____ t. huevo pasado por agua

Commands (Giving Orders or Advice)

Because of the usually formal boss–worker relationship, all commands presented in this book correspond to **usted** and **ustedes**. Commands corresponding to the more familiar **tú** and **vosotros** form and to the **nosotros** and **nosotras** forms are not covered.

Most verbs form the imperative (command) from the first person singular (**yo**) of the present tense. The **o** is dropped, and the following endings are added:

"ar" verbs				Command
Change the **o** to **e**	Example:	hablar (*to speak*)	yo hablo	hable
		pelar (*to peel*)	yo pelo	pele
"er" verbs				
Change the **o** to **a**	Example:	comer (*to eat*)	yo como	coma
		beber (*to drink*)	yo bebo	beba

"ir" verbs

Change the **o** to **a**   Example: surtir (*to stock*)   yo surto   surta

                                            servir (*to serve*)   yo sirvo   sirva

In all cases, to advise or tell someone *not* to do something, **no** is placed before the command. For example: **no hable—no coma—no surta.**

Plural commands (ordering something to more than one person) are formed by adding the letter **n** to the singular command—for example: **hablen—coman— no surtan.**

A few common verbs have irregular command forms:

dar	(*to give*)	dé—den
estar	(*to be*)	esté—estén
ir	(*to go*)	vaya—vayan
ser	(*to be*)	sea—sean

Stem-changing verbs require a stem change when they are used in the imperative mode. Example: **Empiecen a trabajar ahora,** *Start working now.*

In the workplace, commands should be accompanied by the expression **por favor** (*please*). Example: **Por favor, empiecen a trabajar ahora.**

EXERCISE 7.2

Understand the meaning of the following command sentences used in dining room settings and pronounce them in Spanish:

1. Jorge, por favor prepare una mesa para seis personas.
2. Lupita, por favor tome la comanda de la mesa número cinco.
3. Sacudan las sillas antes del almuerzo.
4. No fumen en el restaurante.
5. Juan, sirva las bebidas ahora.
6. Rellene los vasos con limonada.
7. No venga a trabajar mañana.
8. Traiga las chuletas para el banquete, por favor.
9. Surta los aparadores.
10. Barra el piso después de cerrar el comedor.

EXERCISE 7.3

Understand the meaning of the following command sentences used in kitchen settings and pronounce them in Spanish:

1. Antonio, por favor lave la cubertería para la cena.
2. No fume en la cocina.
3. Emplate las chuletas ahora.

4. No ponga los tenedores limpios en la cubeta.

5. Traiga el pescado del almacén.

6. Envuelva dos bistecs para el señor Gómez.

7. Lave la cristalería sucia.

8. Tueste dos rebanadas de pan blanco.

9. Descogele la carne de res para la cena.

10. No derrame la sopa.

EXERCISE 7.4

With a partner, answer the following questions first with a positive and then with a negative, command:
Example: **¿Pelo las peras? Sí, pele las peras; no pele las peras.**

1. ¿Lavo los platos?

2. ¿Frío el pescado?

3. ¿Pongo la mesa?

4. ¿Tengo que cerrar el restaurante?

5. ¿Pelo las papas antes del almuerzo?

6. ¿Puedo hablar con el jefe de cocina?

7. ¿Hago el café para el banquete?

8. ¿Sirvo la fruta a la mesa siete?

9. ¿Pongo la basura en el vertedero?

10. ¿Hay que preparar las ensaladas?

EXERCISE 7.5

Use the correct plural command form (you are talking to more than one person):

1. (separar) la cristalería de la cubertería. _____

2. (asar) las chuletas de cordero ahora. _____

3. (hacer) cincuenta sandwiches de jamón. _____

4. (restregar) las ollas con estropajo y agua jabonosa._____

5. (picar) el perejil para la sopa. _____

6. (freir) los tomates con mucho aceite. _____

7. (cortar) las naranjas en rodajas. _____

8. (hervir) veinticuatro huevos en la marmita grande. _____

9. (servir) el helado de fresa. _____

10. (poner) el salmón en el congelador. _____

EXERCISE 7.6

In pairs, ask and answer the following phrases, making sure that you
understand what you are asking or answering:

Estudiante uno:	¿Surto la estación de servicio ahora?
Estudiante dos:	Sí, surta la estación de servicio antes del almuerzo.
Estudiante uno:	¿Tengo que rellenar los vasos con agua y cubitos de hielo?
Estudiante dos:	No rellene los vasos ahora; por favor, rellene los azucareros.
Estudiante uno:	¿Separo la loza de la cristalería?
Estudiante dos:	Sí, separe la loza de la cubertería en las cubetas.
Estudiante uno:	¿Hago té frío?
Estudiante dos:	Sí, y corte rodajas de limón también.
Estudiante uno:	¿Llevo el trapeador al restaurante?
Estudiante dos:	No, lleve el trapeador a la cocina.
Estudiante uno:	¿Pongo las fresas en los tazones?
Estudiante dos:	No ponga las fresas en los tazones.

EXERCISE 7.7

With a partner, ask and answer the following phrases, making sure that you
understand what you are asking or answering:

Estudiante uno:	¿Tenemos que poner las ensaladas en el refrigerador?
Estudiante dos:	Sí, lleve las ensaladas al refrigerador.
Estudiante uno:	¿Corto la sandía para el banquete?
Estudiante dos:	No corte la sandía, por favor; corte las peras en rodajas.
Estudiante uno:	¿Tengo que mezclar la harina con la leche?
Estudiante dos:	Sí, mezcle la harina con la leche y los huevos.
Estudiante uno:	¿Aso la carne a 450 grados?
Estudiante dos:	No, ase la carne a 300 grados.
Estudiante uno:	¿Frío la masa ahora?
Estudiante dos:	Sí, fría la masa para la cena.
Estudiante uno:	¿Seco los platos?
Estudiante dos:	No seque los platos; seque la cubertería primero.

The Calendar

To ask the date, the following questions can be used:

¿Qué día es hoy?	*What day of the week is today?*
¿Cuál es la fecha?	*What is the date?*

¿Qué fecha es hoy?   *What is today's date?*

¿A cómo estamos hoy?   *What is the day of the month?*

Calendar Vocabulary
🧳

anoche (ah-nóh-cheh)	*last night*
el año (áh-nyoh)	*year*
ayer (ah-yéhr)	*yesterday*
el cumpleaños (coom-pleh-áh-nyohs)	*birthday*
el día (dée-ah)	*day*
el día libre (dée-ah lée-breh)	*day off*
la fecha de nacimiento (féh-chah deh nah-see-mee-éhn-toh)	*date of birth*
el fin de semana (feen deh seh-máh-nah)	*the weekend*
esta mañana, tarde, noche (éhs-tah mah-nyáh-nah, táhr-deh, nóh-cheh)	*this morning, afternoon, evening/night*
hoy (óh-ee)	*today*
mañana (mah-nyáh-nah)	*tomorrow*
mañana por la mañana (mah-nyáh-nah pohr lah mah-nyáh-nah)	*tomorrow morning*
el mes (mehs)	*month*
el minuto (mee-nóo-toh)	*minute*
pasado mañana (pah-sáh-doh mah-nyáh-nah)	*the day after tomorrow*
por la mañana (pohr lah mah-nyáh-nah)	*in the morning*
por la noche (pohr lah nóh-cheh)	*in the evening—at night*
por la tarde (pohr lah táhr-deh)	*in the afternoon*
la semana (seh-máh-nah)	*week*
la semana que viene (seh-máh-nah keh vee-éh-neh)	*next week*
el tiempo (tee-éhm-poh)	*time*
todos los días (tóh-dohs lohs dée-ahs)	*everyday*
las vacaciones (vah-cah-see-óh-nehs)	*vacations*

Days of the Week
🧳

The days of the week (**los días de la semana**) in Spanish are masculine. On Hispanic calendars, the week begins on Monday. To express *on* with days of the week, the articles **el** or **los** are used. Examples: **Trabajo el lunes** (*I work on Monday*), **Pepe no trabaja los sábados** (*Pepe doesn't work on Saturdays*). In Spanish, the days of the week are not capitalized.

lunes (lóo-nehs)	*Monday*
martes (máhr-tehs)	*Tuesday*

miércoles (mee-éhr-coh-lehs)   *Wednesday*
jueves (hoo-éh-vehs)   *Thursday*
viernes (vee-éhr-nehs)   *Friday*
sábado (sáh-bah-doh)   *Saturday*
domingo (doh-méen-goh)   *Sunday*

EXERCISE 7.8

Understand the meaning of the following sentences and pronounce them in Spanish:

1. Trabajo de lunes a viernes pero no trabajo el sábado o el domingo.
2. ¿Qué día es hoy?
3. ¿Qué hace usted los fines de semana?
4. ¿Trabaja Lupita el jueves?
5. No, Lupita no trabaja el jueves; trabaja el miércoles por la mañana.
6. ¿Cuándo trabaja Lupita el miércoles?
7. Lupita trabaja el miércoles por la tarde.
8. ¿Cuándo tenemos el banquete?
9. El banquete es el domingo por la noche.
10. ¿Cuándo es su día libre? Mi día libre es el viernes.

EXERCISE 7.9

Answer the following questions in Spanish using a day of the week:

1. ¿Qué días de la semana trabajo? _____
2. ¿Cierra el restaurante los domingos? _____
3. ¿Cuál es mi día libre?_____
4. ¿Qué día tenemos el banquete? _____
5. ¿Qué días sacude Lupita las sillas en el restaurante? _____
6. ¿Es lunes hoy? _____
7. ¿Va Jorge a Boston el lunes? _____
8. ¿Qué días trabaja usted? _____
9. ¿Hay un banquete el miércoles? _____
10. ¿Es su día libre el jueves? _____

EXERCISE 7.10

In pairs, ask and answer the following phrases, making sure that you understand what you are asking or answering:

Estudiante uno: ¿Qué día limpiamos el almacén?
Estudiante dos: Limpiamos el almacén los lunes.

Estudiante uno:	¿Cuándo preparamos las ensaladas para la semana?
Estudiante dos:	Preparamos las ensaladas los lunes y viernes.
Estudiante uno:	¿Cuándo limpiamos la cocina a fondo?
Estudiante dos:	Limpiamos la cocina a fondo los domingos por la noche.
Estudiante uno:	¿Trabajo el sábado que viene?
Estudiante dos:	No, usted no trabaja este fin de semana.
Estudiante uno:	¿Cuándo frío el pescado?
Estudiante dos:	Fría el pescado mañana por la mañana.
Estudiante uno:	¿Cuándo es mi día libre?
Estudiante dos:	Usted no tiene día libre esta semana.

Months of the Year (los meses del año)

The days of the month are designated by cardinal numbers (**dos, cinco, doce**) except for the first, which is ordinal: **primero** (pree-méh-roh). Examples: **el primero de enero, el dos de febrero.** In Spanish, the months of the year are not capitalized. Thousands are not represented in multiples of hundreds; *nineteen ninety-nine* is translated as **mil novecientos noventa y nueve.** The preposition **de** normally appears twice in a complete date—for example, **Hoy es el doce de diciembre de dos mil seis** (*Today is December 12, 2006*).

el año (áh-nyoh)	*year*
el mes (mehs)	*month*
enero (eh-néh-roh)	*January*
febrero (feh-bréh-roh)	*February*
marzo (máhr-soh)	*March*
abril (ah-bréel)	*April*
mayo (máh-yoh)	*May*
junio (hóo-nee-oh)	*June*
julio (hóo-lee-oh)	*July*
agosto (ah-góhs-toh)	*August*
septiembre (sehp-tee-éhm-breh)	*September*
octubre (ohk-tóo-breh)	*October*
noviembre (noh-vee-éhm-breh)	*November*
diciembre (dee-see-éhm-breh)	*December*

EXERCISE 7.11

Understand the meaning of the following sentences and pronounce them in Spanish:

1. ¿Cuál es la fecha de hoy?
2. Hoy es el veinte de enero.
3. Empiezo a trabajar en el Hotel Royal el cinco de marzo.
4. El cinco de mayo tenemos un banquete para doscientas personas.
5. El restaurante cierra el veinticinco de diciembre.
6. El restaurante abre el veintisiete de diciembre.
7. Mi fecha de nacimiento es el cuatro de abril de mil novecientos ochenta y ocho.
8. Mi cumpleaños es el veintiocho de agosto.
9. El primero de mayo voy a Baltimore.
10. ¿En qué mes es su cumpleaños?

EXERCISE 7.12

In pairs, ask and answer the following phrases, making sure that you understand what you are asking or answering:

Estudiante uno:	¿Cuándo es su cumpleaños?
Estudiante dos:	Mi cumpleaños es el —————.
Estudiante uno:	¿Cuál es su fecha de nacimiento?
Estudiante dos:	Mi fecha de nacimiento es el —— de —— de ——.
Estudiante uno:	¿En qué mes estamos?
Estudiante dos:	Estamos en —————.
Estudiante uno:	¿Qué fecha es hoy?
Estudiante dos:	Hoy es el ————— de —————.
Estudiante uno:	¿Cuándo es el banquete?
Estudiante dos:	El banquete es el jueves por la noche.
Estudiante uno:	¿Cuándo es mi día libre?
Estudiante dos:	Su día libre es el miércoles.

EXERCISE 7.13

Translate the following sentences into Spanish:

1. *My date of birth is November 3, 1987.* _____
2. *My dad's date of birth is July 1, 1960.* _____
3. *Lupita's birthday is October 10.*

4. *Lupita's date of birth is December 3, 1979.*

_____

5. *I go to Venezuela on August 9.*

_____

6. *The banquet is on March 5.*

_____

7. *The restaurant closes from December 27 to January 3.*

_____

8. *My vacation is from July 5 to July 19.*

_____

9. *I don't go on vacation in May.*

_____

10. *Jorge begins his vacation on November 1.*

_____

Las estaciones del año

las estaciones (ehs-tah-see-óh-nehs)   *seasons*
la primavera (pree-mah-véh-rah)   *spring*
el verano (veh-ráh-noh)   *summer*
el otoño (oh-tóh-nyoh)   *fall*
el invierno (een-vee-éhr-noh)   *winter*

EXERCISE 7.14

Understand the meaning of the following sentences and pronounce them in Spanish:

1. ¿Cuántas estaciones tiene el año?
2. Me gusta mucho la primavera.
3. Pepe trabaja esta primavera en Acapulco.
4. En el otoño voy a estudiar alemán.
5. El invierno próximo voy a ir a Nicaragua.
6. ¿Qué estación del año le gusta?
7. No me gusta el invierno.
8. Los veranos trabajo en la cocina del hotel Regis.
9. En el otoño limpio mi casa a fondo.
10. Los meseros mexicanos no vienen esta primavera a San Mateo.

CONVERSATIONAL PROFESSIONAL INTERACTION

In groups of two, translate, practice, and be ready to role-play the following dialogue between a kitchen supervisor and an hourly employee:

Estudiante uno (supervisor):   ¡Hóla, Miguel! ¿Qué días trabaja usted esta semana?

Estudiante dos: (Empleado por hora):   Buenos días, Dolores. Trabajo de lunes a viernes.

Estudiante uno: Bien. Por favor, prepare la cocina para el desayuno.

Estudiante dos: ¿Qué tengo que hacer?

Estudiante uno: Primero, bata doce huevos para hacer huevos revueltos, ponga el tocino en las bandejas y encienda el horno a trescientos grados.

Estudiante dos: De acuerdo. ¿Quién prepara las legumbres para el almuerzo?

Estudiante uno: Yo voy a cortar las zanahorias y hervir las papas.

Estudiante dos: También hay que picar la carne para las hamburguesas y hacer la sopa.

Estudiante uno: Miguel, ¿cuál es su fecha de nacimiento?

Estudiante dos: Mi fecha de nacimiento es el diez y seis de septiembre de mil novecientos ochenta y seis.

Estudiante uno: Yo tengo mi cumpleaños también en septiembre.

Estudiante dos: ¿Sí? ¿Qué día en septiembre?

Estudiante uno: El cinco. Este año el cinco de septiembre es miércoles.

Estudiante dos: ¿Va usted a trabajar ese día?

Estudiante uno: No, voy a tener ese día libre.

Estudiante dos: El tocino está listo. Ahora voy a mezclar harina y leche para hacer panqueques.

Estudiante uno: Bien, Miguel. Usted trabaja muy rápido. Me gusta trabajar con usted.

📋 QUESTIONS TO THE CLASS 📋

Answer the following questions asked by your instructor (or by another student) without looking at your textbook or any class notes:

1. ¿Quién prepara la cocina esta tarde?
2. ¿Tomo la orden de la mesa cinco?
3. ¿Descongelamos los pollos ahora?
4. ¿Qué días trabajo la semana próxima?
5. ¿Le gusta a usted el verano?
6. ¿Cuándo es su cumpleaños?
7. ¿Cuál es su fecha de nacimiento?
8. ¿Cuál es la fecha de nacimiento de su hermano Jorge?
9. ¿Trabaja usted los fines de semana?
10. ¿Puede usted venir a trabajar el lunes y martes?

CULTURAL VIGNETTE

Kitchen workers who come from outside of North America may have a difficult time understanding the temperature required to cook and refrigerate foods. This is because most countries measure temperature in Centigrade (Celsius), not in Fahrenheit degrees. Kitchen supervisors should teach new workers to convert temperatures from Centigrade to Fahrenheit, and vice versa:

- To convert to Fahrenheit: multiply Centigrade degrees by 1.8 and add 32.
- To convert to Centigrade: subtract 32 from Fahrenheit degrees and divide by 1.8.

PART THREE

HOUSEKEEPING OPERATIONS

CHAPTER 8

REFLEXIVE VERBS

"HACE" WITH TIME AND WEATHER EXPRESSIONS

THE WEATHER

OVERVIEW

Chapter 8 deals with Spanish verbs that are used to indicate that the action of the verb is done to the subject. These verbs are particularly difficult for native English-speaking students because they do not correspond to English verbs and sentence structure. This section also covers **hace** with time and weather expressions and lists the most common weather terms.

UNIT CONTENT

Technical Housekeeping Vocabulary (I)   •   The Present Tense of Reflexive Verbs   •   Reflexive Verbs and Commands   •   **Hace** with Time and Weather Expressions   •   The Weather   •   Conversational Professional Interaction   •   Cultural Vignette

Technical Housekeeping Vocabulary (I)

air vent	la rejilla (reh-hée-yah)
A.M. report	el reporte de mañana (reh-póhr-teh deh mah-nyáh-nah)
(to) announce	anunciar (v.) (ah-noon-see-áhr)
armchair	el sillón (see-yóhn)
(to) arrive	llegar (v.) (yeh-gáhr)

ashes	las cenizas (seh-née-sahs)
ashtray	el cenicero (seh-nee-séh-roh)
assistant	el/la asistente (ah-sees-téhn-teh)
attendant (room)	el/la camarista (cah-mah-rées-tah)
babysitter	la niñera (nee-nyéh-rah)
balcony	la terraza (teh-rráh-sah)
basement	el sótano (sóh-tah-noh)
bath mat	el tapete de baño (tah-péh-teh deh báh-nyoh)
bathroom	el baño (báh-nyoh)
bath soap	el jabón de baño (hah-bóhn deh báh-nyoh)
bath towel	la toalla de baño (toh-áh-yah deh báh-nyoh)
bathtub	la bañera (bah-nyéh-rah)
	la tina (tée-nah)
bed	la cama (cáh-mah)
bed linen	los blancos (bláhn-cohs)
bed spread	el cobertor (coh-béhr-tohr)
blackboard	el pizarrón (pee-sah-rróhn)
blanket	la manta (máhn-tah)
	la cobija (coh-bée-hah)
bleach	la lejía (leh-hée-ah)
blocked (room)	bloqueado (*adj.*) (bloh-keh-áh-doh)
bottle opener	el destapador (dehs-tah-pah-dóhr)
bottom sheet	la sábana bajera (sáh-bah-nah bah-héh-rah)
broom	la escoba (ehs-cóh-bah)
brush	el cepillo (seh-pée-yoh)
(to) brush	cepillar (*v.*) (seh-pee-yáhr)
bucket	el balde (báhl-deh)
	el cubo (cóo-boh)
button	el botón (boh-tóhn)
candle	la vela (véh-lah)
carpet	la alfombra (ahl-fóhm-brah)
cart (maid)	el carro de servicio (cáh-rroh deh sehr-vée-see-oh)
ceiling	el techo (téh-choh)
chair	la silla (sée-yah)
(to) check	comprobar (o→ue) (*v.*) (cohm-proh-báhr)
checkout	la salida (sah-lée-dah)
checkout room	el cuarto de salida (coo-áhr-toh deh sah-lée-dah)
cigarette butt	la colilla (coh-lée-yah)
(to) clean	limpiar (*v.*) (leem-pee-áhr)
clean	limpio (*adj.*) (léem-pee-oh)
clean linen	la ropa limpia (róh-pah léem-pee-ah)
cleaning powder	el polvo limpiador (póhl-voh leem-pee-ah-dóhr)
cleaning supplies	los suministros de limpieza (soo-mee-nées-trohs deh leem-pee-éh-sah)
(to) close	cerrar (e→ie) (*v.*) (seh-rráhr)
closed	cerrado (*adj.*) (seh-rráh-doh)

closet	el closet (clóh-seht)
comment card	la tarjeta de comentarios (tahr-héh-tah deh coh-mehn-táh-ree-ohs)
cot	la cama portátil (cáh-mah pohr-táh-teel)
couch	el sofá (soh-fáh)
counter	el mostrador (mohs-trah-dóhr)
courteous	cortés (adj.) (cohr-téhs)
crib	la cuna (cóo-nah)
curtain	la cortina (cohr-tée-nah)
cushion	el cojín (coh-héen)
(to) deep clean	limpiar a fondo (v.) (leem-pee-áhr ah fóhn-doh)
deodorant	el desodorante (deh-soh-doh-ráhn-teh)
department	el departamento (deh-pahr-tah-méhn-toh)
department meeting	la junta de departamento (hóon-tah deh deh-pahr-tah-méhn-toh)
departure room	el cuarto de salida (coo-áhr-toh deh sah-lée-dah)
(to) de-stain	desmanchar (v.) (dehs-mahn-cháhr)
desk	el escritorio (ehs-cree-tóh-ree-oh)
detergent	el detergente (deh-tehr-héhn-teh)
dirt	la mugre (móo-greh)
	la suciedad (soo-see-eh-dáhd)
dirty	sucio (adj.) (sóo-see-oh)
dishwasher (person/ machine)	el lavaplatos (lah-vah-pláh-tohs)
disinfectant	el desinfectante (deh-seen-fehc-táhn-teh)
do not disturb sign	la tarjeta de no molestar (tahr-héh-tah deh noh moh-lehs-táhr)
door	la puerta (poo-éhr-tah)
door stopper	el tope de puerta (tóh-peh deh poo-éhr-tah)
drain	el desagüe (deh-sáh-goo-eh)
(to) draw the curtain	correr la cortina (v.) (coh-rréhr lah cohr-tée-nah)
drawer	el cajón (cah-hóhn)
dresser	el tocador (toh-cah-dóhr)
(to) dry clean	limpiar a seco (v.) (leem-pee-áhr ah séh-coh)
dry cleaning	la limpieza a seco (leem-pee-éh-sah ah séh-coh)
dryer	la secadora (seh-cah-dóh-rah)
dust	el polvo (póhl-voh)
(to) dust	sacudir (v.) (sah-coo-déer)
	desempolvar (v.) (deh-sehm-pohl-váhr)
dustpan	el recogedor (reh-coh-heh-dóhr)
elevator	el elevador (eh-leh-vah-dóhr)
	el ascensor (ahs-sehn-sóhr)
entrance	la entrada (ehn-tráh-dah)

envelope (letter)	el sobre (sóh-breh)
empty	vacío (*adj.*) (vah-sée-oh)
(to) empty	vaciar (*v.*) (vah-see-áhr)
executive housekeeper	el/la ama de llaves (áh-mah deh yáh-vehs)
facial tissue	pañuelos de papel (pah-nyoo-éh-lohs deh pah-péhl)

EXERCISE 8.1

Match the following list of hotel vocabulary words, practice their pronunciation, and be ready to speak them aloud:

1. *envelope*	_____	a. sucio
2. *dresser*	_____	b. elevador
3. *cot*	_____	c. cuna
4. *cigarette butt*	_____	d. escritorio
5. *bottom sheet*	_____	e. carro de servicio
6. *bedspread*	_____	f. silla
7. *bath mat*	_____	g. toalla de baño
8. *executive housekeeper*	_____	h. desagüe
9. *dryer*	_____	i. recogedor
10. *drawer*	_____	j. tapete de baño
11. *chair*	_____	k. cobertor
12. *dustpan*	_____	l. cajón
13. *elevator*	_____	m. cama portátil
14. *crib*	_____	n. colilla
15. *desk*	_____	o. sábana bajera
16. *cart*	_____	p. sobre
17. *drain*	_____	q. secadora
18. *dirty*	_____	r. ama de llaves
19. *bath towel*	_____	s. puerta
20. *door*	_____	t. tocador

The Present Tense of Reflexive Verbs

Some Spanish verbs are used to indicate that the action (of the verb) is done to the subject; these verbs are called reflexive and must be used with a reflexive pronoun. If the infinitive of a verb has the suffix **se** attached (i.e., the verb ends in **se**), the verb is reflexive. For example, the verbs **levantarse** (*to get up*) and **ducharse** (*to* *take a shower*) are reflexive verbs. A reflexive verb must be used with the following "reflexive pronouns":

me (meh)	to be used with yo
se (seh)	to be used with él, ella, usted
nos (nohs)	to be used with nosotros, nosotras
se (seh)	to be used with ellos, ellas, ustedes

Reflexive pronouns always go before the verb in all forms, except the infinitive and affirmative commands where they are placed directly on the end of the verb. The present tense of **levantarse** is:

yo me levanto	*I get up*
él, ella, usted se levanta	*he, she, you gets up*
nosotros, nosotras nos levantamos	*we get up*
ellos, ellas, ustedes se levantan	*they, you get up*

List of Common Reflexive Verbs

acostarse (o→ue)	(ah-cohs-táhr-seh)	*to go to bed*
afeitarse	(ah-feh-ee-táhr-seh)	*to shave*
cepillarse	(seh-pee-yáhr-seh)	*to brush (one's hair or teeth)*
despertarse (e→ie)	(dehs-pehr-táhr-seh)	*to wake up*
divertirse (e→ie)	(dee-vehr-téer-seh)	*to have fun*
dormirse (o→ue)	(dohr-méer-seh)	*to fall asleep*
ducharse	(doo-cháhr-seh)	*to take a shower*
irse	(éer-seh)	*to go away*
lavarse	(lah-váhr-seh)	*to wash oneself*
levantarse	(leh-vahn-táhr-seh)	*to get up*
llamarse	(yah-máhr-seh)	*to be called (one's name)*
peinarse	(peh-ee-náhr-seh)	*to comb/brush (one's hair)*
ponerse	(poh-néhr-seh)	*to put on (clothes/hat/shoes)* *to start doing something*
quitarse	(kee-táhr-seh)	*to take off (clothes/hat/shoes)*
reunirse	(reh-oo-néer-seh)	*to meet/get together*
secarse	(seh-cáhr-seh)	*to dry off*
sentarse (e→ie)	(sehn-táhr-seh)	*to sit down*
vestirse	(vehs-téer-seh)	*to get dressed*

EXERCISE 8.2

In pairs, ask and answer the following phrases with reflexive verbs, making sure that you understand what you are asking or answering:

Estudiante uno:	¿A qué hora se levanta usted?
Estudiante dos:	Me levanto a las ——.
Estudiante uno:	¿Se ducha usted antes del trabajo?
Estudiante dos:	Sí, siempre me ducho antes de trabajar.
Estudiante uno:	¿A qué hora se va usted al hotel?
Estudiante dos:	Me voy a las ocho y media.
Estudiante uno:	¿Se lavan los meseros las manos después de comer?
Estudiante dos:	Sí, ellos se lavan las manos después de comer.
Estudiante uno:	¿A qué hora se reunen ustedes hoy con el jefe de cocina.
Estudiante dos:	Hoy nos reunimos con él a las diez y cuarto.
Estudiante uno:	¿Se divierte usted cuando sale con sus amigos?
Estudiante dos:	Yo siempre me divierto con mis amigos.

EXERCISE 8.3

Understand the meaning of the following sentences and pronounce them in Spanish:

1. Yo me reúno con el jefe de departamento esta tarde a las dos.
2. Yo siempre me despierto a las seis de la mañana.
3. La camarista mexicana se llama Lupita.
4. ¿Cómo se llama usted?
5. Jorge no se acuesta antes de las once de la noche.
6. ¿A qué hora se acuesta usted los fines de semana?
7. Juan no se ducha en la tarde; se ducha por la mañana antes de trabajar.
8. La ama de llaves se pone su uniforme blanco.
9. ¿Lupita, se cepilla usted los dientes (dee-éhn-tehs) (*teeth*) después de desayunar?
10. Nosotros siempre nos cepillamos los dientes después de cenar.

EXERCISE 8.4

Compose statements and form questions with the reflexive verbs provided, using the subjects given on the same line. Example:

cepillarse los dientes   nosotros

Nosotros nos cepillamos los dientes—¿Nos cepillamos los dientes nosotros?

levantarse	la camarista argentina
reunirse	Jorge y Lupita

dormirse	Pepe
llamarse	ustedes
despertarse	usted
ponerse	ellas
secarse	el lavaplatos
vestirse	yo
divertirse	los amigos

EXERCISE 8.5

With a partner, ask and answer the following phrases with reflexive verbs, making sure that you understand what you are asking or answering:

Estudiante uno:	¿Cómo se llama aquella camarista?
Estudiante dos:	Se llama Lupita.
Estudiante uno:	¿Se lava usted las manos con jabón?
Estudiante dos:	Sí, siempre me lavo las manos con jabón.
Estudiante uno:	¿Se afeita usted por la mañana o por la tarde?
Estudiante dos:	Yo siempre me afeito antes de ir al trabajo.
Estudiante uno:	¿Cuándo se va para Mexico?
Estudiante dos:	Me voy el martes que viene.
Estudiante uno:	¿Se cepilla usted el pelo?
Estudiante dos:	No, yo me peino; no me cepillo.
Estudiante uno:	¿A qué hora se levanta usted?
Estudiante dos:	Yo me levanto antes de las siete de la mañana.

Reflexive Verbs and Commands

In affirmative commands, the corresponding reflexive pronoun is attached to the command. For example, **Dúchese antes de trabajar** or **Siéntense, por favor.** In negative commands, the corresponding reflexive pronoun is placed between the negative (**no/nunca**) and the command. For example, **No se duche antes de trabajar** or **No se sienten, por favor.**

EXERCISE 8.6

Understand the meaning of the following commands and pronounce them in Spanish:

1. Lávese las manos después de ir al baño.
2. Levántese de la silla, por favor.
3. Séquense las manos.
4. Póngase su uniforme.
5. Dúchense antes de trabajar.
6. Diviértase esta tarde.
7. Quítese el uniforme ahora.
8. Váyase de la cocina.
9. Péinese.
10. Reúnase con la ama de llaves esta mañana a las diez.

EXERCISE 8.7

In pairs, one student gives the following commands while the other translates their meaning:

1. Por favor, dúchese antes de venir al trabajo.
2. Váyase de la cocina ahora.
3. Péinese, por favor.
4. Levántese de la silla.
5. Reúnase con Jorge en la cafetería de empleados.
6. Quítese el delantal, por favor.
7. Lávese las manos con jabón antes de comenzar a cocinar.
8. Séquese las manos con aquella toalla.
9. Diviértanse.
10. ¡Póngase a trabajar ahorita!

EXERCISE 8.8

Understand the meaning of the following commands and pronounce them in Spanish:

1. No se seque las manos con la servilleta.
2. No se vaya antes de las dos.
3. Levántense, por favor.
4. No se quiten el uniforme.
5. No se vistan en el almacén.
6. No se laven las manos en el fregadero.
7. Por favor, no se reúnan aquí.
8. No se peinen en el restaurante.
9. No se levanten, por favor.
10. No se vayan antes de trapear el piso.

EXERCISE 8.9

Translate the following negative commands into Spanish. Address them to one person and then to two or more persons:

1. *Don't get dressed until 8:30.* _____

   _____

2. *Don't dry your hands with the guests' towels.* _____

   _____

3. *Don't go away, please.* _____
4. *Don't take off your uniform!* _____
5. *Don't brush your hair here!* _____
6. *Don't take a shower now.* _____
7. *Don't meet today; we have two hundred checkouts.* _____

   _____

8. *Don't wash yourself in the storeroom, please!* _____

   _____

9. *Don't go to bed on this couch!* _____
10. *Don't get up, please!* _____

Reflexive Verbs as "Second Verb" in a Sentence

Reflexive pronouns may go before the first verb when the reflexive infinitive is second in a sentence, or it may be attached to the infinitive reflexive. Example: **Me voy a lavar las manos** or **Voy a lavarme las manos** (*I am going to wash my hands*).

EXERCISE 8.10

Understand the meaning of the following sentences and pronounce them in Spanish. (Note that the reflexive verbs are second in the sentence.)

1. ¿Quiere usted lavarse las manos?
2. ¿Se quiere usted lavar las manos?
3. Preferimos sentarnos ahora.
4. No me quiero duchar en el hotel.
5. Me tengo que ir antes de las cuatro.
6. Tengo que irme antes de las cuatro.
7. Jorge y Lupita necesitan irse antes de las dos.
8. Ellos tienen que ponerse sus uniformes antes del banquete.
9. Ellos se tienen que poner sus uniformes antes del banquete.
10. ¿Se tiene usted que ir?

EXERCISE 8.11

With a partner ask and answer the following phrases with reflexive verbs, making sure that you understand what you are asking or answering:

Estudiante uno: ¿Tiene usted que irse ahora?

Estudiante dos: Sí, me tengo que ir ahora.

Estudiante uno: ¿Necesito ducharme antes del almuerzo?

Estudiante dos: Sí, usted necesita ducharse antes del almuerzo.

Estudiante uno: ¿Prefiere usted ponerse el uniforme en el restaurante o en su casa?

Estudiante dos: Prefiero vestirme en mi casa.

Estudiante uno: ¿Tengo que levantarme mañana a las seis?

Estudiante dos: Sí, usted se tiene que levantar a las seis.

Estudiante uno: ¿Debe Lupita peinarse antes del almuerzo?

Estudiante dos: Sí, Lupita debe peinarse antes del almuerzo siempre.

Estudiante uno: ¿Quiere usted reunirse a las dos o a las tres?

Estudiante dos: Prefiero reunirme a las tres.

Impersonal Reflexive Actions

Spanish uses the third person of reflexive verbs to express impersonal actions. These sentences follow the pattern **se** + verb. For example, to say in Spanish *one cleans the ashtrays with a cloth,* the expression **los ceniceros se limpian con un trapo** would be used.

Three special impersonal expressions that are commonly used in general situations are:

se vende (seh véhn-deh)   *for sale*

se alquila (seh ahl-kée-lah)   *for rent*

se habla español (seh áh-blah ehs-pah-nyóhl)   *Spanish spoken*

EXERCISE 8.12

In pairs, ask and answer the following impersonal reflexive phrases, making sure that you understand what you are asking or answering:

Estudiante uno: ¿Se lavan los vasos con jabón?

Estudiante dos: Sí, los vasos se lavan con jabón.

Estudiante uno: ¿Se barren los pasillos por la mañana o por la tarde?

Estudiante dos:	Los pasillos siempre se barren por la tarde.
Estudiante uno:	¿Se limpian los ceniceros con un trapo o se lavan?
Estudiante dos:	Los ceniceros se lavan en el fregadero.
Estudiante uno:	¿Se corren las cortinas en los cuartos?
Estudiante dos:	Sí, las cortinas se corren en los cuartos.
Estudiante uno:	¿Se sacuden los muebles todos los días?
Estudiante dos:	Los muebles se sacuden los lunes y viernes.
Estudiante uno:	¿Dónde se vacían las cenizas?
Estudiante dos:	Se vacían en el inodoro.

EXERCISE 8.13

Understand the meaning of the following impersonal sentences and pronounce them in Spanish:

1. El fregadero se limpia con Ajax.
2. Las ollas se lavan con agua jabonosa.
3. Los cuchillos no se ponen en el fregadero.
4. El almacén se abre a las ocho.
5. Los vasos se enjuagan con agua limpia.
6. ¿Se limpian las bañeras con polvo limpiador?
7. No, las bañeras se limpian con agua jabonosa.
8. ¿A qué hora se cierra el almacén?
9. El almacén se cierra a las diez de la noche.
10. Se vende este hotel.

EXERCISE 8.14

Translate the following impersonal statements into Spanish. (The sentences in English have been modified to better adapt the meaning to the Spanish translation.)

1. *How does one clean cushions?* _____

2. *Does one put deodorant on the carpet?* _____
   _____

3. *When does one wash the linen?* _____
   _____

4. *Where does one put the cleaning supplies?* _____
   _____

5. *When does one close the storeroom?* _____
   _____

6. *At what time does the department open?* _____

_____

7. *A cot is needed now!* _____

8. *Spanish spoken here.* _____

9. *One brushes the couches with the brown brush, not with the yellow brush.* _____

_____

10. *Room for rent.* _____

Hace With Time and Weather Expressions

Hace is the third person singular of the present tense of the verb **hacer** (*to do, to make*), which is used in a variety of idiomatic expressions; for example, in time and weather expressions.

EXERCISE 8.15

Understand the meaning of the following impersonal sentences and pronounce them in Spanish:

1. Hace cinco años que Lupita trabaja en el departamento de ama de llaves.
2. Hace dos horas que Juan cocina la comida para el banquete.
3. ¿Cuánto tiempo hace que trabajan ellas en San Francisco?
4. ¿Cuánto tiempo hace que hierve la sopa?

EXERCISE 8.16

In pairs, ask and answer the following expression with **hace,** making sure that you understand what you are asking or answering:

Estudiante uno:	¿Hace mucho tiempo que vive usted en Iowa?
Estudiante dos:	Hace cinco años que vivo en Iowa.
Estudiante uno:	¿Cuánto tiempo hace que trabaja usted en este hotel?
Estudiante dos:	Hace más de tres meses.
Estudiante uno:	¿Desde cuándo barre Lupita el pasillo?
Estudiante dos:	Desde hace media hora.
Estudiante uno:	¿Desde cuándo no trabaja Antonio?

Estudiante dos:	Antonio no trabaja desde hace dos meses.
Estudiante uno:	¿Hace mucho tiempo que Dolores es camarera de pisos?
Estudiante dos:	Dolores es camarera de pisos desde enero.
Estudiante uno:	¿Cuánto tiempo hace que es usted mozo de pisos?
Estudiante dos:	Soy mozo de pisos desde hace tres años.

The Weather

Spanish uses diverse expressions with **hace** to tell weather. The most common are:

¿Qué tiempo hace? (keh tee-éhm-poh áh-seh).	*What is the weather like?*
Hace buen tiempo (áh-seh boo-éhn tee-éhm-poh).	*The weather is good.*
Hace mal tiempo (áh-seh mahl tee-éhm-poh).	*The weather is bad.*
Hace calor (áh-seh cah-lóhr).	*It is warm.*
Hace frío (áh-seh frée-oh).	*It is cold.*
Hace viento (áh-seh vee-éhn-toh).	*It is windy.*
Hace sol (áh-seh sohl).	*It is sunny.*
Llueve (yoo-éh-veh).	*It is raining.*
Nieva (nee-éh-vah).	*It is snowing.*
Está nublado (ehs-táh noo-bláh-doh).	*It is cloudy.*

EXERCISE 8.17

Understand the meaning of the following weather expressions and pronounce them in Spanish:

1. Hoy hace mal tiempo; llueve.
2. ¿Hace sol?
3. ¿Qué tiempo hace esta mañana?
4. En primavera llueve.
5. En Arizona siempre hace sol.
6. ¿Nieva en invierno en Miami?
7. Está nublado; no hace sol.
8. En el verano hace buen tiempo.
9. Hace viento en el otoño.
10. ¿Hace frío hoy?

EXERCISE 8.18

In pairs, ask and answer the following weather expressions with and without
hace, making sure that you understand what you are asking or answering:

Estudiante uno:	¿Hace calor hoy?
Estudiante dos:	Sí, hace mucho calor.
Estudiante uno:	¿Hace viento en Chicago en enero?
Estudiante dos:	Sí, en Chicago hace viento siempre.
Estudiante uno:	¿Llueve ahora?
Estudiante dos:	No llueve ahorita.
Estudiante uno:	¿Hace frío en Seattle en agosto?
Estudiante dos:	En Seattle nunca hace frío en agosto.
Estudiante uno:	¿Y en febrero?
Estudiante dos:	Sí, en febrero hace mucho frio y llueve siempre.
Estudiante uno:	¿Hace sol en Puerto Rico?
Estudiante dos:	En Puerto Rico hace mucho sol.

EXERCISE 8.19

Ask another student a few questions about today's weather.

CONVERSATIONAL PROFESSIONAL INTERACTION

In groups of two, translate, practice, and be ready to role-play the following dialogue between a housekeeping supervisor and an hourly employee:

Estudiante uno (supervisor):	¡Buenos días, Joaquín! Siéntese, por favor ¿Qué hora es?
Estudiante dos: (empleado por hora):	Son las ocho y media.
Estudiante uno:	Usted tiene que estar en el trabajo a las ocho. ¿A qué hora se levanta usted?
Estudiante dos:	Lo siento. Me levanto a las siete. ¿Qué tengo que hacer hoy?
Estudiante uno:	Hoy tiene que limpiar a fondo el almacén.
Estudiante dos:	¿Tengo que lavar la ropa?
Estudiante uno:	Sí. No tenemos sábanas bajeras. ¿Qué tiempo hace hoy?
Estudiante dos:	Hace buen tiempo. Hace sol.

Estudiante uno:	Póngase su uniforme.
Estudiante dos:	De acuerdo. ¿Hago las camas?
Estudiante uno:	Sí. Haga las camas en los cuartos de salida, pero, por favor, dúchese antes de comenzar.

💼 QUESTIONS TO THE CLASS 💼

Answer the following questions asked by your instructor (or by another student) without looking at your textbook or any class notes:

1. ¿A qué hora se levanta usted?
2. ¿A qué hora se acuesta usted?
3. ¿Se cepilla usted los dientes antes de acostarse?
4. ¿Se limpia el baño en su casa todos los fines de semana?
5. ¿Hace sol hoy?
6. ¿Hace frío en Vancouver en enero?
7. ¿Hace calor en Rio de Janeiro?
8. ¿Hace buen tiempo hoy?
9. ¿Le gusta a usted ir a un restaurante cuando hace viento?
10. ¿Qué tiempo hace hoy?

CULTURAL VIGNETTE

Meals and mealtimes in Hispanic countries differ from those in the United States and Canada. **El desayuno** is usually light, consisting of coffee and milk, toast with butter and jam, or a sweet roll. It is not customary to drink tea for breakfast. **El almuerzo,** eaten late, between 2:00 and 4:00, is the heaviest meal of the day. Wine is usually served with business luncheons. **La cena** is a lighter meal eaten late in the evening. Travelers from Spanish countries are often surprised to discover that they cannot have dinner in most American restaurants after 10:00 P.M.

THE PRETERIT (PAST TENSE)

THE SPANISH "A" BEFORE PERSONS

OVERVIEW

There are two past tenses in Spanish, **el pretérito** and **el imperfecto.** Chapter 9 covers the preterit, which is used to report or express actions that the speaker views as being completed. The imperfect tense will be covered in Chapter 10. Chapter 9 also explains how to use the personal **a** in Spanish.

UNIT CONTENT

Technical Housekeeping Vocabulary (II) • The Preterit of Regular Verbs • The Preterit of Irregular Verbs • Stem Changes in the Preterit Tense • The Use of **a** in Spanish before Persons • Conversational Professional Interaction • Cultural Vignette

Technical Housekeeping Vocabulary (II)

fan	el ventilador (vehn-tee-lah-dóhr)
faucet	el grifo (grée-foh)
fire	el fuego (foo-éh-goh)
floor	el suelo (soo-éh-loh)
	el piso (pée-soh)
floor (story)	el piso (pée-soh)
floor closet	la estación de servicio (ehs-tah-see-óhn deh sehr-vée-see-oh)
floor lamp	la lámpara de pié (láhm-pah-rah deh pee-éh)
floor mop	el trapeador (trah-peh-ah-dóhr)
(to) fold	doblar (*v.*) (doh-bláhr)
friend	el amigo (ah-mée-goh)
	la amiga (ah-mée-gah)
frock, bathrobe	la bata (báh-tah)

front desk	la recepción (reh-sehp-see-óhn)
front desk clerk	el/la recepcionista (reh-sehp-see-oh-nées-tah)
front of the house	las áreas públicas (áh-reh-ahs póo-blee-cahs)
fruit basket	el cesto de frutas (séhs-toh deh fróo-tahs)
fungi	los hongos (óhn-gohs)
furniture	los muebles (moo-éh-blehs)
garbage	la basura (bah-sóo-rah)
general manager	el/la gerente general (heh-réhn-teh heh-neh-ráhl)
germicidal	el germicida (hehr-mee-sée-dah)
glass (pane)	el cristal (crees-táhl)
gloves	los guantes (goo-áhn-tehs)
guest	el/la huésped (oo-éhs-pehd)
guest supplies	los suministros de clientes (soo-mee-nées-trohs deh clee-éhn-tehs)
hand brush	el cepillo de mano (seh-pée-yoh deh máh-noh)
hand soap	el jabón de tocador (hah-bóhn deh toh-cah-dóhr)
hand towel	la toalla de mano (toh-áh-yah deh máh-noh)
hallway	el pasillo (pah-sée-yoh)
(to) hang	colgar (o→ue) (*v.*) (cohl-gáhr)
hanger	el gancho (gáhn-choh)
heating	la calefacción (cah-leh-fahc-see-óhn)
housekeeper (room attendant)	el/la camarista (cah-mah-rées-tah)
housekeeper report	el reporte de camarista (reh-póhr-teh deh cah-mah-rées-tah)
housekeeper room-table-tent	la tarjeta de presentación (tahr-héh-tah deh preh-sehn-tah-see-óhn)
housekeeping department	el departamento de ama de llaves (deh-pahr-tah-méhn-toh deh áh-mah deh yáh-vehs)
housekeeping supervisor	el/la supervisor/a de cuartos (soo-pehr-vee-sóhr deh coo-áhr-tohs)
houseperson	el/la mozo de pisos (móh-soh deh pée-sohs)
ice machine	la máquina de hielo (máh-kee-nah deh ee-éh-loh)
(to) inspect	comprobar (o→ue) (*v.*) (cohm-proh-báhr)
inventory	el inventario (een-vehn-táh-ree-oh)
iron	la plancha (plán-chah)
(to) iron	planchar (*v.*) (plahn-cháhr)
ironer (machine)	la planchadora (plahn-chah-dóh-rah)
ironing board	la tabla de planchar (táh-blah deh plahn-chár)
janitor	el/la limpiador(a) (leem-pee-ah-dóhr)
key	la llave (yáh-veh)
(to) knock at the door	tocar en la puerta (*v.*) (toh-cáhr ehn lah poo-éhr-tah)
	llamar (*v.*) (yah-máhr)

label	la etiqueta (eh-tee-kéh-tah)
laundry bag	la bolsa de lavandería (bóhl-sah deh lah-vahn-deh-rée-ah)
laundry list	la lista de lavandería (lées-tah deh lah-vahn-deh-rée-ah)
laundry room	la lavandería (lah-vahn-deh-rée-ah)
(to) learn	aprender (*v.*) (ah-prehn-déhr)
letterheads	el papel de cartas (pah-péhl deh cáhr-tahs)
light bulb	el foco (fóh-coh)
	la bombilla (bohm-bée-yah)
light switch	el interruptor (een-teh-rroop-tóhr)
linen	la lencería (lehn-seh-rée-ah)
linen folder	el doblador (doh-blah-dóhr)
liquid soap	el jabón líquido (hah-bóhn lée-kee-doh)
(to) live	vivir (*v.*) (vee-véer)
living room	el salón (sah-lóhn)
lobby	el vestíbulo (vehs-tée-boo-loh)
lock	la cerradura (seh-rrah-dóo-rah)
(to) lock	cerrar con llave (*v.*) (seh-rráhr cohn yáh-veh)
locker room (employee)	el vestidor de empleados (vehs-tee-dóhr deh ehm-ple-áh-dohs)
lost and found	los objetos extraviados (ohb-héh-tohs ehs-trah-vee-áh-dohs)
luggage	el equipaje (eh-kee-páh-heh)
luggage rack	el portamaletas (pohr-tah-mah-léh-tahs)
main entrance	la entrada principal (ehn-tráh-dah preen-see-páhl)
(to) make the bed	hacer la cama (*v.*) (ah-séhr lah cáh-mah)
	tender la cama (*v.*) (tehn-déhr lah cáh-mah)
mangle	la planchadora (plahn-chah-dóh-rah)
master key	la llave maestra (yáh-veh máh-ehs-trah)
matches	los cerillos (seh-rée-yohs)
material	el material (mah-teh-ree-áhl)
mattress	el colchón (cohl-chóhn)
mattress pad	el protector de colchón (proh-tehc-tóhr deh cohl-chóhn)
mattress rotation	el volteo de colchón (vohl-téh-oh deh cohl-chóhn)
mirror	el espejo (ehs-péh-hoh)
(to) miter	hacer ingletes (*v.*) (ah-séhr een-gléh-tehs)
mop	el trapeador (trah-peh-ah-dóhr)
(to) mop	trapear (*v.*) (trah-peh-ar)
needle	la aguja (ah-góo-hah)
newspaper	el periódico (peh-ree-óh-dee-coh)
night stand	la mesilla de noche (meh-sée-yah deh nóh-cheh)
(room with) no baggage	sin equipaje (seen eh-kee-páh-heh)
note pad	el bloc de notas (blohc deh nóh-tahs)
occupancy report	el reporte de ocupación (reh-póhr-teh deh oh-coo-pah-see-óhn)

occupied	ocupado (*adj.*) (oh-coo-páh-doh)
office	la oficina (oh-fee-sée-nah)
out of order	fuera de servicio (foo-éh-rah deh sehr-vée-see-oh)
pamphlets	los folletos (foh-yéh-tohs)
paper basket	la papelera (pah-peh-léh-rah)
paper napkin	la servilleta de papel (sehr-vee-yéh-tah deh pah-péhl)
paper towel	la toalla de papel (toh-áh-yah deh pah-péhl)
paperwork	la papelería (pah-peh-leh-rée-ah)

Auxiliary Vocabulary Words

como (cóh-moh)	*as*
preguntar (preh-goon-táhr)	*to ask*
pedir (e→i) (peh-déer)	*to ask for*
anoche (ah-nóh-cheh)	*last night*
el verano pasado (veh-ráh-noh pah-sáh-doh)	*last summer*
la semana pasada (seh-máh-nah pah-sáh-dah)	*last week*
el año pasado (áh-nyoh pah-sáh-doh)	*last year*
ayer (ah-yéhr)	*yesterday*

EXERCISE 9.1

Match the following list of restaurant vocabulary words, practice their pronunciation, and be ready to speak them aloud:

1. *mattress*	_____	a.	toalla de papel
2. *lock*	_____	b.	lencería
3. *hallway*	_____	c.	plancha
4. *gloves*	_____	d.	fuego
5. *front desk*	_____	e.	suministros de clientes
6. *no baggage*	_____	f.	trapear
7. *liquid soap*	_____	g.	llave
8. *general manager*	_____	h.	grifo
9. *light switch*	_____	i.	oficina
10. *mop*	_____	j.	aguja
11. *key*	_____	k.	cerradura
12. *iron*	_____	l.	pasillo
13. *guest supplies*	_____	m.	recepción
14. *linen*	_____	n.	jabón líquido

15. *paper towel*	_____	o. interruptor
16. *office*	_____	p. colchón
17. *(to) mop*	_____	q. sin equipaje
18. *needle*	_____	r. trapeador
19. *faucet*	_____	s. guantes
20. *fire*	_____	t. gerente general

The Preterit of Regular Verbs

The preterit is used in Spanish to report completed actions or events that began and ended in the past. In general, the preterit corresponds to the English simple past (*I cooked, I cleaned, I spoke*), although there are other verb tenses for expressing an action that took place in the past. For example, the sentence *Yesterday I worked until five o'clock* translates into Spanish using the preterit tense, although in English *I did work* can also be used.

Conjugation of the Preterit Tense of Regular Verbs

To form the preterit of regular verbs, drop the **ar** from the infinitive and add the following endings:

	"ar" verbs	"er" verbs	"ir" verbs
yo	**é**	**í**	**í**
él, ella, usted	**ó**	**ió**	**ió**
nosotros, nosotras	**amos**	**imos**	**imos**
ellos, ellas, ustedes	**aron**	**ieron**	**ieron**

Examples: **Ayer yo trabajé hasta las cinco** (*Yesterday I worked until five o'clock*), **Anoche yo comí con Lupita** (*Last night, I ate with Lupita*), **Nosotros freimos las papas ayer** (*We fried the potatoes yesterday*). The **er** and **ir** verbs have identical endings.

In questions and negative statements, *did* is not translated in Spanish. Examples: *Did you sweep the floor?* translates as **¿Barrió usted el suelo?** and *I did not sweep the floor* is translated as **Yo no barrí el suelo.**

EXERCISE 9.2

With a partner, answer the following questions in Spanish using the preterit of regular verbs, making sure that the meaning of each sentence is understood:

1. ¿Dónde trabajó Miguel el año pasado?
2. ¿Con quién cenó usted el lunes?
3. ¿Barrieron los mozos el vestíbulo esta mañana?
4. ¿Preparó la camarista el piso seis?
5. ¿Limpiaron los mozos el vestidor de empleados?
6. ¿Trapeó usted la cocina?
7. ¿Secó Antonio las toallas ayer?
8. ¿Plancharon ustedes las sábanas anoche?
9. ¿Trabajó la camarista nueva bien hoy?
10. ¿Doblaron ustedes las cobijas?

EXERCISE 9.3

Understand the meaning of the following sentences and pronounce them in Spanish:

1. El año pasado yo trabajé en San Diego.
2. Ayer Lupita tendió las camas.
3. Esta mañana Jorge y Antonio trapearon el suelo en el pasillo.
4. ¿Quién preparó los suministros de limpieza ayer?
5. Yo no preparé los suministros de limpieza; yo preparé la lencería.
6. ¿Comprobó Dolores la habitación ciento dos?
7. La semana pasada Juana y yo limpiamos el vestíbulo.
8. ¿Qué cuartos limpiaron las camaristas ayer?
9. Ellas limpiaron del doscientos nueve al doscientos veinte.
10. La supervisora planchó las toallas.

EXERCISE 9.4

With a partner, write two sentences describing what you did last night, two sentences about two activities that you did last summer, and two sentences about two activities that you did last week. Next, make the six sentences negative. Then, make the six sentences interrogative.

EXERCISE 9.5

In pairs, ask and answer the following phrases, making sure that you understand what you are asking or answering:

Estudiante uno: ¿Quién limpió la lavandería ayer?
Estudiante dos: Lupita limpió la lavandería ayer.
Estudiante uno: ¿Lavó Juanita las toallas con detergente?

Estudiante dos:	Sí, Juanita lavó las toallas con detergente.
Estudiante uno:	¿Comprobó Lupita sus cuartos ayer?
Estudiante dos:	Lupita no comprobó sus cuartos.
Estudiante uno:	¿Habló Jorge ayer con la ama de llaves?
Estudiante dos:	No, Jorge habló con la supervisora.
Estudiante uno:	¿Sacudieron ustedes las sillas en el vestíbulo?
Estudiante dos:	Sí, nosotros sacudimos las sillas y los sillones.
Estudiante uno:	¿Quién trapeó el suelo de la cafetería de empleados?
Estudiante dos:	Yo trapeé el suelo y limpié los ceniceros.

The Preterit of Irregular Verbs

Some common irregular verbs, listed in alphabetical order, are:

conducir (cohn-doo-séer)	to drive
decir (deh-séer)	to tell, to say
estar (ehs-táhr)	to be
hacer (ah-séhr)	to make, to do
ir (eer)	to go
poder (poh-déhr)	to be able, can
poner (poh-néhr)	to put
querer (keh-réhr)	to want
saber (sah-béhr)	to know
ser (sehr)	to be
tener (teh-néhr)	to have
traer (trah-éhr)	to bring
venir (veh-néer)	to come

The preterit of these 13 irregular verbs follows. Note that the preterit of the verbs **ir** and **ser** is identical:

Verb		yo	él, ella, usted	nosotros/as	ellos, ellas, ustedes
conducir	to drive	conduje	condujo	condujimos	condujeron
decir	to tell	dije	dijo	dijimos	dijeron
estar	to be	estuve	estuvo	estuvimos	estuvieron
hacer	to make	hice	hizo	hicimos	hicieron
ir	to go	fui	fue	fuimos	fueron
poder	to be able	pude	pudo	pudimos	pudieron
poner	to put	puse	puso	pusimos	pusieron
querer	to want	quise	quiso	quisimos	quisieron
saber	to know	supe	supo	supimos	supieron

ser	*to be*	fui	fue	fuimos	fueron
tener	*to have*	tuve	tuvo	tuvimos	tuvieron
traer	*to bring*	traje	trajo	trajimos	trajeron
venir	*to come*	vine	vino	vinimos	vinieron

EXERCISE 9.6

In pairs, ask and answer the following phrases, making sure that you understand what you are asking or answering:

Estudiante uno: ¿Condujeron Antonio y Miguel a Santa Bárbara ayer?

Estudiante dos: Sí, ellos condujeron allí ayer.

Estudiante uno: ¿Trajo la camarista los suministros?

Estudiante dos: No, Antonia no trajo los suministros.

Estudiante uno: ¿Estuvo Lupita aquí el sábado?

Estudiante dos: No, Lupita estuvo el domingo pero no el sábado.

Estudiante uno: ¿Vinieron ellos a trabajar esta mañana?

Estudiante dos: No, Jorge y Pepe no vinieron.

Estudiante uno: ¿Dónde puso usted el reporte de ocupación?

Estudiante dos: Puse el reporte en el escritorio.

Estudiante uno: ¿Dijo Lupe la verdad?

Estudiante dos: Sí, dijo la verdad. Lupe siempre dice la verdad.

EXERCISE 9.7

Understand the meaning of the following sentences, in which the action was completed in the past, and pronounce them in Spanish:

1. ¿Cuántos días libres tuvo usted la semana pasada?
2. Lupita no vino a trabajar hoy.
3. Jorge condujo a Baltimore ayer.
4. Juan y yo no fuimos a Hawaii el verano pasado.
5. Yo no pude ir a bailar el domingo.
6. ¿Quién hizo las camas en el piso cinco?
7. Juanita y Dolores hicieron las camas.
8. ¿Estuvieron ellas en Albany el martes pasado?
9. Miguel y Dolores estuvieron pero Lupita no estuvo.
10. ¿Puso usted el detergente en el cubo?

EXERCISE 9.8

With a partner, compose five sentences of activities that you did (or didn't do) using irregular verbs in the past tense.

EXERCISE 9.9

In pairs, ask and answer the following phrases, making sure that you understand what you are asking or answering:

Estudiante uno:	¿Hicieron las camaristas las camas bien?
Estudiante dos:	Sí, ellas hicieron las camas muy bien.
Estudiante uno:	¿A qué hora condujo José al hotel?
Estudiante dos:	Él condujo a las once y media.
Estudiante uno:	¿Puso usted el portamaletas en la habitación?
Estudiante dos:	Si, Antonio puso el portamaletas en el cuarto.
Estudiante uno:	¿Fué usted a la lavandería esta mañana?
Estudiante dos:	Sí, fuí a la lavandería a las ocho.
Estudiante uno:	¿Estuvo Juan en Las Vegas en marzo pasado?
Estudiante dos:	No, Juan estuvo en Reno.
Estudiante uno:	¿A qué hora vino Jorge a trabajar hoy?
Estudiante dos:	Jorge vino a las seis.

Stem Changes in the Preterit Tense

There is no stem change in verbs ending in **ar** and **er**. Stem-changing verbs ending in **ir** have a stem change in the **él/ella/usted** and **ellos/ellas/ustedes** forms. The letter **o** becomes **u**, and **e** becomes **i**.

Three common verbs that have stem changes in the preterit are:

dormir (dohr-méer)	*to sleep*	dormí—durmió—dormimos—durmieron
vestir (vehs-téer)	*to dress*	vestí—vistió—vestimos—vistieron
preferir (preh-feh-réer)	*to prefer*	preferí—prefirió—preferimos—prefirieron

EXERCISE 9.10

Understand the meaning of the following sentences with stem-changing verbs in the preterit, and pronounce them in Spanish. (Remember that **nosotros/as** (*we*) doesn't have a stem change.)

1. Jorge durmió bien ayer.
2. Yo no dormí bien anoche.
3. Nosotros nos levantamos esta mañana a las seis y nos vestimos a las seis y media.
4. Los meseros se despertaron y se vistieron antes de las ocho de la mañana.

5. Yo preferí comer en Burger King.

6. La mesera mexicana prefirió comer en Taco Bell porque le gusta la comida mexicana.

7. ¿Durmió usted bien anoche, señor Bell?

8. ¿Prefirieron ellos ir a bailar?

9. Nosotros nos vestimos muy bien antes de ir al hotel el fin de semana pasado.

10. El verano pasado yo preferí ir a Cancún.

EXERCISE 9.11

In pairs, ask and answer the following phrases, making sure that you understand what you are asking or answering:

Estudiante uno:	¿Durmieron ellos bien anoche?
Estudiante dos:	Sí, ellos durmieron muy bien.
Estudiante uno:	¿Prefirió usted las servilletas blancas o las amarillas?
Estudiante dos:	Preferí las blancas porque son más bonitas.
Estudiante uno:	¿A qué hora se vistió usted hoy?
Estudiante dos:	Me vestí a las cinco y diez.
Estudiante uno:	¿Prefirieron ustedes la comida china o la italiana?
Estudiante dos:	Ayer preferimos la comida italiana.
Estudiante uno:	¿Se vistió Lupita bien para el banquete?
Estudiante dos:	Sí, ella se vistió muy bien.
Estudiante uno:	¿A qué hora se acostaron ustedes?
Estudiante dos:	Nos acostamos a las doce.

The Use of **a** in Spanish Before Persons

When a person is the direct object of the action of a verb (a peculiarity of Spanish), speakers use **a** immediately before the direct object if the object is a definite person. This **a** has no equivalent in English. For example, *I saw Carlos yesterday* translates into Spanish as **Yo vi a Carlos ayer.** This "personal a" is not used after forms of **tener.** For example, *We have two Mexican room attendants* is translated as **Tenemos dos camaristas mexicanas.**

EXERCISE 9.12

With a partner, ask and answer the following questions using the "personal **a.**" (Make sure that you understand what you are asking or answering.)

Estudiante uno:	¿A quién vio usted ayer?
Estudiante dos:	Vi a Pepe.
Estudiante uno:	¿A quién preguntó el señor Gómez?
Estudiante dos:	El señor Gómez preguntó a la camarera de pisos.
Estudiante uno:	¿A quién dio usted el reporte de mañana?
Estudiante dos:	A Joaquina.
Estudiante uno:	¿Vio usted a él o a ella?
Estudiante dos:	Vi a los dos.
Estudiante uno:	¿Hizo usted la habitación de salida?
Estudiante dos:	Sí, hice la habitación esta mañana.
Estudiante uno:	¿Preguntó usted al mozo de pisos?
Estudiante dos:	Sí, pregunté a Pepe.

EXERCISE 9.13

Understand the meaning of the following sentences and pronounce them in Spanish:

1. Yo vi a Pepe el verano pasado.
2. ¿Vio usted a la ama de llaves ayer?
3. ¿Tiene este hotel un mozo de pisos puertorriqueño?
4. Preferimos a Juanita como camarista.
5. ¿A quién vio usted en la oficina?
6. Diga a Lupita de barrer el piso.
7. ¿Dijo usted a Jorge de venir a trabajar hoy?
8. Pregunte a Miguel donde está Dolores.
9. Pida las bolsas de lavandería al (a el) mozo de pisos.
10. ¿Pidió usted las bolsas de lavandería a José?

EXERCISE 9.14

Translate the following sentences, using the "personal **a**," into Spanish:

1. *I prefer Pepe as houseperson.* _____
2. *I saw Enrique yesterday.* _____
3. *Did you see Lupita?* _____
4. *Whom did you see last night?* _____
5. *I didn't ask Juan this morning.* _____
6. *Did you ask Jorge to come to work tomorrow?* _____

   _____
7. *Please ask the room attendant for the hand soap.* _____

   _____

8. *Jorge asked the chef for the tablecloths.* _____

9. *Do you prefer the brown uniforms or the white?* _____
_____

10. *We prefer the white.* _____

CONVERSATIONAL PROFESSIONAL INTERACTION

In groups of two, translate, practice, and be ready to role-play the following dialogue between a housekeeping supervisor and an hourly employee:

Estudiente uno (supervisor): ¡Hóla, Joaquín! Ayer fue mi día libre. ¿Qué hizo usted ayer?

Estudiente dos (empleado por hora): Buenos días, jefe. Ayer trabajé en el quinto piso.

Estudiente uno: ¿Cuántos cuartos limpió usted?

Estudiente dos: Limpié quince cuartos. También lavé la lencería y sacudí los muebles en el vestíbulo.

Estudiente uno: ¿Trapeó usted los pasillos?

Estudiente dos: Yo no trapeé los pasillos; Dolores y Miguel trapearon los pasillos y el vestidor de empleados.

Estudiente uno: ¿Vino Juan a trabajar ayer?

Estudiente dos: Yo no sé. Yo no vi a Juan ayer.

Estudiente uno: ¿Vio usted a Lupita ayer?

Estudiente dos: Sí, vi a Lupita en la lavandería.

Estudiente uno: ¿Dobló Lupita los cobertores?

Estudiente dos: No, ella prefirió voltear los colchones.

Estudiente uno: Bueno, Joaquín. Por favor, suba ahora al primer piso y póngase a trabajar en los cuartos ciento doce a ciento veinte y cinco.

Estudiente dos: De acuerdo, jefe. Voy a empezar ahorita.

💼 QUESTIONS TO THE CLASS 💼

Answer the following questions asked by your instructor (or by another student) without looking at your textbook or any class notes:

1. ¿Trabajó usted en Chili's el año pasado?

2. ¿Hizo usted su cama esta mañana?

3. ¿Limpió usted su cocina el fin de semana pasado?

4. ¿Condujo usted a Orlando ayer?

5. ¿Vio usted a George Clooney anoche?

6. ¿Fue usted a un restaurante chino ayer?

7. ¿Cuántos días libres tuvo usted la semana pasada?

8. ¿Durmió usted bien anoche?

9. ¿Preguntó usted a la señorita Smith?

10. ¿Dijo usted la verdad?

CULTURAL VIGNETTE

Spanish and English share words that are similar or identical in form and meaning (*cognates*), although usually they are pronounced differently. Examples of Spanish-English cognates are: **chocolate** (*chocolate*); **supervisor** (*supervisor*); **elegante** (*elegant*).

There are some cognates that are written similarly but have a different meaning in the two languages. Some "false" cognates are:

molestar in Spanish means *to bother* or *tease someone*

estar constipado in Spanish means *to have a cold*

embarazada in Spanish means *being pregnant*

Some words, though spelled the same, have different meanings among Hispanic countries. For example:

tortilla, a thin, round, unleavened pancake in Mexico and Central America, is an *egg omelet* in most other Hispanic countries.

Regadera means *shower* in Mexico but *watering can* in Spain.

Alberca is a swimming pool in Mexico but an *irrigation canal* in Spain.

Carro is an *automobile* in Mexico but a *mule-driven cart* in Spain.

THE IMPERFECT INDICATIVE OF REGULAR AND IRREGULAR VERBS

SPANISH PREPOSITIONS

THE USE OF "POR" AND "PARA"

OVERVIEW

There are two simple tenses in Spanish to express an action that took place in the past. The <u>preterit</u> (covered in Chapter 9) is used to report or express actions that the speaker views as being completed; the <u>imperfect</u> tense is used as another way of talking about the past. Chapter 10 explains how the imperfect is formed and when it is used to express past actions. This chapter also covers Spanish prepositions and explains when to use **por** and **para.**

UNIT CONTENT

Technical Housekeeping Vocabulary (III) • The Imperfect Indicative of Regular and Irregular Verbs • Use of the Imperfect • Spanish Prepositions • The Uses of **por** and **para** • Conversational Professional Interaction • Cultural Vignette

Technical Housekeeping Vocabulary (III)

pass key	la llave de paso (yáh-veh deh páh-soh)
pen (ball point)	el bolígrafo (boh-lée-grah-foh)
pencil	el lápiz (láh-pees)
picture (hanging)	el cuadro (coo-áh-droh)
pillow	la almohada (ahl-moh-áh-dah)

pillowcase	la funda de almohada (fóon-dah deh ahl-moh-áh-dah)
plastic glass	el vaso de plástico (váh-soh deh pláhs-tee-coh)
P.M. report	el reporte de tarde (reh-póhr-teh deh táhr-deh)
poison	el veneno (veh-néh-noh)
(to) polish	pulir (*v.*) (poo-léer)
postcard	la tarjeta postal (tahr-héh-tah pohs-táhl)
public areas	las áreas públicas (áh-reh-ahs póo-blee-cahs)
public bathroom	el baño público (báh-nyoh póo-blee-coh)
queen-sized bed	la cama de matrimonio (cáh-mah deh mah-tree-móh-nee-oh)
quilt	la colcha (cóhl-chah)
radio	la radio (ráh-dee-oh)
rag	el trapo (tráh-poh)
ready-room	el cuarto listo (coo-áhr-toh lées-toh)
ready to rent	listo para alquilar (*adj.*) (lees-toh páh-rah ahl-kee-láhr)
report	el reporte (reh-póhr-teh)
requisition	el pedido (peh-dée-doh)
restroom	el baño (báh-nyoh)
room (guest)	el cuarto (coo-áhr-toh)
	la habitación (ah-bee-tah-see-óhn)
room attendant	el/la camarista (cah-mah-rées-tah)
room division	la división cuartos (dee-vee-see-óhn coo-áhr-tohs)
room section	la sección de cuartos (sehc-see-óhn deh coo-áhr-tohs)
room service	el servicio a cuartos (sehr-vée-see-oh ah coo-áhr-tohs)
(to) rotate	rotar (*v.*) (roh-táhr)
rug	la alfombra (ahl-fóhm-brah)
rug shampooer	la máquina para limpiar alfombras (máh-kee-nah páh-rah leem-pee-áhr ahl-fóhm-brahs)
sanitary bag	la bolsa sanitaria (bóhl-sah sah-nee-táh-ree-ah)
scouring pad	el estropajo (ehs-troh-páh-hoh)
(to) scrape	rascar (*v.*) (rahs-cáhr)
screen	la pantalla (pahn-táh-yah)
section housekeeper	el/la camarista (cah-mah-rées-tah)
security	la seguridad (seh-goo-ree-dáhd)
service	el servicio (sehr-vée-see-oh)
service directory	la guía de servicios (guée-ah deh sehr-vée-see-ohs)
service stairs	la escalera de servicio (ehs-cah-léh-rah deh sehr-vée-see-oh)
(to) sew	coser (*v.*) (coh-séhr)
shampoo	el champú (chahm-póo)
sheers	los visillos (vee-sée-yohs)
sheet	la sábana (sáh-bah-nah)

sheet folder	el doblador de sábanas (doh-blah-dóhr deh sáh-bah-nahs)
shelf	la repisa (reh-pée-sah)
shoes	los zapatos (sah-páh-tohs)
shower	la regadera (reh-gah-déh-rah)
	la ducha (dóo-chah)
shower cap	el gorro de baño (góh-rroh deh báh-nyoh)
shower curtain	la cortina de ducha (cohr-tée-nah deh dóo-chah)
sink (bathroom)	el lavabo (lah-váh-boh)
(to) soak	remojar (*v.*) (reh-moh-háhr)
soap	el jabón (hah-bóhn)
soap dish	la jabonera (hah-boh-néh-rah)
sofa	el sofá (soh-fáh)
soiled linen	la ropa sucia (róh-pah sóo-see-ah)
sponge	la esponja (ehs-póhn-hah)
stain	la mancha (máhn-chah)
stairs	las escaleras (ehs-cah-léh-rahs)
starch	el almidón (ahl-mee-dóhn)
(to) starch	almidonar (*v.*) (ahl-mee-doh-náhr)
stationery	el papel de cartas (pah-péhl deh cáhr-tahs)
suitcase	la maleta (mah-léh-tah)
supervisor	el/la supervisor/a (soo-pehr-vee-sóhr)
supplies	los suministros (soo-mee-nées-trohs)
swing team	el equipo de relevo (eh-kée-poh deh reh-léh-voh)
swimming pool	la alberca (ahl-béhr-cah)
	la piscina (pees-sée-nah)
team	el equipo (eh-kée-poh)
telephone	el teléfono (teh-léh-foh-noh)
telephone book	la guía de teléfonos (guée-ah deh teh-léh-foh-nohs)
television	la televisión (teh-leh-vee-see-óhn)
television-program guide	la guía de televisión (guée-ah deh teh-leh-vee-see-óhn)
television set	el televisor (teh-leh-vee-sóhr)
terry cloth	la felpa (féhl-pah)
thermostat	el termostato (tehr-mohs-táh-toh)
tile	el azulejo (ah-soo-léh-hoh)
toilet bowl	el inodoro (ee-noh-dóh-roh)
toilet paper	el papel higiénico (pah-péhl ee-hee-éh-nee-coh)
towel rack	el toallero (toh-ah-yéh-roh)
trash	la basura (bah-sóo-rah)
trash bag	la bolsa de basura (bóhl-sah deh bah-sóo-rah)
turndown service	el servicio de cortesía (sehr-vée-see-oh deh cohr-teh-sée-ah)
(to) turn off	apagar (*v.*) (ah-pah-gáhr)
(to) turn on	encender (e→ie) (*v.*) (ehn-sehn-déhr)
upholstery	la tapicería (tah-pee-seh-rée-ah)

upstairs	arriba (ah-rrée-bah)
(to) use	usar (*v.*) (oo-sáhr)
vacant	desocupado (*adj.*) (dehs-oh-coo-páh-doh)
vacant and clean (room)	vacío y limpio (*adj.*) (vah-sée-oh ee léem-pee-oh)
vacant and dirty (room)	vacío y sucio (*adj.*) (vah-sée-oh ee sóo-see-oh)
vacant and ready (room)	vacío y listo (*adj.*) (vah-sée-oh ee lées-toh)
(to) vacuum	aspirar (*v.*) (ahs-pee-ráhr)
vacuum cleaner	la aspiradora (ahs-pee-rah-dóh-rah)
valet	el valet (vah-léh)
vanity	el lavabo (lah-váh-boh)
venetian blind	la persiana (pehr-see-áh-nah)
wall	la pared (pah-réhd)
washcloth	la toalla facial (toh-áh-yah fah-see-áhl)
washer	la lavadora (lah-vah-dóh-rah)
wastebasket	el cesto de basura (séhs-toh deh bah-sóo-rah)
wastepaper basket	la papelera (pah-peh-léh-rah)
wax	la cera (séh-rah)
(to) wax	encerar (*v.*) (ehn-seh-ráhr)
white linen	los blancos (bláhn-cohs)
window	la ventana (vehn-táh-nah)
window cleaner	el limpiador de cristales (leem-pee-ah-dór deh crees-táh-lehs)
window sill	el repisón (reh-pee-sóhn)
wood	la madera (mah-déh-rah)
wool	la lana (láh-nah)
workload	la cuota de trabajo (coo-óh-tah deh trah-báh-hoh)
writing pad	la libreta de apuntes (lee-bréh-tah deh ah-póon-tehs)

EXERCISE 10.1

Match the following list of restaurant vocabulary words, practice their pronunciation, and be ready to speak them aloud:

1. *(to) rinse* _____ a. ducha

2. *room attendant* _____ b. alfombra

3. *suitcase* _____ c. almidón

4. *sink* _____ d. división cuartos

5. *postcard* _____ e. coser

6. *room* _____ f. suministros

7. *vacant and ready* _____ g. cuota de trabajo

8. *wastebasket*	_____	h. papel higiénico
9. *window*	_____	i. toallero
10. *shelf*	_____	j. rotar
11. *(to) sew*	_____	k. repisa
12. *towel rack*	_____	l. cesto de basura
13. *workload*	_____	m. vacío y listo
14. *room division*	_____	n. enjuagar
15. *supplies*	_____	o. lavabo
16. *starch*	_____	p. maleta
17. *toilet paper*	_____	q. tarjeta postal
18. *shower*	_____	r. habitación
19. *rug*	_____	s. camarista
20. *(to) rotate*	_____	t. ventana

The Imperfect Indicative of Regular and Irregular Verbs

Usually, the imperfect tense corresponds to the English past progressive (*I was cooking, I was clearing*). One function of the imperfect in Spanish is to provide a background against which a single point action can take place. For example, *when I was cooking the fish* (background continued over a period of time) *I cut my hand with the knife* (a point in time). In Spanish: **cuando cocinaba el pescado** (imperfect) **me corté la mano** (preterit).

To form the imperfect of regular verbs, drop the **ar, er,** or **ir** from the infinitive and add the following endings:

	"ar" verbs	"er" verbs	"ir" verbs
yo	aba	ía	ía
él, ella, usted	aba	ía	ía
nosotros, nosotras	ábamos	íamos	íamos
ellos, ellas, ustedes	aban	ían	ían

The **er** and **ir** verbs have identical endings. There is no stem change in the imperfect tense. Examples:

yo trabajaba	yo comía	yo escribía
ella trabajaba	ella comía	ella escribía
ellos trabajaban	ellos comían	ellos escribían

Only three Spanish verbs have irregular forms in the imperfect:

ir (*to go*)	iba	iba	íbamos	iban
ser (*to be*)	era	era	éramos	eran
ver (*to see*)	veía	veía	veímos	veían

The imperfect form of **hay** is **había/habían** as in **había una toalla aquí** (*there was a towel here*) or **habían toallas allí** (*there were some towels there*).

Use of the Imperfect

While, as we have seen in Chapter 9, the preterit is used to describe actions with a definite beginning and end, the imperfect indicates an unstopped action in the past. Among its English equivalents are *used to* (*dance, work, eat, etc.*) and *was/were* (*dancing, working, eating, etc.*). The imperfect is used mostly to express or describe:

> Age. For example: Cuando yo tenía veinte años yo trabajaba en Taco Bell. (*When I was twenty I used to work at Taco Bell.*)

> Time. For example: Eran las cinco cuando Pepe llegó. (*It was 5 o'clock when Pepe arrived.*)

> Weather. For example. Hacía mucho calor. (*It was very warm.*)

> Physical conditions. For example: Lupita estaba feliz ayer. (*Lupita was happy yesterday.*)

> In actions that used to happen repeatedly. For example: Yo trabajaba mucho en Taco Bell. (*I used to work a lot at Taco Bell.*)

EXERCISE 10.2

Write the imperfect tense using the given pronouns and verb phrases:

nosotras	trabajar en Taco Bell	_____
él	vivir en Cuba	_____
Jorge y Lupita	limpiar las repisas	_____
yo	hacer las camas	_____
el mozo mexicano	aspirar el pasillo	_____
mi amiga y yo	bailar el tango	_____
la señorita Pérez	restregar los baños con jabón	_____
Pepe	ver a su padre los domingos	_____
ustedes	¿ir a Argentina los veranos?	_____
la ama de llaves	escribir inglés bien	_____

EXERCISE 10.3

After completing Exercise 10.2, read the sentences aloud, making sure that you understand their meaning.

EXERCISE 10.4

In pairs, ask and answer the following phrases (make sure that you understand what you are asking or answering):

Estudiante uno: ¿Tenía Juan muchos amigos cuando vivía en Portland?
Estudiante dos: Sí, Juan tenía muchos amigos allí.
Estudiante uno: ¿Era Lupita una camarista cuando trabajaba en Orlando?
Estudiante dos: No, Lupita era cocinera.
Estudiante uno: ¿Estaba el agua del baño fría?
Estudiante dos: Sí, el agua del baño estaba muy fría.
Estudiante uno: ¿Qué desayunaba usted cuando vivía en España?
Estudiante dos: Cuando vivía en España desayunaba tostadas de aceite.
Estudiante uno: ¿Quién era su supervisora cuando trabajaba en Marriott?
Estudiante dos: Mi supervisora era la señorita Esperanza.
Estudiante uno: ¿Cuántos años tenía usted cuando vino de México?
Estudiante dos: Cuando vine de México yo tenía veinte años.

EXERCISE 10.5

Understand the meaning of the following sentences and pronounce them in Spanish:

1. Cuando yo tenía veinte años yo vivía en Costa Rica.
2. ¿Vivía usted en Cuba cuando era niño?
3. Jorge siempre salía del hotel a las siete y media.
4. Estaba nublado siempre que íbamos a Seattle.
5. Cuando Lupita trabajaba como camarista en el hotel ella comía muy bien.
6. ¿Estaba usted en Boston en mil novecientos noventa?
7. Había una escoba aquí ayer.
8. Siempre hacía mucho viento cuando vivíamos en Chicago.
9. Cuando Lupita vivía en México siempre escribía a su amiga Dolores.
10. ¿Era usted camarista cuando trabajaba en el hotel Royal?

EXERCISE 10.6

Translate the following sentences into Spanish using the imperfect tense:

1. *Jorge was living in Tucson when he was a waiter.* (use **ser**) _____

_____

2. *It was two o'clock when the room attendant arrived.* _____

_____

3. *The water was cold.* (use **estar**) _____

4. *There was a broom in the storeroom last weekend.* _____

_____

5. *When I was ten years old, I used to clean my room very well.* _____

_____

6. *When I was vacuuming the hallway, I saw Jorge.* _____

_____

7. *Jorge was a supervisor* (use **ser**) *when Lupita used to work in the hotel.*

_____

8. *Jorge and Lupita always used to work the morning shift.* _____

_____

9. *The executive housekeeper was* (use **ser**) *a room attendant when she used to work in San Francisco.* _____

_____

10. *The houseman used to live in Peru when he was twenty years old.* _____

_____

Spanish Prepositions

Prepositions are words that introduce phrases that tell about condition, time, place, manner, association, and degree. It is difficult to master the use of prepositions in Spanish because very few of them correspond exactly with English prepositions. Of the nineteen prepositions in Spanish, the following are used frequently:

a (ah)	*to, at*
con (cohn)	*with*
contra (cóhn-trah)	*against*
de (deh)	*of, from*
desde (déhs-deh)	*from, since*
en (ehn)	*in, on, at*
entre (éhn-treh)	*between*
hasta (áhs-tah)	*until*
para (páh-rah)	*for, to, in order to, by*
por (pohr)	*for, by, per, through*
sin (seen)	*without*

EXERCISE 10.7

With a partner, ask and answer the following phrases (make sure that you understand what you are asking or answering):

Estudiante uno: ¿Dónde están los vasos de plástico?

Estudiante dos:	Están en las cajas verdes.
Estudiante uno:	¿Con quién trabajó usted ayer?
Estudiante dos:	Trabajé con Jorge y Fabiola.
Estudiante uno:	¿Pongo las sillas contra la pared?
Estudiante dos:	Sí, ponga las sillas contra la pared, por favor.
Estudiante uno:	¿De dónde es usted?
Estudiante dos:	Soy de Ensenada; y usted ¿de dónde es?
Estudiante uno:	¿Trabajó Juan el domingo entre las cinco y las seis?
Estudiante dos:	No, él trabajó entre las dos y las tres.
Estudiante uno:	¿Por dónde se va al sótano?
Estudiante dos:	Se va por el pasillo a la derecha.

EXERCISE 10.8

Understand the meaning of the following sentences and pronounce them in Spanish:

1. La llave de paso está en el cajón.
2. ¡Hasta mañana, clase!
3. La semana que viene voy a ir con Jorge a Yuma.
4. El balde está contra la pared.
5. La máquina de refrescos está entre el piso primero y el piso segundo.
6. Estos trapos son para limpiar el suelo.
7. Por favor, use agua sin detergente.
8. ¿Desde cuando trabaja usted en el departamento de ama de llaves?
9. Venga por aquí, por favor.
10. Lupita trabaja como camarista desde febrero.

EXERCISE 10.9

Fill the blanks with one of the prepositions listed above:

1. Antonio, usted trabaja mañana _____ las ocho y las tres.
2. Antonio, usted trabaja mañana _____ las ocho a las tres.
3. El escurridor está _____ la pared.
4. Los trapos están _____ la mesa.
4. Estas sábanas son _____ Lupita.
5. La camarista chilena trabaja _____ Pepe.
6. ¡_____ el lunes, Dolores!
7. El mozo de pisos está _____ San Diego ahora.
8. Las mantas _____ este hotel son _____ lana.

9. No trabajo _____ el verano próximo.

10. Soy camarista en este hotel _____ el año pasado.

EXERCISE 10.10

Translate the following sentences into Spanish using the correct preposition:

1. *Give the sheers to your supervisor.* _____

2. *Please, clean the sinks with cleaning powder.* _____

3. *Are the chairs against the table?* _____

4. *These pillowcases are* (use **ser**) *for Jorge.* _____

5. *Those sheets are Jorge's.* _____

6. *The executive housekeeper is in the office now.* _____

7. *Tomorrow, you work between 8 and 3.* _____

8. *I'll see you later!* _____

9. *Please wash the towels without starch.* _____

10. *I am here since 9 o'clock!* _____

Pronouns Used as Objects of Prepositions

When used with **con** (*with*), the first person singular object takes the special form of **conmigo** (*with me*). The rest of the persons don't have a special form: **con él, con ella, con usted, con nosotros/as, con ellos/as, con ustedes.**

EXERCISE 10.11

Understand the meaning of the following sentences and pronounce them in Spanish:

1. Iré con ella a casa del supervisor.

2. Juan vendrá conmigo a firmar la solicitud de empleo.

3. ¿Trabajará usted conmigo mañana?

EXERCISE 10.12

Translate the following sentences into Spanish:

1. *Lupita will take the aptitude test with me.* _____

2. *She doesn't want to train with him.* _____

3. *I will not work tomorrow with them.* _____

The Uses Of **Por** And **Para**

The preposition **para** can be translated as *for, to, in order to,* and *by* in English. In general, **para** conveys the idea of purpose, use, and destination. Examples:

Estas almohadas son para Antonia.	*These pillows are for Antonia.*
Estos trapos son para limpiar el suelo.	*These cloths are to clean the floor.*
Para limpiar la bañera, use detergente.	*In order to clean the bathtub, use detergent.*
Lave los blancos para las cinco.	*Wash the linen by 5 o'clock.*

The preposition **por** can be translated as *for, by, per,* and *through.* It has a wider range of uses than **para**. In general, **por** conveys the underlying idea of a cause, reason, or source behind an action. Examples:

Dolores fue a España por dos años.	*Dolores went to Spain for two years.*
Pedro va por el pasillo.	*Pedro is going (walking) by the hall way.*
cinco por ciento.	*5 percent.*
Por favor, venga por esta puerta.	*Please come through this door.*

Por is also used in several idiomatic expressions, as in the following examples:

por ahora	*for now*
por ciento	*percent*
¡por Dios!	*for Heaven's sake!*
por ejemplo	*for example*
por el momento	*for the time being*
por eso	*therefore, for that reason*
por favor	*please*
¡por fin!	*at last!*
por lo menos	*at least*
por lo visto	*apparently*

EXERCISE 10.13

Understand the meaning of the following sentences with the preposition **para** and pronounce them in Spanish:

1. Estas mantas de lana son para la habitación 105.
2. Esos directorios de servicios son para los cuartos del tercer piso.
3. El uniforme es para Angel.

4. Las toallas son para los clientes; no son para limpiar el piso.
5. Tenga su sección de cuartos lista para las cuatro.
6. Las fundas de almohada son para él.
7. Voy para el almacén ahora.
8. Esté lista para comenzar el trabajo a las ocho.
9. Venga para aquí, por favor.
10. A Antonia le gusta trabajar para Dolores.

EXERCISE 10.14

With a partner, ask and answer the following phrases (make sure that you understand what you are asking or answering):

Estudiante uno:	¿Para quién son estos suministros?
Estudiante dos:	Son para Jorge.
Estudiante uno:	¿Son aquellos cubos para mí?
Estudiante dos:	Sí, son para usted.
Estudiante uno:	¿Tengo que lavar los blancos para las diez?
Estudiante dos:	Sí, por favor lave los blancos para las diez.
Estudiante uno:	¿Uso las toallas para secar la alfombra?
Estudiante dos:	Nunca use las toallas para secar la alfombra.
Estudiante uno:	¿Para dónde va usted?
Estudiante dos:	Voy para Los Angeles.
Estudiante uno:	¿Para quién son estos periódicos?
Estudiante dos:	Son para el cliente del cuarto tres uno cero.

EXERCISE 10.15

Understand the meaning of the following sentences with the preposition **por** and pronounce them in Spanish:

1. Por aquí, por favor.
2. Vaya al almacén ahora, ¡por Dios!
3. Por lo visto, Juan está en Colombia ahora.
4. Sí, fué a Medellín por dos semanas.
5. ¡Ah! por eso no vino a trabajar hoy.
6. Por el momento no tenemos blancos.
7. Hoy, Pepe trabaja por Lupita.
8. Por lo menos hay trescientos huéspedes en el hotel hoy.
9. Miguel vino a los Estados Unidos por dos años.
10. Ella trabaja como camarista por ahora.

EXERCISE 10.16

In pairs, ask and answer the following phrases (make sure that you understand what you are asking or answering):

Estudiante uno: ¿Por dónde está la recepción del hotel?

Estudiante dos: Por aquí, por favor.

Estudiante uno: ¿Llegaron las sábanas?

Estudiante dos: Sí, por fin llegaron.

Estudiante uno: ¿Trabaja usted por Juan hoy?

Estudiante dos: Sí, hoy trabajo por él.

Estudiante uno: ¿Cuántos cuartos tenemos mañana?

Estudiante dos: Tendremos por lo menos cincuenta.

Estudiante uno: ¿Tengo que limpiar el lavabo ahora?

Estudiante dos: Por el momento no.

Estudiante uno: ¿Cómo restriego las baldosas?

Estudiante dos: Por ejemplo, puede usar un cepillo.

EXERCISE 10.17

Fill the gaps with the preposition **por** or **para**:

1. Este espejo es _____ el cuarto 303.
2. Aquellos trapos son _____ limpiar el piso.
3. Los cuartos 101 a 110 están listos _____ los huéspedes.
4. ¿ _____ cuanto tiempo está usted en los Estados Unidos?
5. Tenemos _____ lo menos cincuenta cuartos de salida.
6. Estábamos listos _____ hacer los cuartos pero no teníamos sábanas.
7. No use los tapetes de baño _____ limpiar las bañeras.
8. ¿ _____ quién son estas toallas?
9. ¿ _____ dónde voy _____ ir al sótano?
10. ¿ _____ dónde empiezo a limpiar mi sección de cuartos?

CONVERSATIONAL PROFESSIONAL INTERACTION

In groups of two, translate, practice, and be ready to role-play the following dialogue between a housekeeping supervisor and an hourly employee:

Estudiante uno (supervisor):   !Hóla, Lupe! Por favor, prepare su carro de servicio y empiece a trabajar en el quinto piso.

Estudiante dos (empleado por hora):   Bien. ¿Por dónde empiezo?

Estudiante uno: Empiece a limpiar los cuartos de salida primero.

Estudiante dos: De acuerdo. ¿Tenemos sábanas y toallas listas?

Estudiante uno: Sí. Vaya a la lavandería y pida los blancos para su sección de cuartos.

Estudiante dos: ¿Para qué son estos suministros de limpieza?

Estudiante uno: El polvo limpiador es para fregar el piso de los baños y el jabón líquido es para limpiar los lavabos.

Estudiante dos: ¿Con qué limpio las bañeras?

Estudiante uno: Limpie las bañeras con el detergente con la etiqueta roja.

Estudiante dos: Señora Rosario, ¿dónde trabajaba usted cuando era camarista?

Estudiante uno: Cuando yo era camarista, trabajaba para Marriott.

Estudiante dos: ¿Le gustaba a usted trabajar para Marriott?

Estudiante uno: Sí, también yo tenía muchos amigos cuando era camarista.

Estudiante dos: Y ahora, ¿usted no tiene amigos?

Estudiante uno: No puedo. Ahora tengo cuatro niños.

Estudiante dos: ¡Por Dios, señora Rosario! ¿Dónde está el reporte de camarista?

Estudiante uno: Su reporte está en el cajón de la derecha.

Estudiante dos: ¿Hablaba usted español cuando era camarista en Miami?

Estudiante uno: Sí, en el hotel de Miami todos hablábamos español.

Estudiante dos: Yo quiero aprender a hablar español.

Estudiante uno: Cuando yo tenía quince años yo iba a la escuela para aprender español.

Estudiante dos: Yo tengo que empezar a ir a la escuela para aprender inglés.

Estudiante uno: Lupe, póngase a trabajar. Súbase al quinto piso ahorita.

📖 QUESTIONS TO THE CLASS 📖

Answer the following questions asked by your instructor (or by another student) without looking at your textbook or any class notes:

1. ¿Tenía usted amigos cuando vivía en Billings?

2. ¿Estaba el agua caliente cuando se duchó?

3. ¿Cuándo trabajaba usted en Taco Bell, era usted mesero o cocinero?

4. ¿Estaba usted en Guatemala en mil novecientos noventa y nueve?

5. ¿Están las sillas contra la pared?

6. ¿Trabajó Lupita ayer entre las dos y las ocho?

7. ¿Para qué es este libro?

8. ¿Por dónde viene usted a la universidad?

9. ¿Quiere usted bailar conmigo esta noche?

10. ¿Le gusta salir a los bares con ella?

CULTURAL VIGNETTE

There is a great variety of food specialties among Hispanic countries. For example, people from Cuba often eat rice dishes cooked with special ingredients. In Argentina, the local specialty is beef on the grill, whereas in Mexico tortillas are served with many different fillings. In Spain, foods that are viewed as exotic by North Americans are served on a daily basis—for instance, **pulpo** (octopus), **calamares** (squid), and **riñones** (beef or lamb kidneys). Main meals in Hispanic countries are often prepared inexpensively with legumes, particularly using **lentejas** (lentils), **garbanzos** (chickpeas), and **frijoles** (dry beans).

PART FOUR

ENGINEERING OPERATIONS

CHAPTER 11

"SER" AND "ESTAR"

THE PRESENT PROGRESSIVE TENSE

OVERVIEW

The Spanish verbs **ser** and **estar** cover most of the meanings of the English verb *to be*. Each expresses different concepts, and, for this reason, they cannot be interchangeable. In general, **ser** is used to express an inherent characteristic or quality, whereas **estar** is used to express a condition or state that is often susceptible to change. This chapter also deals with the present progressive tense, which is used to express an action going on at the moment the statement is made.

UNIT CONTENT

Technical Engineering Vocabulary (I) • Uses of **ser** • Uses of **estar** •
Ser versus **estar** • *To Be* Substituted by **Tener** • The Present Progressive
Tense • Uses of the Present Progressive Tense • Conversational
Professional Interaction • Cultural Vignette

Technical Engineering Vocabulary (I)

air-conditioned	el aire acondicionado (áh-ee-reh ah-cohn-dee-see-oh-náh-doh)
air exhaust	el extractor de aire (ehs-trahc-tóhr deh áh-ee-reh)
algae	las algas (áhl-gahs)
algicide	el alguicida (ahl-guee-sée-dah)
ant	la hormiga (ohr-mée-gah)
beach	la playa (pláh-yah)
bee	la abeja (ah-béh-hah)
belt (motor)	la correa (coh-rréh-ah)
blade (tool)	la hoja (óh-hah)
board (wood)	la tabla (táh-blah)

boiler	la caldera (cahl-déh-rah)
branch (tree)	la rama (ráh-mah)
breakdown	
(equipment)	la avería (ah-veh-rée-ah)
brick	el ladrillo (lah-drée-yoh)
broken	roto (*adj.*) (róh-toh)
broom	la escoba (ehs-cóh-bah)
brush	el cepillo (seh-pée-yoh)
bush	el arbusto (ahr-bóos-toh)
cable	el cable (cáh-bleh)
carpenter	el carpintero (cahr-peen-téh-roh)
carpet	la alfombra (ahl-fóhm-brah)
cement	el cemento (seh-méhn-toh)
chain saw	la motosierra (móh-toh see-éh-rrah)
chemicals	productos químicos (proh-dóoc-tohs kée-mee-cohs)
chisel	el cincel (seen-séhl)
chlorine	el cloro (clóh-roh)
cockroach	la cucaracha (coo-cah-ráh-chah)
coil	el serpentín (sehr-pehn-téen)
compressor	el compresor (cohm-preh-sóhr)
concrete	el hormigón (ohr-mee-góhn)
courtyard	el patio (páh-tee-oh)
curtain	la cortina (cohr-tée-nah)
(to) dig	cavar (*v.*) (cah-váhr)
ditch	la zanja (sáhn-hah)
drain	la coladera (coh-lah-déh-rah)
drainage	el drenaje (dreh-náh-heh)
duct	el conducto (cohn-dóoc-toh)
electrician	el electricista (eh-lehc-tree-sées-tah)
electricity	la electricidad (eh-lehc-tree-see-dáhd)
electricity plate	
(on wall)	la placa (plāh-cah)
elevator	el elevador (eh-leh-vah-dóhr)
	el ascensor (ahs-sehn-sóhr)
emergency	la emergencia (eh-mehr-héhn-see-ah)
emergency lighting	las luces de emergencia (lóo-sehs deh eh-mehr-héhn-see-ah)
enamel	el esmalte (ehs-máhl-teh)
engineering	la ingeniería (een-heh-nee-eh-rée-ah)
erosion	la erosión (eh-roh-see-óhn)
exit	la salida (sah-lée-dah)
exit light	la luz de salida (loos deh sah-lée-dah)
fan	el ventilador (vehn-tee-lah-dóhr)
faucet	el grifo (grée-foh)
fence	la cerca (séhr-cah)
(to) fertilize	abonar (*v.*) (ah-boh-náhr)

fertilizer	el abono (ah-bóh-noh)
filter	el filtro (féel-troh)
fire detector	el detector de fuego (deh-tehc-tóhr deh foo-éh-goh)
fire extinguisher	el extinctor (es-teenc-tóhr)
flat roof	la azotea (ah-soh-téh-ah)
float	el flotador (floh-tah-dóhr)
flower	la flor (flohr)
flower pot	la maceta (mah-séh-tah)
fluorescent tube	el tubo fluorescente (tóo-boh floo-oh-rehs-séhn-teh)
fountain	la fuente (foo-éhn-teh)

Auxiliary Vocabulary Words

el/la abuelo/a (ah-boo-éh-loh/ah)	*grandfather/grandmother*
cerca (séhr-cah)	*near*
el/la esposo/a (ehs-póh-soh/ah)	*husband/wife*
la familia (fah-mée-lee-ah)	*family*
el/la hermano/a (ehr-máh-noh/ah)	*brother/sister*
el/la hijo/a (ée-hoh/ah)	*son/daughter*
la madre (máh-dreh)	*mother*
la mamá (mah-máh)	*mommy*
el padre (páh-dreh)	*father*
los padres (páh-drehs)	*parents*
el papá (pah-páh)	*daddy*
el tío/a (tée-oh/ah)	*uncle/aunt*

List of Adjectives Commonly Used with **Ser** (less commonly, some of these adjectives can also be used with **estar**)

bonito/a (boh-née-toh/ah)	*pretty*
delgado/a (dehl-gáh-doh/dah)	*thin*
difícil (dee-fée-seel)	*difficult*
elegante (eh-leh-gáhn-teh)	*elegant*
fácil (fáh-seel)	*easy*
guapo/a (goo-áh-poh)	*handsome/pretty*
inteligente (een-teh-lee-héhn-teh)	*intelligent*
interesante (een-teh-reh-sáhn-teh)	*interesting*
rico/a (rée-coh/ah)	*rich (moneywise)*

List of Adjectives Commonly Used with **Estar** (less commonly, some of these adjectives can also be used with **ser**) (*continued*)

🧳

cansado/a (cahn-sáh-doh/dah)	*tired*
casado/a (cah-sáh-doh/dah)	*married*
contento/a (cohn-téhn-toh/ah)	*glad, pleased*
enfadado/a (ehn-fah-dáh-doh/dah)	*angry*
enfermo/a (ehn-féhr-moh/mah)	*sick, ill*
rico/a (rée-coh/ah)	*tasty, yummy (things to eat)*

EXERCISE 11.1

Match the following list of restaurant vocabulary words, practice their pronunciation, and be ready to speak them aloud:

1. *fan*	_____	a.	zanja
2. *breakdown*	_____	b.	luces de emergencia
3. *cable*	_____	c.	ladrillo
4. *air-conditioned*	_____	d.	playa
5. *fluorescent tube*	_____	e.	grifo
6. *drainage*	_____	f.	abono
7. *electrician*	_____	g.	luz de salida
8. *fire detector*	_____	h.	correa
9. *chlorine*	_____	i.	carpintero
10. *branch*	_____	j.	patio
11. *emergency lighting*	_____	k.	drenaje
12. *exit light*	_____	l.	ventilador
13. *ditch*	_____	m.	tubo fluorescente
14. *fertilizer*	_____	n.	rama
15. *carpenter*	_____	o.	cable
16. *courtyard*	_____	p.	avería
17. *brick*	_____	q.	cloro
18. *faucet*	_____	r.	detector de fuego
19. *beach*	_____	s.	aire acondicionado
20. *belt*	_____	t.	electricista

Uses of **Ser**

As we know from previous chapters, the present, imperfect, and preterit tenses of **ser** are:

	Present	Imperfect	Preterit
yo	soy	era	fui
él, ella, usted	es	era	fue
nosotros/as	somos	éramos	fuimos
ellos, ellas, ustedes	son	eran	fueron

were   *used to be*

In general, **ser** is used to:

1. Identify people, places, and things. Examples:

¿Quién es usted?	*Who are you?*
Soy el mozo nuevo.	*I am the new houseperson.*
¿Qué es esto?	*What is this?*
Es un trapeador.	*It is a mop.*

2. Express where people and things are from (origin):

¿De dónde es Jorge?	*Where is Jorge from?*
Jorge es de España.	*Jorge is from Spain.*
Jorge es español.	*Jorge is Spanish.*

3. Express time of day:

¿Qué hora era?	*What time was it?*
Eran las tres de la tarde	*It was 3:00 P.M.*
¿A qué hora es la salida?	*What is the checkout time?*
La salida es a las doce.	*Checkout time is 12 o'clock.*

4. Indicate possession with **de:**

¿De quién es esta escoba?	*Whose broom is this?*
Es de Eduardo.	*It is Eduardo's.*

5. Link subjects with adjectives perceived as being of "permanent" condition:

Juan es alto.	*Juan is tall.*
¿Es el hotel bueno?	*Is the hotel a good one?*

6. Express impersonal statements:

Es importante.	*It is important.*
Era necesario.	*It was necessary.*
Es posible.	*It is possible.*
Es probable	*It is probable.*

7. Indicate a profession:

¿Es su hermano electricista?	*Is your brother an electrician?*
Sí, Juan es electricista.	*Yes, Juan is an electrician.*

EXERCISE 11.2

Understand the meaning of the following sentences with the verb **ser** and pronounce them in Spanish:

1. La señora López es la esposa de Miguel.
2. ¿Es Eduardo de Colombia?
3. Es necesario reparar ahora los grifos en el baño público.
4. Mi jefe es muy inteligente.
5. Yo soy moreno, pero mi tía es muy rubia.
6. ¿Es el banquete a las once o a las doce?
7. ¿Es el esmalte rojo caro?
8. No, el esmalte rojo es muy barato.
9. ¿Son los mozos de pisos guatemaltecos?
10. Sí, son de Guatemala.

EXERCISE 11.3

Fill in the blanks with the appropriate form of the verb **ser:**

1. El carpintero elegante _____ de Venezuela.
2. ¿De quién _____ aquel uniforme?
3. Aquel uniforme _____ mío.
4. ¿ _____ usted mesero o electricista?
5. _____ electricista.
6. ¿A qué hora _____ el desayuno?
7. El desayuno _____ de siete y media a diez.
7. ¿Quién _____ su padre?
8. Mi padre _____ el señor que trabaja en la playa del hotel.
9. ¿ _____ Lupita elegante?
10. Sí, Lupita _____ muy elegante.

EXERCISE 11.4

In pairs, ask and answer the following questions using the Spanish verb **ser,** making sure that you understand the meaning of each sentence:

1. ¿Qué hora es?
2. ¿Es el electricista nuevo de Chile o de Cuba?
3. ¿Es su mamá rubia o morena?
4. ¿Quién es ese señor elegante?

5. ¿A que hora fue el banquete anoche?

6. ¿Es necesario reparar el cable ahora?

7. ¿Es el trabajo aquí fácil o difícil?

8. ¿Es el tío de Lupita mexicano o puertorriqueño?

9. ¿Fue la avería en el ventilador o en la motosierra?

10. ¿Fue el banquete por la mañana o por la tarde?

11. ¿Por qué es importante este trabajo?

EXERCISE 11.5

With a partner, ask and answer the following phrases, making sure that you understand what you are asking or answering:

Estudiante uno:	¿Era usted carpintero cuando trabajaba en Boston?
Estudiante dos:	No, cuando yo trabajaba en Boston era plomero.
Estudiante uno:	¿A qué hora fue el banquete ayer?
Estudiante dos:	El banquete fue a la una y cuarto.
Estudiante uno:	¿Es Jorge inteligente?
Estudiante dos:	Sí, Jorge es muy inteligente.
Estudiante uno:	¿Es posible reparar el refrigerador ahora?
Estudiante dos:	Lo siento, no es posible porque no tenemos tiempo.
Estudiante uno:	¿Son las tres ya?
Estudiante dos:	Todavía no son las tres.
Estudiante uno:	¿Quién es la supervisora nueva?
Estudiante dos:	La señora Benigna es la supervisora nueva.

Uses of **Estar**

As we know from previous chapters, the present, imperfect, and preterit tenses of **estar** are:

	Present	Imperfect	Preterit
yo	estoy	estaba	estuve
él, ella, usted	está	estaba	estuvo
nosotros/as	estamos	estábamos	estuvimos
ellos, ellas, ustedes	están	estaban	estuvieron

In general, **estar** is used to express relational or temporary conditions:

1. To indicate location. Examples:

¿Dónde está Antonio?	*Where is Antonio?*
Antonio está en el almacén.	*Antonio is in the storeroom.*

2. To express health conditions. Examples:

Ella estuvo enferma ayer.	*She was sick yesterday.*
Estoy bien, gracias.	*I am well, thank you.*

3. To express temporary emotional conditions. Examples:

Juan estaba enfadado.	*Juan was feeling angry.*
Ellas están contentas.	*They are pleased/happy.*

4. To describe a quality that is usually subject to change. Examples:

El té está caliente.	*The tea is hot.*
Este pastel está rico.	*This cake is yummy.*
El ventilador está roto.	*The fan is broken.*
La luz está encendida.	*The light is on.*

EXERCISE 11.6

Understand the meaning of the following sentences with the verb **estar** and pronounce them in Spanish:

1. Este ventilador está estropeado.
2. El electricista estuvo enfermo ayer.
3. Juan no está en el hotel este fin de semana.
4. ¿Dónde están sus padres ahora?
5. ¿Está bien su hijo?
6. Mi hijo y mi esposa están muy bien, gracias.
7. El carpintero está muy enfadado con el cajero.
8. El agua en la alberca está fría.
9. Yo no voy a estar en mi oficina esta tarde.
10. ¿Está Jorge contento en el hotel?

EXERCISE 11.7

Fill the blanks with the appropriate form of the verb **estar:**

1. Pepe no _____ bien hoy.
2. El jefe de cocina _____ en México ahora.
3. Jorge y Lupita _____ enfermos ayer.
4. Las sábanas _____ aquí esta mañana pero ahora no _____.
5. ¿Cómo _____ usted?

6. ¿Dónde _____ los cepillos?

7. La azotea _____ en el piso doce.

8. Estos pasteles _____ muy ricos (*someone is in the act of eating them*).

9. ¿Por qué _____ contentas las camaristas?

10. Los cuartos _____ listos a las cuatro.

EXERCISE 11.8

In pairs, ask and answer the following questions using the Spanish verb **estar,** making sure that you understand the meaning of each sentence:

1. ¿Está el electricista enfadado hoy?

2. ¿Estuvo usted enferma ayer?

3. ¿Estaba Juana en el almacén cuando usted la vio?

4. ¿Cuándo está la ama de llaves en su oficina?

5. ¿Está el carpintero enfermo?

6. ¿Dónde está el sótano?

7. ¿Están contentos los huéspedes?

8. ¿Estuvo Jorge en Providence el verano pasado?

9. ¿Está su padre en Tucson ahora?

10. ¿Por qué está enfadada María?

EXERCISE 11.9

With a partner, ask and answer the following phrases, making sure that you understand what you are asking or answering:

Estudiante uno:	¿Dónde está su familia ahora?
Estudiante dos:	Mi familia está en Zacatecas, México.
Estudiante uno:	¿Estuvo usted en Arkansas el verano pasado?
Estudiante dos:	No estuve en Arkansas; estuve en Carolina del Norte.
Estudiante uno:	¿Están las luces encendidas en el comedor?
Estudiante dos:	Sí, están encendidas; las encendí yo a las tres.
Estudiante uno:	¿Está la sopa caliente?
Estudiante dos:	Sí, la sopa está muy caliente.
Estudiante uno:	¿Están ricos estos pasteles?
Estudiante dos:	Los pasteles están muy ricos.
Estudiante uno:	¿Cómo está su tío Zacarías?
Estudiante dos:	Mi tío Zacarías está muy bien, gracias.

Ser Versus Estar

Both **ser** (*to be*) and **estar** (*to be*) can be used before adjectives. In general, *ser* is used when the quality to be expressed is a fundamental characteristic of the person or thing; **estar** is used if the quality expressed is a state or condition that is subject to change. However, in some cases the choice of **ser** or **estar** depends on the kind of description we wish to make. If we wish to make a factual, impersonal statement, we use **ser.** The statement **Esas peras son verdes** means that the pears are green in color. The statement **Esas peras están verdes** means that the pears are not ripe. In some cases, when **ser** and **estar** are used with adjectives, the meaning of what is said changes by using one or the other verb. For example, **Lupita es guapa** means that she is really cute, while the sentence **Lupita está guapa** means that she looks cute today.

EXERCISE 11.10

Fill in the blanks with the appropriate form of **ser** or **estar:**

1. Pepe no _____ bien hoy.
2. El electricista _____ de Perú.
3. El jardinero _____ en Des Moines hoy.
4. Jorge _____ cansado.
5. ¿ _____ Josefina en el almacén ahora?
6. ¿De quién _____ este cepillo?
7. ¿Dónde _____ las tablas?
8. ¿ _____ usted el plomero nuevo?
9. ¿Cuál uniforme _____ el mío?
10. Miguel _____ en el patio.

EXERCISE 11.11

Fill in the blanks using the appropriate form of **ser** or **estar:**

1. Este pastel _____ muy rico.
2. Lupita _____ morena y muy bonita.
3. ¿ _____ usted cansada hoy?
4. María, hoy _____ usted muy elegante.
5. María _____ una persona elegante.
6. Dos cocineros _____ enfermos hoy.
7. ¿Por qué _____ enfadada Lupita?
8. Juan no _____ casado con Micaela.
9. ¿ _____ casado Juan?
10. _____ importante hablar español.

EXERCISE 11.12

Let's learn about Lupita! With a partner, translate the following information about her:

Lupita is from San Diego. She is pretty, dark-haired, and very intelligent. Her family is in Los Angeles where her father is a plumber in a hotel. Her mother is a cook in a restaurant. Today Lupita is tired. She is angry because Jorge did not clean the storeroom well. Lupita is in Tijuana today where she has an aunt. Her aunt is married to a Cuban. He is very rich!

To Be Substituted by Tener

To express certain physical and mental conditions, the verb **tener** (*to have*) is used with nouns in Spanish instead of the English equivalent of *to be* with adjectives. For example, the statement *I am hungry* in English is expressed in Spanish as **Tengo hambre,** where *hungry* is an adjective and **hambre** is a noun.

Common idioms with **tener** are:

tener hambre/apetito	*to be hungry*
tener sed	*to be thirsty*
tener sueño	*to be sleepy*
tener calor	*to be warm*
tener frío	*to be cold*
tener razón	*to be right*
tener ____ años	*to be ____ years old*
tener ganas de	*to be eager/to desire*
tener cuidado	*to be careful*
tener suerte	*to be lucky*
tener miedo	*to be afraid*
tener prisa	*to be in a hurry*

EXERCISE 11.13

Understand the meaning of the following sentences with idioms of **tener** and pronounce them in Spanish:

1. Por favor, tenga cuidado cuando use la motosierra.
2. El plomero tiene sed; quiere un vaso de agua.

3. Yo trabajé mucho ayer; ahora tengo mucho sueño.
4. Tengo calor cuando trabajo cerca de la caldera.
5. Hoy tengo prisa; tengo que limpiar los filtros en la alberca.
6. ¡Juan siempre tiene suerte!
7. Eso no es verdad, usted no tiene razón.
8. ¿Tiene usted frío cuando trabaja en la azotea?
9. Son las once, tengo ganas de tomar un café.
10. ¿Tiene Pedro razón?

EXERCISE 11.14

With a partner, answer the following questions using **tener** (instead of **ser** or **estar**):

1. Son las doce y media, ¿tiene usted hambre?
2. ¿Tiene Pepe apetito?
3. ¿Tiene Juanito prisa hoy?
4. ¿Tienen ustedes sed?
5. ¿Tienen Juan y Jorge sueño?
6. ¿Debe el carpintero tener cuidado con la sierra de cadena?
7. ¿Tiene su papá suerte cuando conduce por Los Angeles?
8. ¿Cuántos años tienen sus hijos?
9. ¿Tenía usted frío cuando vivía en Vancouver?
10. ¿Tiene usted ganas de beber una cerveza?

EXERCISE 11.15

In pairs, ask and answer the following phrases, making sure that you understand what you are asking or answering:

Estudiante uno:	¿Tiene prisa el señor Robinson hoy?
Estudiante dos:	Sí, él tiene mucha prisa hoy.
Estudiante uno:	¿Tiene usted sed?
Estudiante dos:	No tengo sed ahorita.
Estudiante uno:	¿Tiene la señorita Esperanza razón?
Estudiante dos:	Sí, ella siempre tiene razón; es muy inteligente.
Estudiante uno:	¿Tiene usted frío?
Estudiante dos:	Tengo mucho frío. Necesito una cobija.
Estudiante uno:	¿Cuántos años tiene su hija Fabiola?
Estudiante dos:	Mi hija Fabiola tiene doce años.
Estudiante uno:	¿Tenía sueño Lupita ayer?
Estudiante dos:	Sí, porque ella fue a una fiesta de cumpleaños.

EXERCISE 11.16

With a partner, translate the following sentences into Spanish using **tener** idioms:

1. *Are you in a hurry today?* _____

2. *Yes, I am in a hurry because I have to fertilize the flower pots.* _____
   _____

3. *Don't be afraid! There is time for that!* _____
   _____

4. *Be careful with that cable!* _____

5. *Pepe is right; today is Monday, not Tuesday.* _____
   _____

6. *I am very sleepy today; yesterday I drove to New York.* _____
   _____

7. *Lupita is twenty years old, and her brother Antonio is twenty-five.* _____
   _____

8. *Are you eager to dig in the courtyard now?* _____
   _____

9. *I am not eager; it is very hot today.* _____
   _____

10. *Are you thirsty? Do you want a beer?* _____
    _____

The Present Progressive Tense

In English, the progressive tense consists of the verb *to be* plus the *ing* form of the main verb in the sentence—for example, *Pedro is fertilizing the flowers.* In Spanish, the progressive tense is formed with the verb **estar** plus the present participle of the main verb in the sentence. For example, **Pedro está fertilizando las flores.**

To form the present participle of verbs in Spanish, drop the ending of the infinitive form and add **ando** for verbs ending in **ar** and **iendo** for verbs ending in **er** or **ir.** The present participle does not change to agree with the subject of the sentence and always ends in **o.**

ar verbs:	trabajar	trabaj + ando	*working*
er verbs:	comer	com + iendo	*eating*
ir verbs:	escribir	escrib + iendo	*writing*

Examples:

Pepe está trabajando ahora en el patio, *Pepe is working now in the courtyard.*

El electricista está comiendo con Juan, *The electrician is eating with Juan.*

Lupita está escribiendo a su abuelo, *Lupita is writing to her grandfather.*

There is only one exception to the above rule: When an unstressed **i** occurs between two vowels, it changes to **y,** for example:

| ir | yendo | *going* |
| traer | trayendo | *bringing* |

EXERCISE 11.17

Understand the meaning of the following present progressive sentences and pronounce them in Spanish:

1. Juan y Enrique están cavando el drenaje para la fuente.
2. Lupe está cortando las ramas.
3. ¿Quién está trabajando en la cerca?
4. El carpintero está trabajando en la cerca.
5. Estoy viendo una cucaracha en el sofá.
6. ¿Está Juan aspirando la piscina?
7. No, Juan está barriendo la cocina.
8. Ayer vi a Lupita cortando los arbustos.
9. ¿Con quién está comiendo Isabel?
10. La camarista está haciendo las camas en la habitación 110.

EXERCISE 11.18

In pairs, ask and answer the following phrases, making sure that you understand what you are asking or answering:

Estudiante uno:	¿Quién está cavando los arbustos?
Estudiante dos:	Pedro está cavando los arbustos.
Estudiante uno:	¿Está Lupita cepillando los sillones en el vestíbulo?
Estudiante dos:	No, Lupita está barriendo el suelo.
Estudiante uno:	¿Qué está haciendo el carpintero?
Estudiante dos:	Eduardo está barnizando las sillas en el comedor.
Estudiante uno:	¿Quién está fertilizando las macetas?
Estudiante dos:	El jardinero está fertilizando las macetas.
Estudiante uno:	¿Está usted trabajando en Red Lobster?
Estudiante dos:	No, ahorita estoy trabajando en Olive Garden.
Estudiante uno:	¿Qué está bebiendo Lupe?
Estudiante dos:	Lupe está bebiendo una coca-cola.

Uses of the Present Progressive Tense

Generally, the present progressive tense is used only to describe an action that is happening at this very moment. If the action is not happening right now, the simple present tense is used as shown in the following statements in which the action is not taking place now:

English	Spanish
This week I am working on Monday.	Esta semana trabajo el lunes.
Tomorrow I am working.	Trabajo mañana.
They are coming to dinner tonight.	Vienen a cenar esta noche.

EXERCISE 11.19

With a partner, answer the following questions in Spanish:

1. ¿Trabaja usted la semana que viene?
2. ¿Dónde está trabajando usted ahora?
3. ¿Están Jorge y Fernando fertilizando las flores?
4. ¿Va usted a fertilizar las flores esta tarde?
5. ¿Quién está cortando los arbustos?
6. ¿Va a cortar usted los arbustos esta semana?
7. ¿Vive Joaquín en Santa Fe?
8. ¿Qué está haciendo Lupita?
9. ¿Qué va a hacer Lupita esta tarde?
10. ¿Está el carpintero fumando o trabajando?

EXERCISE 11.20

Understand the meaning of the following present progressive sentences and pronounce them in Spanish:

1. Estamos fertilizando las flores.
2. Vamos a fertilizar las flores mañana.
3. Mañana fertilizamos las flores.
4. Juan y Antonio están cortando los arbustos en el patio.
5. Juan y Antonio van a cortar los arbustos en el patio el lunes.
6. Juan y Antonio cortan los arbustos en el patio los miércoles.
7. Lupita está viviendo con su abuela Marta.
8. Lupita y su abuela viven en El Cajón.
9. Luisa está comiendo con sus amigas en el comedor.
10. Luisa va a comer con sus amigas a las doce y media.

EXERCISE 11.21

In pairs, ask and answer the following phrases, making sure that you understand what you are asking or answering:

Estudiante uno:	¿Quién va a cortar las ramas?
Estudiante dos:	Federico va a cortar las ramas.
Estudiante uno:	¿Quién come con el jefe hoy?
Estudiante dos:	Yo como con él a las doce.
Estudiante uno:	¿Quién está trabajando en el almacén?
Estudiante dos:	El mozo de pisos está trabajando allí.
Estudiante uno:	¿Quién va a limpiar la piscina?
Estudiante dos:	Ellos van a limpiar la piscina.
Estudiante uno:	¿Va a trabajar Felipe el turno de noche mañana?
Estudiante dos:	No, Felipe va a trabajar el turno de tarde.
Estudiante uno:	¿Va usted a pintar la cerca el lunes?
Estudiante dos:	Sí, voy a pintar la cerca el lunes por la mañana.

CONVERSATIONAL PROFESSIONAL INTERACTION

In groups of two, translate, practice, and be ready to role-play the following dialogue between an engineering supervisor and an hourly employee:

Estudiante uno (supervisor):   Buenas tardes, Enrique. Tenemos que cortar los arbustos.

Estudiante dos (empleado por hora):   De acuerdo. ¿Dónde está la sierra de cadena?

Estudiante uno:	Está en el almacén. ¿Está usted cansado hoy?
Estudiante dos:	Sí, porque ayer fui a una fiesta.
Estudiante uno:	¿Dónde fue la fiesta?
Estudiante dos:	Fue en casa de Lupita. ¿Tiene usted frío?
Estudiante uno:	No tengo frío pero tengo sed.
Estudiante dos:	Vamos a tomar una coca-cola.
Estudiante uno:	No. Tenemos que trabajar ahora.
Estudiante dos:	¿De dónde es el carpintero nuevo?
Estudiante uno:	Es de Colombia. Está viviendo con sus padres.
Estudiante dos:	¿Dónde viven sus padres?
Estudiante uno:	Viven cerca del hotel.
Estudiante dos:	¿Cuántos años tiene su padre?

Estudiante uno:	Tiene sesenta años. Es electricista.
Estudiante dos:	¿Dónde trabaja?
Estudiante uno:	Está trabajando en un restaurante como lavaplatos.
Estudiante dos:	¿Dónde dijo usted que estaba la sierra de cadena?
Estudiante uno:	Dije que estaba en el almacén. Ahora vaya a trabajar.
Estudiante dos:	Está bien. No tenga usted prisa, yo trabajo rápido.

📬 QUESTIONS TO THE CLASS 📬

Answer the following questions asked by your instructor (or by another student) without looking at your textbook or any class notes:

1. ¿De dónde es usted?
2. ¿Dónde está su familia ahora?
3. ¿Está usted cansado(a)?
4. ¿Tiene usted sed?
5. ¿Está usted trabajando en un restaurante o en un hotel?
6. ¿Estuvo usted enfermo(a) la semana pasada?
7. ¿Es usted plomero?
8. ¿Es su papá electricista o carpintero?
9. ¿Tiene usted sueño?
10. ¿Por qué tiene usted sueño? ¿Porqué está cansado(a)?

CULTURAL VIGNETTE

Sports are as important to Hispanics as they are to North Americans. The favorite sport in Hispanic countries is soccer, in which touching the ball with the hands is forbidden.

In Cuba, Mexico, Spain, and in Florida, **jai alai** is also a popular sport. Jai alai is played in a court with three walls. The players throw a hard ball against a wall using a curved, long, narrow basket attached to their arms. Basketball and baseball are now quite popular in Mexico, Cuba, Puerto Rico, and the Dominican Republic from where many star players in American Major League Baseball have originated.

Object Pronouns

Adverbs of Time

OVERVIEW

Chapter 12 deals with object pronouns. Pronouns are related to nouns and take their place, referring to persons or objects without giving their names. This chapter also covers adverbs of time.

UNIT CONTENT

Technical Engineering Vocabulary (II)

fuse	el fusible (foo-sée-bleh)
game room	el salón de juegos (sah-lóhn deh hoo-éh-gohs)
garbage disposal	el triturador (tree-too-rah-dóhr)
garden	el jardín (hahr-déen)
garden path	el andador (ahn-dah-dóhr)
gardener	el/la jardinero/a (hahr-dee-néh-roh/ah)
gas	la gasolina (gah-soh-lée-nah)
gloves	los guantes (goo-áhn-tehs)
graft	el injerto (een-héhr-toh)
(to) graft	injertar (*v.*) (een-hehr-táhr)
grass	la hierba (ee-éhr-bah)
gravel	el cascajo (cahs-cáh-hoh)
grease	la grasa (gráh-sah)
grease trap	la trampa de grasa (tráhm-pah deh gráh-sah)

guest room	la habitación (ah-bee-tah-see-óhn)
hammer	el martillo (mahr-tée-yoh)
heating	la calefacción (cah-leh-fac-see-óhn)
hedge	el seto (séh-toh)
herbicide	el herbicida (ehr-bee-sée-dah)
hinge	la bisagra (bee-sáh-grah)
hoe	el azadón (ah-sah-dóhn)
hole	el agujero (ah-goo-héh-roh)
hole (in the ground)	el hoyo (óh-yoh)
hose	la manguera (mahn-guéh-rah)
insect	el insecto (een-séhc-toh)
insecticide	el insecticida (een-sehc-tee-sée-dah)
irrigation water	el agua para riego (áh-goo-ah páh-rah ree-éh-goh)
lawn	el césped (séhs-pehd)
lawn mower	la cortadora de césped (cohr-tah-dóh-rah deh séhs-pehd)
leaf	la hoja (óh-hah)
leak	la fuga de agua (fóo-gah deh áh-goo-ah)
light	la luz (loos)
light bulb	la bombilla (bohm-bée-yah)
	el foco (fóh-coh)
light switch	el apagador (ah-pah-gah-dóhr)
	el interruptor (een-teh-rroop-tóhr)
lime (not the fruit)	la cal (cahl)
lock	la cerradura (seh-rrah-dóo-rah)
locker room	el vestidor (vehs-tee-dóhr)
(to) lubricate	lubricar (*v.*) (loo-bree-cáhr)
maintenance	el mantenimiento (mahn-teh-nee-mee-éhn-toh)
maintenance department	el departamento de mantenimiento (deh-pahr-tah-méhn-toh deh mahn-teh-nee-mee-éhn-toh)
maintenance shop	el taller (tah-yéhr)
manure	el estiércol (ehs-tee-éhr-cohl)
money	el dinero (dee-néh-roh)
motor	el motor (moh-tóhr)
mouse (rodent)	el ratón (rah-tóhn)
mousetrap	la ratonera (rah-toh-néh-rah)
(to) mow the lawn	cortar el césped (cohr-táhr ehl séhs-pehd)
nail	el clavo (cláh-voh)
(to) nail	clavar (*v.*) (clah-váhr)
natural gas	el gas ciudad (gahs see-oo-dád)
nozzle	la boquilla (boh-kée-yah)
out of order	fuera de servicio (*adj.*) (foo-éh-rah deh sehr-vée-see-oh)
paint	la pintura (peen-tóo-rah)
(to) paint	pintar (*v.*) (peen-táhr)
palm tree	la palmera (pahl-méh-rah)

(to) park	aparcar (*v.*) (ah-pahr-cáhr)
parking lot	el estacionamiento (ehs-tah-see-oh-nah-mee-éhn-toh)
part	la pieza (pee-éh-sah)
pest control	el control de plagas (cohn-tróhl deh pláh-gahs)
pesticide	el pesticida (pehs-tee-sée-dah)
pipe	el tubo (tóo-boh)
piping	la tubería (too-beh-rée-ah)
plant	la planta (pláhn-tah)
(to) plant	plantar (*v.*) (plahn-táhr)
plaster	el yeso (yéh-soh)
playground	el área de juegos (áh-reh-ah deh hoo-éh-gohs)
pliers	los alicates (ah-lee-cáh-tehs)
plumber	el plomero (ploh-méh-roh)
potable water	el agua potable (áh-goo-ah poh-táh-bleh)
pressure	la presión (preh-see-óhn)
pressure gage	el manómetro (mah-nóh-meh-troh)
preventive maintenance	el mantenimiento preventivo (mahn-teh-nee-mee-éhn-toh preh-vehn-tée-voh)
(to) prune	podar (*v.*) (poh-dáhr)
pulley	la polea (poh-léh-ah)
pump	la bomba (bóhm-bah)

EXERCISE 12.1

Match the following list of restaurant vocabulary words, practice their pronunciation, and be ready to speak them aloud:

1. *gloves*	_____	a. bisagra
2. *mouse*	_____	b. cal
3. *pressure gage*	_____	c. fuera de servicio
4. *pipe*	_____	d. alicates
5. *heating*	_____	e. hierba
6. *garden path*	_____	f. martillo
7. *light*	_____	g. estiércol
8. *nail*	_____	h. vestidor
9. *(to) plant*	_____	i. pintura
10. *plumber*	_____	j. lubricar
11. *grass*	_____	k. guantes
12. *hammer*	_____	l. calefacción
13. *lime*	_____	m. ratón
14. *locker room*	_____	n. clavo
15. *pliers*	_____	o. tubo

16. *paint*	_____	p. plomero
17. *out of order*	_____	q. plantar
18. *manure*	_____	r. andador
19. *(to) lubricate*	_____	s. luz
20. *hinge*	_____	t. manómetro

Direct Object Pronouns

In Spanish, object pronouns are always joined in speech to a verb. As is the case with reflexive pronouns, object pronouns immediately precede the verb, whereas in affirmative commands they follow the verb. These pronouns may precede or follow the infinitive and the present progressive tense. Generally, direct object pronouns refer to people or things for which they substitute in order to avoid repeating names. Direct object pronouns are usually placed immediately before the verb. (Exceptions will be given later.)

Direct Object Pronouns

	Singular	Plural
me (meh)	*me*	nos (nohs) *us*
lo (loh)	*you, him, it*	los (lohs) *you, them*
la (lah)	*you, her, it*	las (lahs) *you, them*

Example: **Juan planta las flores** (*Juan plants the flowers*) can also be expressed as **Juan las planta** (*Juan plants them*). As you can see, in affirmative statements, the pronoun *them* in English follows the verb whereas the pronoun **las** in Spanish precedes it.

EXERCISE 12.2

Translate the following sentences into English. (The nouns in parentheses have been substituted by direct object pronouns.)

1. Yo lo veo (el hotel). _____
2. El jardinero los barre (los andadores). _____
3. ¿Las tiene usted (las llaves)? _____
4. No, Juan las tiene (las llaves). _____
5. Juan lo aspira (el pasillo). _____
6. ¿Quién los corta (los arbustos)? _____
7. El plomero no los corta (los arbustos). _____
8. Ellos las están limpiando (las cortinas). _____
9. Raúl lo cava (el hoyo). _____
10. Usted la enciende (la luz). _____

EXERCISE 12.3

Substitute the nouns in bold with the appropriate direct object pronoun:

1. Jorge pinta la **pared** una vez al año. _____
2. Las camaristas limpiaron los **cuartos** ayer. _____
3. En este hotel lavamos los **blancos** por la mañana. _____
4. Él está preparando el **aire acondicionado** para el banquete de esta tarde. _____
5. Lupita llama a sus **padres** dos veces por semana. _____
6. El jefe de departamento necesita de **mí.** _____
7. El jefe de departamento necesita de **Jorge y yo.** _____
8. El carpintero está clavando los **clavos** en la cerca. _____
9. Antonia siempre limpia el **vestidor de empleados** entre las diez y las doce. _____
10. El jardinero poda las **palmeras** en la primavera. _____

EXERCISE 12.4

Answer the following questions using direct object pronouns instead of the nouns in bold:

1. ¿Tenemos **espejos** en el almacén? _____
2. ¿Hay **un martillo** en ese cajón? _____
3. ¿Corta el jardinero **flores** para el comedor? _____
4. ¿Tiene el plomero **los alicates?** _____
5. ¿Planta el jardinero **plantas** cada verano? _____
6. ¿Quién pinta las **paredes** en el bar este fin de semana? _____
7. ¿Quién reparó la **bomba?** _____
8. ¿Lubricó Juan el **motor?** _____
9. ¿Lubrica Juan el **motor** mañana? _____
10. ¿Trajo el electricista la **llave maestra** al taller? _____

EXERCISE 12.5

In pairs, ask and answer the following phrases, making sure that you understand what you are asking or answering:

Estudiante uno: ¿Quién lleva las flores al restaurante?

Estudiante dos: Jorge las lleva.

Estudiante uno: ¿Tiene Jorge que vaciar los cubos de basura?

Estudiante dos: Sí, Jorge los tiene que vaciar.

Estudiante uno:	¿Está Carmen haciendo las camas?
Estudiante dos:	Sí, Carmen las está haciendo.
Estudiante uno:	¿Tiene usted la llave del almacén?
Estudiante dos:	Sí, yo la tengo.
Estudiante uno:	¿Quién tiene la cortadora de césped?
Estudiante dos:	El jardinero la tiene.
Estudiante uno:	¿Habla usted español?
Estudiante dos:	Sí, lo hablo muy bien.

Indirect Object Pronouns

Generally, indirect object pronouns tell to whom or for whom the action of the verb is done. As with direct object pronouns, indirect object pronouns are usually placed immediately before the verb. (Exceptions will be given later.) Because **le** and **les** can refer to different subjects, Spanish speakers may add the expressions **a él, a Juan, a ella, a Lupita, a ellos, a Juan y Lupita, a ellas, a Lupita y Antonia** to the sentence for clarification or emphasis.

Indirect Object Pronouns

Singular	Plural
me (meh) *to/for/from me*	nos (nohs) *to/for/from us*
le (leh) *to/for/from you*	les (lehs) *to/for/from you*
le (leh) *to/for/from him/her/it*	les (lehs) *to/for/from them*

Example: **Juan escribe a Lupita** (*Juan writes to Lupita*) can also be expressed as **Juan le escribe** (*Juan writes to her*). As with direct object pronouns, in affirmative statements the indirect *to her* in English follows the verb, whereas the pronoun **le** in Spanish precedes it.

EXERCISE 12.6

Translate the following sentences into English. (The nouns in parentheses have been substituted by indirect object pronouns.)

1. Antonio le pide los focos (a Jorge). _____

   _____

2. Antonio les pide los focos (a Jorge y Raúl). _____

   _____

3. ¿Quién nos escribió? (a nosotros). _____

   _____

4. Juanita nos escribió (a nosotros). _____

5. Yo le hago siempre el desayuno (a ella). _____
   _____

6. Ella no me hace el desayuno nunca (a mí). _____
   _____

7. ¿Les quiere usted (a sus hijos)? _____

8. El plomero mexicano me preguntó (a mí). _____
   _____

9. Yo le contesté (a él). _____

10. Su mamá les envía ropa limpia cada semana (a ellos). _____
    _____

EXERCISE 12.7

Substitute the nouns in bold with the appropriate indirect object pronoun:

1. Jorge envía dinero **(a su mamá).** _____

2. Antonio prepara los productos químicos antes del turno **(a nosotros).**
   _____

3. El ama de llaves dio uniformes **(a los electricistas).** _____

4. Su tío escribió una carta **(a Lupita).** _____

5. Él da un cepillo **(al mozo).** _____

6. Yo envié la alfombra **(al señor González).** _____

7. El señor González envió el yeso **(a Juan).** _____

8. Yo podé los arbustos **(a Luís).** _____

9. La semana pasada, Luís podó los arbustos **(a mí).** _____

10. Ayer, el jefe del departamento de mantenimiento pidió el reporte
    (a ellos). _____

EXERCISE 12.8

In pairs, ask and answer the following phrases, making sure that you understand what you are asking or answering:

Estudiante uno:	¿Les trae ella los cepillos?
Estudiante dos:	Sí, ella les trae los cepillos.
Estudiante uno:	¿Le dio usted los focos al electricista?
Estudiante dos:	Sí, le di los focos ayer.
Estudiante uno:	¿Cuándo le enviará usted flores a Lupita?
Estudiante dos:	Le enviaré flores el martes.
Estudiante uno:	¿Le escribirá Jorge a Lupita una carta?
Estudiante dos:	Sí, él le escribirá una carta desde Acapulco.
Estudiante uno:	¿Le preguntó usted a Dolores?

Estudiante dos:	No le pregunté a Dolores.
Estudiante uno:	¿Preparó usted los cuartos para los huéspedes?
Estudiante dos:	Sí, les preparé los cuartos antes de las cinco.

Direct and Indirect Pronouns Used Together in the Same Sentence

Often, direct and indirect pronouns are used together in the same sentence. In this case, the indirect pronoun is always placed before the direct pronoun with no words between them. Example: *He gave me the gloves* will translate, using pronouns, as **él me los dio.** In this case, **me** is the indirect pronoun used instead of *to me*, and **los** is the direct pronoun used instead of *the gloves* (**los guantes**). The indirect object pronouns **le** and **les** always change to **se** when they are used with the direct object pronouns **lo, la, los,** and **las.** Example: *He gave them to* translates as **él se los dio.**

EXERCISE 12.9

Understand the meaning of the following sentences and pronounce them in Spanish:

1. Él me lo da.   2. Ellos nos las dan.   3. El electricista se lo prepara (a usted).   4. Juan se los envía (a ellos).   5. Ellos se la piden (a ella).
6. Yo se los podo (a él).   7. Lupita se las hace (a ellos).   8. ¿Me los quiere preparar, por favor?   9. Se los preparé mañana.   10. ¿Me la escribió usted?

EXERCISE 12.10

Substitute the nouns in bold for direct and indirect pronouns:

1. Jorge prepara los **productos químicos** para **Juan.** _____
2. El carpintero pide el **cable** al **electricista.** _____
3. Lupita hace las **camas** para los **huéspedes.** _____
4. El jardinero corta las **flores** para el **ama de llaves.** _____
5. Antonia lava los **uniformes** para los **electricistas.** _____
6. El jardinero prepara un **hoyo** para el **electricista.** _____
7. Nosotros dimos la **pintura** a **Juan** esta mañana. _____
8. La mesera está sirviendo las **bebidas** a los **clientes.** _____
9. ¿Quién pidió la **ratonera** al **carpintero?** _____
10. Joaquín pidió la **ratonera** al **carpintero.** _____

EXERCISE 12.11

With a partner, ask and answer the following phrases, making sure that you understand what you are asking or answering:

Estudiante uno:	¿Preparan los cocineros el almuerzo para los clientes?
Estudiante dos:	Sí, ellos se lo preparan.
Estudiante uno:	¿Pidió Jorge las llaves a Lupita?
Estudiante dos:	Sí, se las pidió esta mañana.
Estudiante uno:	¿Cuándo le enviará usted flores a Lupita?
Estudiante dos:	Se las enviaré el martes.
Estudiante uno:	¿Quién le pidió a usted los azadones?
Estudiante dos:	Antonio y Federico me los pidieron.
Estudiante uno:	¿Escribirá Jorge a Lupita una carta?
Estudiante dos:	Sí, él se la escribirá desde Portland.
Estudiante uno:	¿Preparó usted los cuartos para los huéspedes?
Estudiante dos:	Sí, se los preparé antes de las cinco.

Object Pronouns and Commands

Object pronouns are attached to affirmative commands. If the command is negative, the pronouns precede the command. As with statements, the indirect object pronoun is always placed before the direct object pronoun. Examples:

Affirmation Command

Dé la motosierra a Pedro.	*Give the chain saw to Pedro* (no pronouns).
Déla a Pedro.	*Give it to Pedro* (direct pronoun).
Déle la motosierra.	*Give him the chain saw* (indirect pronoun).
Désela.	*Give it to him* (indirect + direct pronouns)

Negative Commands

No dé la motosierra a Pedro.
No la dé a Pedro.
No le dé la motosierra.
No se la dé.

EXERCISE 12.12

Understand the meaning of the following sentences and pronounce them in Spanish:

1. Escríbale una carta.
2. Escríbala a Juan.
3. Escríbasela.
4. No le escriba una carta.

5. No la escriba a Juan.
6. No se la escriba.
7. Pídale una escoba.
8. Pídala a Jorge.
9. Pídasela.
10. No se la pida.

EXERCISE 12.13

With a partner, ask and answer the following phrases, making sure that you understand what you are asking or answering:

Estudiante uno: ¿Pelo las patatas para el jefe?
Estudiante dos: Sí, péleselas, por favor.
Estudiante uno: ¿Pongo el cloro en la alberca?
Estudiante dos: Sí, póngalo.
Estudiante uno: ¿Llevo el cable al electricista?
Estudiante dos: No se lo lleve; yo se lo llevaré después.
Estudiante uno: ¿Podo las ramas de los árboles cerca de la cerca?
Estudiante dos: Sí, pódelas antes del miércoles.
Estudiante uno: ¿Envío las flores a Lupita?
Estudiante dos: Sí, envíeselas hoy.
Estudiante uno: ¿Pinto las paredes en el salón de juegos?
Estudiante dos: No las pinte hoy, píntelas el jueves.

Object Pronouns with the Infinitive Form and the Present Progressive Tense

When used with the infinitive form or with the present progressive tense, object pronouns may be placed before the verb or attached to the end of it. Examples: *I am going to give the mop to Lupita* can be translated, using pronouns, as **voy a dárselo** and **se lo voy a dar.** Similarly, *Lupita is making the beds for the guests* can be translated, using pronouns, as **Lupita está haciéndoselas** and **Lupita se las está haciendo.**

EXERCISE 12.14

Understand the meaning of the following sentences and pronounce them in Spanish:

1. Juan no quiere dárselas.
2. Lupita se las está pidiendo.

3. Yo necesito comprarlas.
4. Yo las necesito preparar.
5. Ellos prefieren no dárselas.
6. Lupita está haciéndoselas.
7. Es importante barrerlos ahora.
8. No puedo contarlas hasta pasado mañana.
9. ¿Quiere usted cortársela, por favor?
10. Lo siento; no se la puedo cortar ahora.

EXERCISE 12.15

Translate the following sentences, substituting the nouns in bold for object pronouns:

1. *I cannot vacuum it now* **(the swimming pool).** _____

_____

2. *Do you want to paint them* **(the walls)?** _____

_____

3. *I prefer to paint them tomorrow* **(the walls).** _____

_____

4. *Lupita doesn't want to send them to him* **(the curtains).** _____

_____

5. *I prefer to write it to her next month* **(the note).** _____

_____

6. *Do you need to send them to them today* **(the hinges)?** _____

_____

7. *I prefer to send them to them tomorrow* **(the hinges).** _____

_____

8. *Is he washing them* **(the sheets)?** _____

9. *Yes, he is washing them for her* **(the sheets).** _____

_____

10. *Lupita doesn't want to clean them* **(the hallways).** _____

_____

Adverbs of Time

As in English, Spanish adverbs are words used to qualify or limit a verb, an adjective, or another adverb. Adverbs are often formed in English by adding the suffix *ly* to an adjective. In Spanish, many adverbs are formed by adding the suffix **mente** to the feminine form of adjectives. Example: **rápido** (ráh-pee-doh) meaning *quick* becomes **rápidamente** (ráh-pee-dah-mehn-teh) meaning *quickly*. In the sentence, adverbs should be placed as near the verb as possible.

EXERCISE 12.16

Form adverbs from the following adjectives:

1. excelente _____
2. estupendo _____
3. bueno _____
4. actual _____
5. necesario _____
6. especial _____
7. malo _____
8. rápida _____
9. claro _____
10. natural _____

Adverbs of Time (These adverbs do not end in *ly* in English, nor do they end in **mente** in Spanish.)

ahora (ah-óh-rah)	*now*
ahorita (ah-oh-rée-tah)	*right now*
anoche (ah-nóh-cheh)	*last night*
antes (áhn-tehs)	*before*
ayer (ah-yéhr)	*yesterday*
después (dehs-poo-éhs)	*later/after*
en seguida (ehn seh-guée-dah)	*at once*
hoy (óh-ee)	*today*
mañana (mah-nyáh-nah)	*tomorrow*
nunca (nóon-cah)	*never*
siempre (see-éhm-preh)	*always*
tarde (táhr-deh)	*late*
temprano (tehm-práh-noh)	*early*
todavía (toh-dah-vée-ah)	*still/yet*
todavía no (toh-dah-vée-ah noh)	*not yet*
ya (yah)	*already*

EXERCISE 12.17

Understand the meaning of the following sentences containing adverbs of time and pronounce them in Spanish:

1. ¿Fue usted anoche al hotel?
2. Sí, fui antes de las diez.
3. Ayer tuvimos ciento cincuenta clientes.

4. Por favor, prepare los filtros después de limpiar el conducto.

5. De acuerdo, voy a prepararlos en seguida.

6. ¿Está abierto el departamento de mantenimiento hoy?

7. No está abierto hasta mañana.

8. Jorge, nunca barra los andadores con escoba; use siempre un cepillo.

9. Lupita llegó tarde al trabajo ayer pero hoy llegó temprano.

10. Todavía tenemos una fuga en el cuarto ciento dos.

EXERCISE 12.18

With a partner, ask and answer the following phrases, making sure that you understand what you are asking or answering:

Estudiante uno: ¿Está el primer piso fuera de servicio todavía?

Estudiante dos: Sí, todavía está fuera de servicio.

Estudiante uno: ¿Llegó usted tarde al trabajo hoy?

Estudiante dos: No, yo siempre llego al trabajo temprano.

Estudiante uno: ¿Hago las camas ahora?

Estudiante dos: No, hágalas después.

Estudiante uno: ¿Fue Juan a una fiesta anoche?

Estudiante dos: No, Juan estuvo estudiando español anoche.

Estudiante uno: ¿Podrá usted trabajar el turno de noche mañana?

Estudiante dos: Sí, mañana podré trabajar el turno de noche.

Estudiante uno: ¿Está usted limpiando los baños públicos todavía?

Estudiante dos: Sí, todavía los estoy limpiando.

CONVERSATIONAL PROFESSIONAL INTERACTION

In groups of two, translate, practice, and be ready to role-play the following dialogue between an engineering supervisor and an hourly employee:

Estudiante uno (supervisor):   Hola, Enrique. Por favor, esta mañana pode las palmeras.

Estudiante dos (empleado por hora):   Juan las podó ayer por la tarde.

Estudiante uno: Lo siento, no lo sabía. Barra el aparcamiento, por favor.

Estudiante dos: ¿Necesito ponerme los guantes?

Estudiante uno: Sí. Póngaselos siempre antes de empezar a trabajar.

Estudiante dos: ¿Qué debo hacer después de barrer el aparcamiento?

Estudiante uno: Tiene que poner cloro en la piscina.

Estudiante dos: ¿Y el alguicida, tengo que ponérselo también?

Estudiante uno: No, Juan se lo puso ayer.

Estudiante dos: ¿Trabaja hoy el plomero?

Estudiante uno: Sí, está poniéndole una pieza a la caldera.

Estudiante dos: Hay una fuga en la manguera del jardín.

Estudiante uno: Dígale al plomero que ponga una manguera nueva.

Estudiante dos: De acuerdo. Voy a decírselo ahora. ¿Quién corta el césped hoy?

Estudiante uno: Usted tiene que cortarlo.

Estudiante dos: Hoy tengo mucho trabajo. Voy a empezar ahorita.

📖 QUESTIONS TO THE CLASS 📖

Answer the following questions asked by your instructor (or by another student) without looking at your textbook or any class notes:

1. ¿Le escribe usted a su mamá frecuentemente?
2. ¿Les envía usted flores a sus amigos en Navidad?
3. ¿Le pide usted dinero a su papá cada mes?
4. ¿Le hace usted la cama a su hermano(a) cuando está en casa?
5. ¿Le compra usted chocolates a su profesor(a) todos los lunes?
6. Cuando cocina su mamá camarones para usted, ¿los come usted?
7. ¿Le gustan las naranjas a usted?
8. Cuando su profesor le habla en español, ¿le entiende usted?
9. Cuando su profesor habla español ¿lo comprende usted?
10. Por favor, ¿quiere usted darle este libro a Britney?

CULTURAL VIGNETTE

As the number of Spanish-speaking people in the United States continues to increase, more and more radio and television programs, printed publications, and advertising agencies are attempting to appeal to the Hispanic market. The fact is that the Hispanic presence in North America constitutes an important cultural and economic force. While many employers of Spanish-speaking workers insist that employees use only English in the workplace, others are seeking front-line individuals that can accommodate the increasing numbers of Hispanics. Because it appears to be a difficult and touchy issue, perhaps the answer lies in American employers learning Spanish while insisting that their workers become fluent in English as soon as they possibly can. Business would be wise to provide Spanish classes for their managers and line supervisors as well as English classes for those employees who don't understand the language well.

THE PRESENT PERFECT TENSE

ADVERBS OF MANNER

ADVERBS AND THE COMPARISON
OF ADJECTIVES

OVERVIEW

Chapter 13 covers the present perfect tense, which is used to talk about actions and conditions that have or have not happened in the relatively recent past. The chapter also presents the most commonly used adverbs of manner and discusses the use of adverbs in the comparison of adjectives or other adverbs.

UNIT CONTENT

Technical Engineering Vocabulary (III) • The Present Perfect Tense •
Adverbs of Manner • Comparison of Adjectives, Adverbs, and Nouns •
Conversational Professional Interaction • Cultural Vignette

Technical Engineering Vocabulary (III)

rake	el rastrillo (rahs-trée-yoh)
rat	la rata (ráh-tah)
register box	la caja de registro (cáh-hah deh reh-hées-troh)
(to) repair	reparar (*v.*) (reh-pah-ráhr)
rock	la piedra (pee-éh-drah)
rodent	el roedor (roh-eh-dóhr)
root	la raíz (rah-ées)

rototiller	el aflojador de tierra (ah-floh-hah-dóhr deh tee-éh-rrah)
rubber boots	las botas de goma (bóh-tahs deh góh-mah)
rubber gloves	los guantes de goma (goo-áhn-tehs deh góh-mah)
sand	la arena (ah-réh-nah)
saw	la sierra (see-éh-rrah)
screen (wire)	la tela de alambre (téh-lah deh ah-láhm-breh)
screw	el tornillo (tohr-née-yoh)
screwdriver	el destornillador (dehs-tohr-nee-yah-dóhr)
screw nut	la tuerca (too-éhr-cah)
screw valve	la válvula de cierre (váhl-voo-lah deh see-éh-rreh)
(to) seed	sembrar (*v.*) (sehm-bráhr)
short circuit	el cortocircuito (cohr-toh-seer-coo-ée-toh)
shovel	la pala (páh-lah)
shower	la regadera (reh-gah-déh-rah)
	la ducha (dóo-cha)
shut-off valve	la llave de paso (yáh-veh deh páh-soh)
sink (kitchen)	el fregadero (freh-gah-déh-roh)
sink (guest room)	el lavabo (lah-váh-boh)
smoke	el humo (óo-moh)
smoke detector	el detector de humo (deh-tehc-tóhr deh óo-moh)
soil	la tierra (tee-éh-rrah)
spider	la araña (ah-ráh-nyah)
(to) spray	rociar (*v.*) (roh-see-áhr)
sprinkler	el rociador (roh-see-ah-dóhr)
stone	la piedra (pee-éh-drah)
strainer	el filtro (feél-troh)
(to) strain	filtrar (*v.*) (feel-tráhr)
swimming pool	la piscina (pees-sée-nah)
	la alberca (ahl-béhr-cah)
tank	el tanque (táhn-keh)
tennis court	la pista de tenis (pées-tah deh téh-nees)
	la cancha de tenis (cáhn-chah deh téh-nees)
thermostat	el termostato (tehr-mohs-táh-toh)
tile	la baldosa (bahl-dóh-sah)
toilet bowl	el inodoro (ee-noh-dóh-roh)
tool	la herramienta (eh-rrah-mee-éhn-tah)
tool box	la caja de herramientas (cáh-hah deh eh-rrah-mee-éhn-tahs)
(to) transplant	transplantar (*v.*) (trahns-plahn-táhr)
trash	la basura (bah-sóo-rah)
trash bag	la bolsa de basura (bóhl-sah deh bah-sóo-rah)
trash can	el cubo de basura (cóo-boh deh bah-sóo-rah)
tree	el árbol (áhr-bohl)
trench	la zanja (sáhn-hah)
valve	la válvula (váhl-voo-lah)
varnish	el barniz (bahr-nées)

(to) varnish	barnizar *(v.)* (bahr-nee-sáhr)
voltage	el voltaje (vohl-táh-heh)
wallpaper	el papel tapiz (pah-péhl tah-pées)
wasp	la avispa (ah-vées-pa)
waste	el desperdicio (dehs-pehr-dée-see-oh)
waste water	las aguas negras (áh-goo-ahs néh-grahs)
(to) water	regar (e→ie) *(v.)* (reh-gáhr)
(to) weed	escardar *(v.)* (ehs-cahr-dáhr)
wheelbarrow	la carretilla (cah-rreh-tée-yah)
wire	el alambre (ah-láhm-breh)
wood	la madera (mah-déh-rah)
work order	la orden de trabajo (óhr-dehn deh trah-báh-hoh)

EXERCISE 13.1

Match the following list of restaurant vocabulary words, practice their pronunciation, and be ready to speak them aloud:

1. *(to) water*	_____	a. herramienta
2. *shower*	_____	b. rastrillo
3. *screw*	_____	c. sierra
4. *trench*	_____	d. rociar
5. *tile*	_____	e. regadera
6. *wheelbarrow*	_____	f. madera
7. *rubber boots*	_____	g. guantes de goma
8. *screen*	_____	h. bolsa de basura
9. *soil*	_____	i. barniz
10. *wasp*	_____	j. papel tapiz
11. *wood*	_____	k. carretilla
12. *(to) spray*	_____	l. tierra
13. *tool*	_____	m. baldosa
14. *trash bag*	_____	n. zanja
15. *sprinkler*	_____	o. regar
16. *wallpaper*	_____	p. rociador
17. *rake*	_____	q. botas de agua
18. *rubber gloves*	_____	r. tornillo
19. *saw*	_____	s. tela de alambre
20. *varnish*	_____	t. avispa

The Present Perfect Tense

The present perfect is a compound tense that is formed and used almost exactly as in English. The Spanish equivalent of the English auxiliary verb *have* is **haber.** The present perfect is formed by taking the present of **haber** and the past participle of a verb. The past participle is formed by dropping the infinitive ending and adding **ado** for **ar** verbs and **ido** for **er** and **ir** verbs. The past participle always ends in **o.**

Present Tense Forms of "Haber"

yo	he (eh)	*I have*
él, ella, usted	ha (ah)	*he, she, you, it has*
nosotros, nosotras	hemos (éh-mohs)	*we have*
ellos, ellas, ustedes	han (ahn)	*they, you have*

Examples of past participles:

trabajar	trabajado
comer	comido
servir	servido

The irregular past participle may end in **to** and **cho.** Common irregular past participles are:

abrir	abierto
cubrir	cubierto
decir	dicho
escribir	escrito
freir	frito
hacer	hecho
poner	puesto
ser	sido
ver	visto
volver	vuelto

Examples: *I have fried the fish* translates as **Yo he frito el pescado,** and *Lupita has made the beds* as **Lupita ha hecho las camas.**

Object pronouns and the negative **no** are placed directly before the form of **haber.** Examples: **Yo no he visto a Juan hoy** (*I haven't seen Juan today*). **El electricista ha reparado el motor; lo ha reparado muy bien** (*The electrician has repaired the motor; he has repaired it very well*).

EXERCISE 13.2

Understand the meaning of the following present perfect sentences and pronounce them in Spanish:

1. El jardinero ha plantado las flores en el jardín.
2. Yo no he hecho mi cama esta mañana.
3. Juan ha visto a Pepe en el taller.
4. El jardinero ha puesto la manguera en el almacén.
5. Jorge y Lupita han trabajado mucho hoy.
6. El plomero ha reparado el fregadero en la cocina; lo ha reparado muy bien.
7. Esperanza no ha escrito a sus padres esta semana.
8. El electricista no ha podido reparar el cortocircuito todavía.
9. No lo hemos reparado porque no hemos tenido tiempo.
10. No han abierto el restaurante todavía.

EXERCISE 13.3

With a partner, answer the following questions using the present perfect tense:

1. ¿A qué hora se ha levantado usted hoy?
2. ¿Se ha duchado usted?
3. ¿Han terminado ustedes de limpiar los baños públicos?
4. ¿Cuántas tuercas han comprado?
5. ¿Ha vuelto el jefe del departamento de mantenimiento ya?
6. ¿Se ha puesto usted las botas de agua?
7. ¿Dónde ha puesto Pepe la caja de herramientas?
8. ¿Quién ha barnizado estas sillas?
9. ¿Por qué no han regado ustedes el césped?
10. ¿Lo ha hecho usted bien?

EXERCISE 13.4

With a partner, ask and answer the following phrases, making sure that you understand what you are asking or answering:

Estudiante uno: ¿Ha reparado Felipe los detectores de humo?
Estudiante dos: Sí, los ha reparado ya.
Estudiante uno: ¿Ha regado el jardinero las plantas ya?
Estudiante dos: Sí, las ha regado y ha cortado los arbustos también.
Estudiante uno: ¿Ha visto usted al electricista?
Estudiante dos: Sí, lo vi esta mañana temprano.
Estudiante uno: ¿Quién ha puesto la gasolina cerca de la caldera?
Estudiante dos: Lo siento, jefe. Yo la he puesto.
Estudiante uno: ¿Dónde han puesto ustedes los uniformes?
Estudiante dos: Los hemos puesto en el vestidor de empleados.

Estudiante uno: ¿Por qué no ha reparado usted el ventilador?

Estudiante dos: No lo he reparado porque no he tenido tiempo.

Adverbs of Manner

Some common adverbs of manner are:

así	*thus/in this way/so*
así así	*so-so*
bien	*well*
despacio	*slowly*
mal	*badly*
mejor	*better*
peor	*worse*
rápido	*fast*

EXERCISE 13.5

Understand the meaning of the following sentences containing adverbs of manner and pronounce them in Spanish:

1. Por favor, haga las camas rápido.
2. Usted trabaja muy bien, Alberto.
3. ¿Es mejor hacerlo por la mañana?
4. No, es peor hacerlo por la mañana.
5. Pepe, usted debe regar las macetas despacio.
6. Ellos escriben mal inglés pero escriben bien español.
7. ¿Cómo esta usted, Sr. Natali? Estoy así así hoy.
8. Jorge lo hizo mal ayer.
9. Hoy tiene que hacerlo mejor.
10. Así es mejor que como usted lo está haciendo.

EXERCISE 13.6

In pairs, ask and answer the following phrases, making sure that you understand what you are asking or answering:

Estudiante uno: ¿Cómo está usted hoy?

Estudiante dos: Estoy así así; estoy un poco enfermo.

Estudiante uno: ¿Qué madera prefiere?

Estudiante dos: Prefiero ésta; es mejor que aquella.

Estudiante uno: ¿Trabaja Juan rápido?
Estudiante dos: Sí, Juan es un trabajador muy rápido.
Estudiante uno: ¿Lo hago rápido?
Estudiante dos: No, por favor hágalo despacio.
Estudiante uno: ¿Pintó Juan las paredes bien?
Estudiante dos: Sí, Juan las pintó muy bien.
Estudiante uno: ¿Lo hago así?
Estudiante dos: No lo haga así; así es peor.

Comparison of Adjectives, Adverbs, and Nouns

To compare people, things, or ideas in English, *more* or *less* is used with an adjective or the suffix *er* is added to the adjective. In Spanish, to compare adjectives and adverbs, the following expressions are used:

más . . . .que	*more, (. . . er) . . . .than*
menos . . . .que	*less, (. . . er), fewer . . . .than*
tan . . . .como	*as . . . .as*

Examples: Yo trabajo más rápido que Jorge. Este cable es menos caro que aquel cable. Estos cepillos son tan buenos como ésos.

To compare nouns, **tan** becomes **tanto/a/os/as** (**tanto** must agree in number and gender with the noun it modifies). Examples: **Yo tengo tantos amigos como Juan. Juan tiene tantas amigas como Pedro.**

The word **de** is used before a number as the equivalent of *than*. Example: **Ellas han limpiado más de veinte cuartos hoy.**

EXERCISE 13.7

Understand the meaning of the following sentences and pronounce them in Spanish:

1. Juan es más rápido que Pepe.
2. Pepe es tan rápido como Juan.
3. Yo tengo menos clavos que usted.
4. Mi tío Enrique tiene tanto dinero como usted.
5. Yo no tengo tantos dólares como mi tío Enrique.
6. ¿Ha podado usted tantas palmeras como Jorge?
7. No, yo he podado menos que él.
8. Juan barnizó ayer más de diecinueve sillas.
9. Josefina es tan buena como su padre.
10. ¿Tiene usted tanto dinero como ella?

EXERCISE 13.8

In pairs, answer the following questions in Spanish:

1. ¿Tiene Juan más hijos que Feliciano?
2. ¿Quién tiene menos, Juan o Feliciano?
3. ¿Trabajó ella tanto como él?
4. ¿Limpiaron ustedes más de diez cuartos?
5. ¿Es el jardinero nuevo tan rápido como Jorge?
6. ¿Tiene aquel hotel tantos árboles como el nuestro?
7. ¿Compró el electricista más de cinco cables?
8. ¿Ha cavado el jardinero más de cuatro zanjas?
9. ¿Tiene su abuelo más de cien mil dólares?
10. ¿Sabe usted tanto español como yo?

EXERCISE 13.9

With a partner, ask and answer the following phrases, making sure that you understand what you are asking or answering:

Estudiante uno:	¿Cuántos rastrilladores tenemos?
Estudiante dos:	Tenemos menos de diez.
Estudiante uno:	¿Tienen ellos abono?
Estudiante dos:	Sí, tienen tanto como el año pasado.
Estudiante uno:	¿Hay tornillos en el cajón?
Estudiante dos:	Sí, hay más que la semana pasada.
Estudiante uno:	¿Cuántas camas ha hecho Carmen?
Estudiante dos:	Ha hecho menos que Lupita.
Estudiante uno:	¿Tiene Filomena más sábanas que Josefina?
Estudiante dos:	Josefina tiene menos sábanas que Filomena.
Estudiante uno:	¿Cuántos clientes tenemos hoy?
Estudiante dos:	Tenemos más de trescientos.

Conversational Professional Interaction

In groups of two, translate, practice, and be ready to role-play the following dialogue between an engineering supervisor and an hourly employee:

Estudiante uno (supervisor):   ¿Ha reparado usted el inodoro del baño público?

Estudiante dos (empleado por hora):   No lo he podido reparar todavía.

Estudiante uno: ¿A qué hora podrá usted repararlo?

Estudiante dos:	Lo podré reparar después del almuerzo.
Estudiante uno:	De acuerdo. ¿Qué está usted haciendo ahora?
Estudiante dos:	Estoy arreglando la regadera del cuarto 205.
Estudiante uno:	Por favor, arréglela rápido.
Estudiante dos:	¿Ha comprado Juan el detector de humo para el comedor?
Estudiante uno:	Sí, lo ha comprado esta mañana.
Estudiante dos:	Bien. Lo voy a poner en el comedor esta tarde.
Estudiante uno:	¿Tiene usted clavos para ponerlo?
Estudiante dos:	Sí, tengo más de veinte en mi caja de herramientas.
Estudiante uno:	Dígale a Pedro que tiene que limpiar la alberca.
Estudiante dos:	Pedro ya la ha limpiado.
Estudiante uno:	¿Qué está haciendo ahora?
Estudiante dos:	Está rellenando la piscina y poniéndole cloro.
Estudiante uno:	De acuerdo. Hasta luego Antonio.

💼 QUESTIONS TO THE CLASS 💼

Answer the following questions asked by your instructor (or by another student) without looking at your textbook or any class notes:

1. ¿Ha estudiado usted español hoy?
2. ¿Ha hecho su tarea también?
3. ¿Ha llamado usted a su familia por teléfono esta semana?
4. ¿Ha dado usted chocolates a su profesor(a) hoy?
5. ¿Ha enviado usted flores a su amigo(a)?
6. ¿Está usted bien hoy?
7. ¿Escribe usted español bien o mal?
8. ¿Tiene usted tantos años como yo?
9. ¿Puede hablar usted inglés rápido?
10. ¿Soy yo más alto(a) que usted?

CULTURAL VIGNETTE

Hospitality managers should be familiar with the **fiesta de la quinceañera.** Celebrating this **fiesta** acknowledges a girl's transition into adulthood. In the **quinceañera** celebration relatives and close friends are invited to a party that includes dancing, food, drinks, and conversation. The party may be celebrated as a gala event in a hotel or more simply at home. In Latin America, the event may be featured in the society pages of the local newspaper. If workers ask permission to have a day off to attend this fifteenth birthday celebration for one of their daughters, managers should try their best to accommodate them.

PART FIVE

HUMAN RESOURCES (PERSONNEL DEPARTMENT)

THE FUTURE TENSE

THE PRESENT SUBJUNCTIVE

ADVERBS OF PLACE

 OVERVIEW

Chapter 14 covers the future indicative and the present tense of the subjunctive mode. The future tense is indicated in English by *shall* and *will*. In Spanish, the subjunctive is used to express actions involving suggestions, requests, or wishes for events that speakers want to happen; to express opinions, attitudes, hopes, doubts, or fears; to express approval or disapproval; and to react emotionally to happenings taking place around the speaker. The subjunctive is used much more commonly in Spanish than it is in English. The chapter also presents the most commonly used adverbs of place in Spanish.

UNIT CONTENT

Technical Human Resources Vocabulary (I) • The Future Tense •
The Present Subjunctive Tense • Uses of the Present Subjunctive • Adverbs
of Place • Conversational Professional Interaction • Cultural Vignette

Technical Human Resources Vocabulary (I)

absenteeism	la ausencia excesiva (ah-oo-séhn-see-ah ehx-seh-sée-vah)
address	la dirección (dee-rehc-see-óhn)
alcoholic beverages	las bebidas alcohólicas (beh-bée-dahs ahl-coh-óh-lee-cahs)

application form	la solicitud de ingreso (soh-lee-see-tóod deh een-gréh-soh)
appointment	la cita (sée-tah)
appraisal	la evaluación (eh-vah-loo-ah-see-óhn)
apprenticeship	el aprendizaje (ah-prehn-dee-sáh-heh)
aptitude test	el test de aptitud (tehst deh ahp-tee-tóod)
attitude	la actitud (ahc-tee-tóod)
ballpoint pen	el bolígrafo (boh-lée-grah-foh)
benefits	los beneficios (beh-neh-fée-see-ohs)
bicycle	la bicicleta (bee-see-cléh-tah)
birthday	el cumpleaños (coom-pleh-áh-nyohs)
break (rest)	el descanso (dehs-cáhn-soh)
bus	el autobús (ah-oo-toh-bóos)
call	la llamada (yah-máh-dah)
(to) call	llamar (*v.*) (yah-máhr)
car	el carro (cáh-rroh)
	el coche (cóh-cheh)
change	cambiar (*v.*) (cahm-bee-áhr)
change of address	el cambio de dirección (cáhm-bee-oh deh dee-rehc-see-óhn)
citizen	el/la ciudadano/a (see-oo-dah-dáh-noh/ah)
citizenship	la ciudadanía (see-oo-dah-dah-née-ah)
city	la ciudad (see-oo-dáhd)
(to) clock	
(in and out)	marcar (*v.*) (mahr-cáhr)
coach	el/la entrenador/a (ehn-treh-nah-dóhr)
(to) coach	entrenar (ehn-treh-náhr)
company	la empresa (ehm-préh-sah)
	la compañía (cohm-pah-nyée-ah)
competent	competente (*adj.*) (cohm-peh-téhn-teh)
computer	el ordenador (ohr-deh-nah-dóhr)
contract	el contrato (cohn-tráh-toh)
county	el condado (cohn-dáh-doh)
date	la fecha (féh-chah)
(to) date	fechar (*v.*) (feh-cháhr)
dental insurance	el seguro dental (seh-góo-roh dehn-táhl)
dentist	el dentista (dehn-tées-tah)
department head	el/la jefe/a de departamento (héh-feh/ah deh deh-pahr-tah-méhn-toh)
disciplinary action	la acción disciplinaria (ahc-see-óhn dees-see-plee-náh-ree-ah)
doctor	el doctor (dohc-tóhr)
	el médico (méh-dee-coh)
driver's license	la licencia para manejar (lee-séhn-see-ah páh-rah mah-neh-háhr)
	el permiso para conducir (pehr-mée-soh páh-rah cohn-doo-séer)

drugs	las drogas (dróh-gahs)
education	la educación (eh-doo-cah-see-óhn)
employee	el/la empleado/a (ehm-pleh-áh-doh/ah)
employee appraisal	la evaluación de empleados (eh-vah-loo-ah-see-óhn deh ehm-pleh-áh-dohs)
employee cafeteria	la cafetería de empleados (cah-feh-teh-rée-ah deh ehm-pleh-áh-dohs)
employee entrance	la entrada de empleados (ehn-tráh-dah deh ehm-pleh-áh-dohs)
employee exit	la salida de empleados (sah-lée-dah deh ehm-pleh-áh-dohs)
employee handbook	el manual de empleados (mah-noo-áhl deh ehm-pleh-áh-dohs)
employee locker room	el vestidor de empleados (vehs-tee-dóhr deh ehm-pleh-áh-dohs)
employee lounge	el salon de descanso (sah-lóhn deh dehs-cáhn-soh)
employer	el empleador (ehm-pleh-ah-dóhr) el patrón (pah-tróhn)
equal-opportunity employer	empresa de igual oportunidad (ehm-préh-sah deh ee-goo-áhl oh-pohr-too-nee-dáhd)
experience	la experiencia (ehcs-peh-ree-éhn-see-ah)
felony	la felonía (feh-loh-née-ah)
(to) fill out	rellenar (v.) (reh-yeh-náhr)
first name	el nombre (nóhm-breh)
free meal	la comida gratis (coh-mée-dah gráh-tees)
full-time job	el empleo de tiempo completo (ehm-pléh-oh deh tee-éhm-poh cohm-pléh-toh)
green card	la tarjeta verde (tahr-héh-tah véhr-deh)
grooming	la apariencia personal (ah-pah-ree-éhn-see-ah pehr-soh-náhl)
(to) help	ayudar (v.) (ah-yoo-dáhr)
high school diploma	el diploma de estudios secundarios (dee-plóh-mah deh ehs-tóo-dee-ohs seh-coon-dáh-ree-ohs)
(to) hire	contratar (v.) (cohn-trah-táhr)
holiday	el día festivo (dée-ah fehs-tée-voh)
honesty	la honradez (ohn-rah-déhs)
human resources	los recursos humanos (reh-cóor-sohs oo-máh-nohs)
hygiene	la higiene (ee-hee-éh-neh)
idea	la idea (ee-déh-ah)
identification card	la tarjeta de identificación (tahr-héh-tah deh ee-dehn-tee-fee-cah-see-óhn)
immigrant	el/la inmigrante (een-mee-gráhn-teh)
immigration agency (INS)	la agencia de inmigración (ah-héhn-see-ah deh een-mee-grah-see-óhn)
insubordination	la insubordinación (een-soo-bohr-dee-nah-see-óhn)
insurance	el seguro (seh-góo-roh)
interview	la entrevista (ehn-treh-vées-tah)

EXERCISE 14.1

Match the following list of restaurant vocabulary words, practice their pronunciation, and be ready to speak them aloud:

1. *holiday*	_____ a. nombre
2. *employee lounge*	_____ b. tarjeta de identificación
3. *insurance*	_____ c. seguro dental
4. *company*	_____ d. cita
5. *apprenticeship*	_____ e. recursos humanos
6. *city*	_____ f. descanso
7. *employee*	_____ g. salida de empleados
8. *grooming*	_____ h. comida gratis
9. *citizen*	_____ i. licencia para manejar
10. *date*	_____ j. cambio de dirección
11. *human resources*	_____ k. seguro
12. *first name*	_____ l. día festivo
13. *dental insurance*	_____ m. empleada
14. *break*	_____ n. ciudad
15. *driving license*	_____ o. empresa
16. *appointment*	_____ p. aprendizaje
17. *change of address*	_____ q. fecha
18. *employee exit*	_____ r. salón de descanso
19. *identification card*	_____ s. ciudadana
20. *free meal*	_____ t. apariencia personal

The Future Tense

You have already learned to express actions or ideas that are going to occur in the future by using **ir + a + infinitive.** Both in English and in Spanish, the present tense can also be used to express the idea of futurity. Yet another way to express the future is by using the future tense. The three conjugations of regular verbs form the future tense using the straight infinitive as stem and adding the endings **é, á, emos, án.** There are no stem changes in the future form.

Examples of the future tense of regular verbs are:

	"ar," "er," "ir" verbs		
yo	hablaré	comeré	escribiré
él, ella, usted	hablará	comerá	escribirá
nosotros, nosotras	hablaremos	comeremos	escribiremos
ellos, ellas, ustedes	hablarán	comerán	escribirán

Examples: **Mañana yo trabajaré el turno de tarde** (*Tomorrow I will work the evening shift*). **Ella lavará la lencería el lunes próximo** (*She will wash the linen next Monday.*)

Conjugation of the Future Tense of Irregular Verbs

Some irregular verbs require a modified form of the infinitive before adding the same endings used with regular verbs. The future tense endings of some common irregular verbs are:

decir (*to tell*)	diré—dirá—diremos—dirán
hacer (*to do, to make*)	haré—hará—haremos—harán
poder (*can, be able to*)	podré—podrá—podremos—podrán
poner (*to put*)	pondré—pondrá—pondremos—pondrán
querer (*to want*)	querré—querrá—querremos—querrán
saber (*to know*)	sabré—sabrá—sabremos—sabrán
salir (*to leave*)	saldré—saldrá—saldremos—saldrán
tener (*to have*)	tendré—tendrá—tendremos—tendrán
valer (*to be worth, to cost*)	valdré—valdrá—valdremos—valdrán
venir (*to come*)	vendré—vendrá—vendremos—vendrán

The future of **hay** (*there is, there are*) is **habrá.**

EXERCISE 14.2

Understand the meaning of the following sentences and pronounce them in Spanish:

1. Juan trabajará con Pepe mañana.
2. Después, él comerá con Lupita.
3. No podré almorzar con Domingo mañana.
4. Ellas no harán las camas antes de las once.
5. Mi amigo Timoteo irá a Portland este fin de semana.
6. Nosotros viajaremos a España el verano que viene.
7. Enrique conducirá a México con su amigo Jaime.
8. Ellos no comenzarán su aprendizaje hasta la semana próxima.
9. Yo tendré una entrevista con el jefe del departamento de alimentos y bebidas el viernes.

EXERCISE 14.3

With a partner, answer the following questions in Spanish:

1. ¿Me llamarán ustedes mañana?
2. ¿Firmaremos el contrato hoy?

3. ¿Saldrá Lupita con Jorge este fin de semana?
4. ¿A qué hora comenzará el banquete?
5. ¿Tendremos muchas personas para la cena esta tarde?
6. ¿Quién vendrá a trabajar mañana?
7. ¿Se lavarán ustedes las manos con jabón antes de comenzar su turno?
8. ¿Dónde viajará usted esta primavera?
9. ¿Sabrá usted cocinar el pescado bien?
10. ¿Cuántos manteles lavará Lupita?

EXERCISE 14.4

With a partner, ask and answer the following phrases, making sure that you understand what you are asking or answering:

Estudiante uno: ¿Llegarán ellos temprano hoy?

Estudiante dos: Sí, Julio y Jesús llegarán a las siete.

Estudiante uno: ¿Quién reparará los grifos en el baño?

Estudiante dos: Yo los repararé esta tarde.

Estudiante uno: ¿Cuándo le dirá usted a Pepe de limpiar la piscina?

Estudiante dos: Se lo diré el domingo.

Estudiante uno: ¿Podrán ustedes trabajar mañana?

Estudiante dos: No, porque tendremos el día libre.

Estudiante uno: ¿Irá Lupita a San Mateo este verano?

Estudiante dos: No, Lupita y su hermano irán a Baja California.

Estudiante uno: ¿Trabajarán Miguel y Paco esta tarde?

Estudiante dos: Sí, ellos van a trabajar el turno de 4 a 12.

The Present Subjunctive Tense

The subjunctive is seldom used in English, but it is quite frequent and important in Spanish. The present subjunctive forms of most Spanish verbs are similar to command forms. To form the present subjunctive of most verbs, drop the **o** or **oy** ending of the present indicative **yo** form and add the following endings:

"ar" verbs: **e, e, emos, en**

Example:	yo	trabaje
	él, ella, usted	trabaje
	nosotros, nosotras	trabajemos
	ellos, ellas, ustedes	trabajen

<u>**"er/ir" verbs:**</u>   **a, a, amos, an**

Example: yo   coma   escriba
                  él, ella, usted   coma   escriba
                  nosotros, nosotras   comamos   escribamos
                  ellos, ellas, ustedes   coman   escriban

As with commands, verbs that are irregular in the first person singular of the present indicative are irregular in the subjunctive. For example, **decir—digo—diga** (command).

The only two verbs that have irregular subjunctives are:

	ir	**dar**
yo	vaya	dé
él, ella, usted	vaya	dé
nosotros, nosotras	vayamos	demos
ellos, ellas, ustedes	vayan	den

Stem-changing verbs require a stem change in the present subjunctive. Example:

<u>almorzar</u>

almuerce
almuerce
almorcemos
almuercen

Uses of the Present Subjunctive

The Subjunctive to Express Wishes and Requests

In Spanish, the subjunctive is required when a subject attemps to influence the behavior of others. Generally, if the verb in the main clause is in the present, future, or command form, the subjunctive verb in the subordinate clause will be in the present tense. Examples: The expression *I want you to clean Room 102* translates in Spanish as **Quiero que usted *limpie* el cuarto 102** (literally, I want that you clean Room 102); *I prefer for you to come to work tomorrow* translates as **Prefiero que usted *venga* a trabajar mañana** (literally, *I prefer that you come to work tomorrow*).

Here are some "influencing verbs" commonly used to persuade others to do something. (Each verb is given with an example in which the main clause is in the present indicative form, with the present subjunctive in the subordinate clause.)

desear (*to wish*)	Pedro desea que usted *vaya* a su casa hoy.
insistir (*to insist*)	Insisto que Lupita *trabaje* mañana.
invitar (*invite*)	Les invitamos a que *almuercen* ustedes con nosotros.
necesitar (*need*)	Necesito que usted *limpie* el pasillo.
pedir (*to request*)	Le pido a usted que no *fume* en el taller.
permitir (*to permit*)	No les permito que *fumen* ustedes en el taller.

preferir (*to prefer*)   Juan, prefiero que no *trabaje* mañana.
prohibir (*to forbid*)   Le prohibo que *vea* la televisión en los cuartos.
querer (*to want*)   La supervisora quiere que *lavemos* las sábanas ahora.
recomendar
  (*to recommend*)   Nos recomiendan que *almorcemos* a las doce.
sugerir (*to suggest*)   Lupita me ha sugerido que *coma* más fruta.

EXERCISE 14.5

Understand the meaning of the following statements containing the present subjunctive form and pronounce them in Spanish:

1. Le prohibo que tome bebidas alcoholicas en el trabajo.
2. No está permitido que bebamos vino con el almuerzo.
3. El gerente sugiere que vengamos a trabajar en autobús.
4. Le recomiendo que coma muchas legumbres.
5. Lupita me ha invitado a que vaya a su casa esta tarde.
6. Le pido que no llegue tarde a su turno.
7. El supervisor insiste en que lavemos los blancos ahora.
8. Ella prefiere que usemos detergente sin lejía.
9. Quiero que ayude usted a Joaquín en la lavandería.
10. El cliente desea que le traiga usted un vaso de agua.

EXERCISE 14.6

With a partner, ask and answer the following questions using the present subjunctive tense:

1. ¿Está prohibido que llamemos por teléfono durante el descanso?
2. ¿Permiten aquí que fumemos en la cafetería de empleados?
3. ¿Le ha sugerido usted a Pepe que trabaje más rápido?
4. ¿Le ha recomendado usted que tome un test de aptitud?
5. ¿Nos ha invitado el gerente a que almorcemos con él?
6. ¿Ha pedido usted a Juan que limpie el lobby?
7. ¿Insiste usted en que yo venga a trabajar mañana?
8. ¿Prefiere usted que hable con el jefe de departamento?
9. ¿Quiere el supervisor que firme la solicitud de ingreso ahora?
10. ¿Desea usted que comience a trabajar hoy o el lunes?

EXERCISE 14.7

With a partner, ask and answer the following phrases, making sure that you understand what you are asking or answering:

Estudiante uno:	¿Quiere usted que yo venga a trabajar mañana?
Estudiante dos:	Sí, necesito que usted venga a trabajar a las ocho.
Estudiante uno:	¿Por qué insiste Juan que lavemos las sábanas ahora?
Estudiante dos:	Insiste porque no tenemos sábanas limpias.
Estudiante uno:	¿Prefiere usted que firme la solicitud de ingreso ahora?
Estudiante dos:	No, prefiero que la firme usted después.
Estudiante uno:	¿Necesita usted que le ayude?
Estudiante dos:	No necesito que me ayude en este momento.
Estudiante uno:	¿Está prohibido que fumemos en la cocina?
Estudiante dos:	Sí, el jefe no quiere que fumemos durante el trabajo.
Estudiante uno:	¿Me recomienda usted que vaya ahora?
Estudiante dos:	No, prefiero que vaya usted el sábado.

The Subjunctive after Expressions of Emotion

Spanish speakers use the present subjunctive tense to express their feelings or emotions about a circumstance or an event involving others. In this case, the verb of emotion (main clause) in the present indicative tense is followed by **que,** with the second verb (dependent clause) in the present subjunctive form. Examples: The expression *I hope that you see Lupita tomorrow* translates in Spanish as **Espero que usted *vea* a Lupita mañana;** *I am afraid that she is sick* translates as **Temo que ella *esté* enferma.**

Here are some "verbs of emotion" commonly used with the subjunctive to express emotion about certain people and things. (Each verb is given with an example.)

alegrarse (de)	(*to be glad about*)	Me alegro de que *esté* usted bien.
esperar	(*to hope*)	Espero que *encuentre* usted su carro.
gustar	(*to like*)	A Lupita le gusta que usted la *invite* a almorzar.
molestar	(*to bother*)	¿Le molesta a usted que *fume*?
quejarse de	(*to complain about*)	Ella se queja de que usted no la *llame* nunca.
sentir (→ie)	(*to be sorry*)	Siento que ellos no *puedan* venir hoy.
temer	(*to fear/dread*)	Temo que Carlos no *venga* a trabajar hoy.
tener miedo	(*to be afraid*)	Juan tiene miedo que Lupita *esté* enferma.

EXERCISE 14.8

Understand the meaning of the following statements containing the present subjunctive form and pronounce them in Spanish:

1. Tengo miedo que no tengamos servilletas para el banquete.

2. El supervisor teme que Pepe no venga a trabajar mañana.
3. Espero que trabaje usted el domingo.
4. Siento que no pueda usted ir a Nueva York.
5. A la supervisora le molesta que las camaristas fumen en el salón de descanso.
6. Me gusta que usted trabaje bien.
7. Esperamos que Juan nos llame hoy.
8. Me alegro de que usted pueda trabajar los fines de semana.
9. ¿Por qué no se queja usted de que Pepe fume en la lavandería?
10. No me gusta que usted use lejía para lavar las fundas de almohada.

EXERCISE 14.9

In pairs, ask and answer the following phrases, making sure that you understand what you are asking or answering:

Estudiante uno:	¿No quieren que fumemos en la cafetería de empleados?
Estudiante dos:	Los supervisores no quieren que fumemos.
Estudiante uno:	¿Espera usted que Pepe venga a trabajar hoy?
Estudiante dos:	Sí, espero que Pepe venga hoy a trabajar.
Estudiante uno:	¿Tiene usted miedo de que Pepe no venga a trabajar?
Estudiante dos:	Sí, temo que Pepe no venga a trabajar hoy.
Estudiante uno:	¿Le molesta que fume?
Estudiante dos:	Sí, me molesta que usted fume en la cocina.
Estudiante uno:	¿Le gusta a usted que Jorge hable con Lupita?
Estudiante dos:	Sí, me gusta que hable con ella.
Estudiante uno:	¿Siente usted que Pepe se vaya para Nicaragua?
Estudiante dos:	Sí, siento que se vaya porque Pepe es un buen trabajador.

The Subjunctive after Ojalá

Another way of expressing feelings of hope and desires is to use the expression **ojalá que** with the subjunctive. This expression can be translated in English as *I hope that . . . , let's hope that . . . .* Example: **Ojalá que Juan venga a trabajar hoy** means *I hope that Juan will come to work today.*

EXERCISE 14.10

Understand the meaning of the following statements containing the present subjunctive form and pronounce them in Spanish:

1. Ojalá que Juan pueda encontrar trabajo.
2. Ojalá que abran el restaurante a las ocho.

3. Ojalá que los clientes lleguen temprano.
4. Ojalá que Antonia venga en este autobús.
5. Ojalá que haga buen tiempo la semana próxima.
6. Ojalá que haya un banquete esta noche.
7. Ojalá que Lupita haga las camas bien hoy.
8. Ojalá que no haga mucho calor este verano.
9. Ojalá que los mozos limpien las escaleras de servicio.
10. Ojalá que mi mamá me envíe dinero.

EXERCISE 14.11

Translate the following sentences into Spanish using the present subjunctive tense:

1. *I hope that Juan will be able to work in this restaurant.* _____
   _____

2. *I hope that we have a banquet today.* _____
   _____

3. *I hope that she finished the laundry before 5 o'clock.* _____
   _____

4. *Let's hope that Jorge knows how to fry fish.* _____
   _____

5. *I hope that Juan knows how to grill meat also.* _____
   _____

6. *Let's hope that Lupita speaks English.* _____
   _____

7. *I hope that she writes Spanish well.* _____
   _____

8. *I hope that you clock in before your shift.* _____
   _____

9. *I hope that you drive well.* _____
   _____

10. *Let's hope that the manager is good.* _____
    _____

The Subjunctive after Impersonal Expressions

When impersonal expressions are followed by a different subject in the subordinate clause, **que** is used followed by the present subjunctive. Example: *It is important that you sweep the floor in the afternoon* translates as **Es importante que usted barra el piso por la tarde.**

Some important impersonal expressions are:

es importante	*it's important*
no es importante	*it isn't important*

es imposible	it's impossible
es necesario	it's necessary
es posible	it's possible
es probable	it's probable

EXERCISE 14.12

Understand the meaning of the following statements containing the present subjunctive form and pronounce them in Spanish:

1. Es importante que los estudiantes hablen en español.
2. No es necesario que los estudiantes escriban en inglés.
3. Es imposible que Juan venga a trabajar hoy.
4. Es posible que tengamos muchos clientes esta noche.
5. No es probable que Juan esté enfermo.
6. Es necesario que Lupita doble las sábanas ahorita.
7. No es posible que usted tenga su día libre los viernes.
8. No es necesario que vaya usted al almacén todavía.
9. Es necesario que usted lave los platos en la cocina.
10. Es importante que usted firme el contrato antes del miércoles.

EXERCISE 14.13

In pairs, ask and answer the following phrases, making sure that you understand what you are asking or answering:

Estudiante uno:	¿Es probable que el restaurante abra temprano?
Estudiante dos:	Sí, es probable que abra antes de las seis.
Estudiante uno:	¿Es posible que Juan doble las sábanas para las doce?
Estudiante dos:	Sí, Juan trabaja rápido. Es posible que las doble.
Estudiante uno:	¿Es necesario que yo venga a trabajar esta tarde?
Estudiante dos:	Sí, es necesario que venga porque tenemos un banquete.
Estudiante uno:	¿Es posible que yo tenga mi día libre el domingo?
Estudiante dos:	Sí, es posible porque no hay mucho trabajo ese día.
Estudiante uno:	¿Es importante que Ernesto vaya a Vermont?
Estudiante dos:	Sí, es muy importante que él vaya mañana.
Estudiante uno:	¿Es necesario que limpie el baño ahora?
Estudiante dos:	Sí, es necesario que lo limpie ahorita.

The Subjunctive after Expressions of Doubt, Denial, and Uncertainty

Spanish speakers use the subjunctive to express doubt, denial, and uncertainty. Example: **Dudo que Juan termine su trabajo antes de las once** translates as *I doubt that Juan finishes his work before 11 o'clock.*

Some verbs and expressions that are used in Spanish to express doubt, uncertainty, or denial are:

dudar + que	(*to doubt*)
no creer + que	(*not to believe*)
no estar seguro + que	(*not to be sure*)
tal vez	(*maybe*)
quizás	(*perhaps*)

EXERCISE 14.14

Understand the meaning of the following statements containing the present subjunctive form and pronounce them in Spanish:

1. Juan duda que Pepe pueda cocinar los camarones.
2. Tal vez Pepe venga mañana.
3. No creo que contraten en este hotel.
4. Quizás me den trabajo aquí.
5. Martín no está seguro que este restaurante sea bueno.
6. El gerente duda que tengamos más de cincuenta clientes en el banquete hoy.
7. Ellos no creen que yo pueda servir cinco mesas sin ayuda.
8. Tal vez Pepe venga a Albuquerque para mi cumpleaños.
9. No estoy seguro que Lupita haga veinte camas en su turno.
10. ¿Irá usted al hotel? No sé, quizás vaya.

EXERCISE 14.15

With a partner, ask and answer the following phrases, making sure that you understand what you are asking or answering:

Estudiante uno:	¿Duda usted que yo sea norteamericano?
Estudiante dos:	No dudo que usted lo sea.
Estudiante uno:	¿No cree usted que el jefe hable español?
Estudiante dos:	No creo que lo hable bien.
Estudiante uno:	¿No está usted seguro que Emilio le compre flores?
Estudiante dos:	Dudo que Emilio las compre.
Estudiante uno:	¿Cree usted que tal vez tengamos mucho trabajo hoy?
Estudiante dos:	Creo que tal vez lo tengamos.
Estudiante uno:	¿Quizás me invite usted a bailar en la fiesta?
Estudiante dos:	Sí, quizás lo haga.
Estudiante uno:	¿Cree usted que Juan llegue a tiempo?
Estudiante dos:	Sí, creo que Juan llegue a las cinco.

The Subjunctive after Expressions of Time

The subjunctive is required after some expressions of time in which a situation may or may not take place or will probably occur. The indicative is used, however, to describe a habitual or completed action. Examples (the indicative is used in the following sentence because it is a habitual occurrence): **Generalmente, yo llego tarde al trabajo porque no tengo carro** (*Generally, I arrive late to work because I don't have a car*). The subjunctive is needed in the following sentence because it may or may not happen: **Yo nunca llegaré tarde al trabajo cuando tenga carro** (*I will never arrive to work late when I have a car*).

The following conjunctions of time require the subjunctive when the situation may take place or will probably happen:

antes (de) que	*before*
cuando	*when*
después (de) que	*after*
en cuanto	*as soon as*
hasta que	*until*
tan pronto como	*as soon as*

EXERCISE 14.16

Understand the meaning of the following statements containing the present subjunctive form and pronounce them in Spanish:

1. Siempre preparo la cena antes de que él llegue a casa.
2. Por favor, llame a Pedro cuando vaya a Salt Lake City.
3. En cuanto termine este trabajo, quiero que empiece usted a pintar las paredes.
4. Sí, empezaré a pintar las paredes después de que termine este trabajo.
5. Cuando rellene usted la solicitud de empleo, llévela al departamento de recursos humanos.
6. Sí, la llevaré después de que la rellene.
7. En cuanto terminen, por favor lávense las manos con jabón.
8. De acuerdo, nos lavaremos las manos en cuanto terminemos.
9. Por favor, lave los platos hasta que llegue Pedro.
10. Bien, los lavaré hasta que llegue.

EXERCISE 14.17

In pairs, ask and answer the following phrases, making sure that you understand what you are asking or answering:

Estudiante uno: ¿Va usted a poner la mesa antes de que lleguen?

Estudiante dos:	Sí voy a ponerla antes de que los clientes lleguen.
Estudiante uno:	¿Puede secar los platos tan pronto como los lave?
Estudiante dos:	Sí, cuando los lave los secaré.
Estudiante uno:	¿Puede hacer las camas después de que aspire el suelo?
Estudiante dos:	Sí, las haré después de que aspire el suelo.
Estudiante uno:	¿Irá usted a México cuando tenga dinero?
Estudiante dos:	Sí, iré a México cuando lo tenga.
Estudiante uno:	¿Hablará Jason español cuando venga de Venezuela?
Estudiante dos:	Sí, lo hablará bien cuando vuelva.
Estudiante uno:	¿Se lava usted las manos cuando pica la carne de res?
Estudiante dos:	Sí, siempre me las lavo cuando trabajo con carne.

Adverbs of Place

Some adverbs of place commonly used in Spanish are:

abajo (ah-báh-hoh)	*down, downstairs*
adentro (ah-déhn-troh)	*inside*
afuera (ah-foo-éh-rah)	*outside*
ahí (ah-ée)	*there (closer)*
allá (ah-yáh)	*there (farther)*
allí (ah-yée)	*there (farther)*
alrededor (de) (ahl-reh-deh-dóhr)	*around*
aquí (ah-kée)	*here*
arriba (ah-rrée-bah)	*up, upstairs*
cerca (séhr-cah)	*near*
enfrente (de) (ehn-fréhn-teh)	*opposite, in front of*
lejos (de) (léh-hohs)	*far, far away*

EXERCISE 14.18

Understand the meaning of the following statements containing adverbs of place and pronounce them in Spanish:

1. El sótano está abajo.
2. La azotea está arriba.
3. Ponga las escobas aquí.
4. El almacén está cerca de la cocina.
5. Por favor, no ponga los productos químicos cerca de la comida.
6. La playa no está muy lejos del hotel.

7. Por favor, firme la solictud de ingreso aquí.

8. Hay una cerca alrededor de la pista de tenis.

9. Vaya allí y compruebe el motor.

10. El restaurante Taco Bell está enfrente del hotel.

EXERCISE 14.19

In pairs, ask and answer the following phrases, making sure that you understand what you are asking or answering:

Estudiante uno:	¿Dónde están los formularios?
Estudiante dos:	Están ahí, sobre el escritorio.
Estudiante uno:	¿Adónde quiere que vaya?
Estudiante dos:	Venga aquí, por favor.
Estudiante uno:	¿Están las piscinas lejos?
Estudiante dos:	No, están muy cerca, a la izquierda de la cancha de tenis.
Estudiante uno:	¿Pongo las sillas afuera?
Estudiante dos:	No, póngalas adentro.
Estudiante uno:	¿Dónde está Jorge?
Estudiante dos:	Está allí, hablando con Lupita.
Estudiante uno:	¿Adónde voy?
Estudiante dos:	Vaya arriba.

CONVERSATIONAL PROFESSIONAL INTERACTION

In groups of two, translate, practice, and be ready to role-play the following dialogue between a personnel department supervisor and an hourly employee:

Estudiante uno (supervisor):   Buenos días. Por favor, siéntese.

Estudiante dos (empleado por hora):   Gracias. ¿Necesitan cocineros para su restaurante?

Estudiante uno: Sí. Necesitamos un cocinero que sepa cocinar pescado. ¿Sabe usted cocinar pescado?

Estudiante dos: Sí. Yo he trabajado en un restaurante en Chula Vista por dos años.

Estudiante uno: Bien. Por favor, rellene esta solicitud de ingreso y fírmela.

Estudiante dos: Aquí la tiene. Ya la he rellenado.

Estudiante uno: ¿Tiene usted diploma de educación secundaria?

Estudiante dos: Sí. Yo prefiero empleo de tiempo completo.

Estudiante uno: Este empleo es para cuarenta horas a la semana.

Estudiante dos:	Está bien. ¿Qué beneficios tienen los empleados de esta empresa?
Estudiante uno:	Tienen una comida gratis por turno de ocho horas.
Estudiante dos:	¿No tienen seguro dental?
Estudiante uno:	No. Pero lo tendremos próximamente.
Estudiante dos:	¿Cuándo puedo empezar a trabajar?
Estudiante uno:	Después de esta entrevista tiene que tomar un test de aptitud. ¿Tiene usted tarjeta verde?
Estudiante dos:	Sí. Vivo en los Estados Unidos desde mil novecientos noventa.
Estudiante uno:	De acuerdo. Firme aquí por favor. Cuando venga a trabajar el lunes, traiga zapatos de tenis. También, su aseo personal debe ser excelente.
Estudiante dos:	¿Quién es mi jefe?
Estudiante uno:	Su jefe es el señor Molina. Espero que le guste. Sabe hablar español muy bien. Es de Sonora.
Estudiante dos:	De acuerdo. Muchas gracias. Le veré el lunes a las siete de la mañana. Adiós.

📰 QUESTIONS TO THE CLASS 📰

Answer the following questions asked by your instructor (or by another student) without looking at your textbook or any class notes:

1. ¿Quiere que hable español con usted?
2. ¿Cuándo irá usted a Francia?
3. ¿Vendrá usted a la clase de español mañana?
4. ¿Escribirá usted a su profesor(a) en Navidad?
5. ¿Desea usted que yo le compre flores?
6. ¿Le gusta al (a la) profesor(a) que hablemos en clase?
7. ¿Es importante que hablemos español?
8. ¿Es necesario que usted viaje a España este verano?
9. ¿Duda usted que yo trabaje en Taco Bell?
10. ¿Cree usted que tal vez yo baile con Julia Roberts esta noche?

CULTURAL VIGNETTE

Whether or not Hispanic individuals are religious, they make frequent references to the Virgin Mary, the saints, heaven, and God. Someone might respond to a question such as *Do you plan to stay in the United States to live?* with **Si Dios quiere** (*If God is willing*). A way of saying God grant . . . is **ojalá** taken from the Arabic. (Can you hear the word "Allah" in there?) One could say there are two ways of translating **Ojalá que pueda ir a México el año próximo:** The literal translation is *God grant that I can go to Mexico next year,* but a secular translation would be *I hope I can go to Mexico next year.*

THE CONDITIONAL TENSE

THE IMPERFECT SUBJUNCTIVE TENSE

ADVERBS OF INTENSITY

 **OVERVIEW**

Chapter 15 presents the conditional and imperfect (past) subjunctive tenses. The conditional tense is indicated in English by the word *would*. The imperfect subjunctive tense has two forms, often referred to as the **ra** and **se** forms. This chapter also presents the most commonly used adverbs of intensity in Spanish.

 **UNIT CONTENT**

Technical Human Resources Vocabulary (II) • The Conditional Tense • The Imperfect Subjunctive Tense (Past Subjunctive) • Adverbs of Intensity • Conversational Professional Interaction • Cultural Vignette

Technical Human Resources Vocabulary (II)

job	el trabajo (trah-báh-hoh)
job application	la solicitud de empleo (soh-lee-see-tóod deh ehm-pléh-oh)
job description	la descripción del puesto (dehs-creep-see-óhn dehl poo-éhs-toh)
job experience	la experiencia de trabajo (ehs-peh-ree-éhn-see-ah deh trah-báh-hoh)
job opening	la vacante (vah-cáhn-teh)
legal immigrant	el/la inmigrante legal (een-mee-gráhn-teh leh-gáhl)
legal resident	el/la residente legal (reh-see-déhn-teh leh-gáhl)

letter	la carta (cáhr-tah)
life insurance	el seguro de vida (seh-góo-roh deh vée-dah)
(to) look for	buscar (*v.*) (boos-cáhr)
lunch break	el descanso para el almuerzo (dehs-cáhn-soh páh-rah ehl ahl-moo-éhr-soh)
mailing address	la dirección postal (dee-rehc-see-óhn pohs-táhl)
manager	el director (dee-rehc-tóhr)
	el gerente (heh-réhn-teh)
	el manejador (mah-neh-hah-dóhr)
medical insurance	el seguro médico (seh-góo-roh méh-dee-coh)
message	el mensaje (mehn-sáh-heh)
minimum wage	el salario mínimo (sah-láh-ree-oh mée-nee-moh)
money	el dinero (dee-néh-roh)
name (first)	el nombre (nóhm-breh)
name (last)	el apellido (ah-peh-yée-doh)
name tag	la etiqueta con su nombre (eh-tee-kéh-tah cohn soo nóhm-breh)
nickname	el apodo (ah-póh-doh)
(to) notify	notificar (*v.*) (noh-tee-fee-cáhr)
no smoking	no fumar (*v.*) (noh foo-máhr)
(to) offer	ofrecer (*v.*) (oh-freh-séhr)
office	la oficina (oh-fee-sée-nah)
(job) opening	la vacante (vah-cáhn-teh)
overtime	el tiempo extra (tee-éhm-poh éhs-trah)
pants	los pantalones (pahn-tah-lóh-nehs)
(to) park	aparcar (*v.*) (ah-pahr-cáhr)
parking	el aparcamiento (ah-pahr-cah-mee-éhn-toh)
part-time job	el empleo de tiempo parcial (ehm-pléh-oh deh tee-éhm-poh pahr-see-áhl)
party	la fiesta (fee-éhs-tah)
(to) pay	pagar (*v.*) (pah-gáhr)
paycheck	el cheque salarial (chéh-keh sah-lah-ree-áhl)
payday	el día de pago (dée-ah deh páh-goh)
pay raise	el aumento salarial (ah-oo-méhn-toh sah-lah-ree-áhl)
permanent work	el empleo permanente (ehm-pléh-oh pehr-mah-néhn-teh)
personal hygiene	la higiene personal (ee-hee-éh-neh pehr-soh-náhl)
personal information	los datos personales (dáh-tohs pehr-soh-náh-lehs)
personnel department	el departamento de personal (deh-pahr-tah-méhn-toh deh pehr-soh-náhl)
phone	el teléfono (teh-léh-foh-noh)
physical examination	el examen médico (ehc-sáh-mehn méh-dee-coh)
police	la policía (poh-lee-sée-ah)
police officer	el/la agente de policía (ah-héhn-teh deh poh-lee-sée-ah)

position (work)	el puesto (poo-éhs-toh)
probationary period	el período de prueba (peh-rée-oh-doh deh proo-éh-bah)
professional test	el test profesional (tehst proh-feh-see-oh-náhl)
punctual	puntual (*adj.*) (poon-too-áhl)
punctuality	la puntualidad (poon-too-ah-lee-dáhd)
quiz	la prueba (proo-éh-bah)
recruiting	el reclutamiento (reh-cloo-tah-mee-éhn-toh)
reference	la recomendación (reh-coh-mehn-dah-see-óhn)
reliable	seguro (*adj.*) (seh-góo-roh)
responsibility	la responsabilidad (rehs-pohn-sah-bee-lee-dáhd)
resumé	el curriculum vitae (coo-rrée-coo-loom vée-tah)
retirement plan	el plan de retiro (plahn deh reh-tée-roh)
raise (wage)	el aumento (ah-oo-méhn-toh)

EXERCISE 15.1

Match the following list of restaurant vocabulary words, practice their pronunciation, and be ready to speak them aloud:

1. *permanent job*	_____	a. gerente
2. *nickname*	_____	b. apellido
3. *life insurance*	_____	c. plan de retiro
4. *probationary period*	_____	d. teléfono
5. *lunch break*	_____	e. trabajo
6. *opening*	_____	f. dinero
7. *letter*	_____	g. seguro
8. *personnel department*	_____	h. aumento
9. *name (first)*	_____	i. solicitud de empleo
10. *pay raise*	_____	j. puntualidad
11. *pay raise*	_____	k. aumento salarial
12. *phone*	_____	l. período de prueba
13. *job*	_____	m. nombre
14. *manager*	_____	n. seguro de vida
15. *job application*	_____	o. apodo
16. *last name*	_____	p. descanso para el almuerzo
17. *punctuality*	_____	q. departamento de personal
18. *retirement plan*	_____	r. empleo permanente
19. *money*	_____	s. carta
20. *reliable*	_____	t. vacante

The Conditional Tense

In English, we express conditional actions or states using the word *would* with a verb. For example: *I would like to go with you.* Spanish speakers express these ideas also by using the conditional tense. The construction of this tense is quite similar to that of the future tense, except that it has different endings. Regular verbs form the conditional tense using the straight infinitive as stem and adding the endings **ía, ía, íamos,** and **ían.** As with the future, there are no stem changes in the conditional form. Examples of the conditional tense of regular verbs:

	"ar," "er," "ir" verbs
yo	hablaría
él, ella, usted	comería
nosotros, nosotras	escribiríamos
ellos, ellas, ustedes	trabajarían

Examples: **Mañana yo trabajaría el turno de tarde, pero no puedo** (*Tomorrow I would work the evening shift, but I cannot*). **Ella lavaría la lencería, pero no tiene tiempo** (*She would wash the linen, but she has no time*).

Conjugation of the Conditional Tense of Irregular Verbs

As with the future, some irregular verbs require a modified form of the infinitive before adding the same endings used with regular verbs. The following list gives the conditional tense of most common irregular verbs.

decir (*to tell*)	diría—diría—diríamos—dirían
hacer (*to do, to make*)	haría—haría—haríamos—harían
poder (*can, be able to*)	podría—podría—podríamos—podrían
poner (*to put*)	pondría—pondría—pondríamos—pondrían
querer (*to want*)	querría—querría—querríamos—querrían
saber (*to know*)	sabría—sabría—sabríamos—sabrían
salir (*to leave*)	saldría—saldría—saldríamos—saldrían
tener (*to have*)	tendría—tendría—tendríamos—tendrían
valer (*to be worth, to cost*)	valdría—valdría—valdríamos—valdrían
venir (*to come*)	vendría—vendría—vendríamos—vendrían

The conditional of **hay** (*there is, there are*) is **habría.**

EXERCISE 15.2

Understand the meaning of the following conditional sentences and pronounce them in Spanish:

1. Yo iría a Taos mañana, pero no tengo carro.

2. Pepe vendría a la fiesta esta noche, pero trabaja.

3. Ellos irían a España este verano, pero no tienen dinero.

4. El jefe del departamento de personal le contrataría, pero no hay vacantes.

5. Nos gustaría saber inglés, pero no tenemos mucho tiempo para estudiar.

6. Juan escribiría una carta al director del hotel, pero no sabe inglés.

7. ¿Podría usted venir a trabajar mañana?

8. Me gustaría venir a trabajar, pero mi hijo está enfermo.

9. Yo conduciría a la playa, pero mi coche está roto.

10. Mi tía Filomena vendría a trabajar por mí, pero no puede.

EXERCISE 15.3

In pairs, answer the following questions using the conditional tense:

1. ¿Podría usted trabajar el miércoles, Juanita? _____

2. ¿Iría usted a Guadalajara con Lupita este fin de semana? _____

3. ¿Trabajaría usted en este hotel en tiempo completo? _____

4. ¿Le gustaría a usted cocinar en el restaurante en tiempo parcial? _____

5. ¿Tendría usted tiempo para tomar un test de aptitud esta tarde? _____

6. ¿Podría usted llamarme por teléfono mañana por la mañana? _____

7. ¿Sabría usted decirme donde está la oficina de recursos humanos? ____

8. ¿Podría usar este teléfono para llamar a mi hermana? _____

9. ¿Sería usted tan amable de poner su nombre en la solicitud de ingreso?

10. ¿Pagarían ustedes más del salario mínimo después de trabajar en el hotel tres meses? _____

EXERCISE 15.4

With a partner, ask and answer the following phrases, making sure that you understand what you are asking or answering:

Estudiante uno: ¿Le gustaría trabajar como camarista?

Estudiante dos:	No, preferiría trabajar como cocinera.
Estudiante uno:	¿Podría Fernando empezar a trabajar el día seis?
Estudiante dos:	Creo que él podría empezar el día seis.
Estudiante uno:	¿Iría usted a Chile?
Estudiante dos:	Sí, yo iría a Chile.
Estudiante uno:	¿Llamaría usted mañana si pudiera?
Estudiante dos:	Naturalmente que llamaría.
Estudiante uno:	¿Trabajaría usted de tiempo completo?
Estudiante dos:	Sí, me gustaría mucho.
Estudiante uno:	¿Pagarían ustedes siete dólares por hora?
Estudiante dos:	No, solo pagaríamos el salario mínimo.

The Imperfect Subjunctive (Past Subjunctive)

In most cases, the imperfect subjunctive is used under the same conditions as the present subjunctive, except that the point of view is in the past. For example, *I want you to go* translates in Spanish as **Quiero que usted vaya.** To say *I wanted you to go,* the past subjunctive is needed, **Quise que usted fuera.** The imperfect subjunctive is formed from the third person plural of the preterit tense by dropping the **ron** of the **ellos** form and adding **ra, ra, ramos, ran,** or **se, se, semos, sen.** There are no exceptions. Some examples are:

Verb	Uds. Form of Preterit	Past Subjunctive
usar	usaron	usara, usara, usáramos, usaran
pedir	pidieron	pidiese, pidiese, pidiésemos, pidiesen
ir	fueron	fuera, fuera, fuéramos, fueran
hacer	hicieron	hiciese, hiciese, hiciésemos, hiciesen

The past subjunctive of **hay** (there is, there are) is **hubiera.**

EXERCISE 15.5

Understand the meaning of the following past subjunctive sentences and pronounce them in Spanish:

1. Yo iría a Venezuela este verano si tuviera dinero.
2. Pepe se ducharía si hubiera agua.
3. Ellas trabajarían más si esta compañía pagara siete dólares por hora.
4. Federico escribiría a Juanita si tuviera su dirección.
5. Dije a Pepe que cocinara los camarones.
6. Ella llegó al trabajo antes de que su hermano llegara.

7. Mi papá me envió cien dólares para que me divirtiera.

8. Yo fui al hotel después que empezara el banquete.

9. Cuando trabajábamos en ese hotel, era importante que habláramos con los huéspedes.

10. El jefe de cocina pidió al cocinero que cortara las legumbres.

EXERCISE 15.6

With a partner, answer in Spanish using the past subjunctive tense:

1. ¿Irían ustedes a Tierra del Fuego si tuvieran dinero? _____

   _____

2. ¿Viajarían ustedes a La Jolla si tuvieran coche? _____

   _____

3. ¿Trabajaría usted en este hotel si pudiera? _____

   _____

4. ¿Le gustaría a Samuel invitar a Lupita si tuviera una fiesta? _____

   _____

5. ¿Vendrían ellos a San Francisco si los invitáramos? _____

   _____

6. ¿Me pagarían el salario mínimo si trabajara aquí? _____

   _____

7. ¿Me escribiría usted una carta si se lo pidiera? _____

   _____

8. ¿Le enviaría su hermana dinero si fuera rica? _____

   _____

9. ¿Harían ellas las camas si se lo pidiéramos? _____

   _____

10. ¿Le gustarían viajar a los Estados Unidos si tuvieran tiempo? _____

   _____

EXERCISE 15.7

With a partner, ask and answer the following phrases, making sure that you understand what you are asking or answering:

Estudiante uno:	¿Trabajaría usted en Pierre si le pagaran bien?
Estudiante dos:	No me gustaría trabajar en Pierre, hace mucho frío.
Estudiante uno:	¿Era necesario que hablaran solo español?
Estudiante dos:	Sí, era necesario que habláramos solo en español.
Estudiante uno:	¿Iría usted a Honolulu si tuviese dinero?
Estudiante dos:	Sí, yo iría a Honolulu si tuviera dinero.
Estudiante uno:	¿Si tuviera usted un Cadillac, conduciría usted a Reno?
Estudiante dos:	Si tuviese un Cadillac no iría a Reno, iría a Las Vegas.

Estudiante uno:	¿Si tuviera Lupita una fiesta, iría usted?
Estudiante dos:	Si Lupita tuviese una fiesta, yo no iría.
Estudiante uno:	¿Se ducharía usted si tuviera tiempo?
Estudiante dos:	No me ducharía porque me duché esta mañana.

Adverbs of Intensity

The following adverbs of intensity are commonly used in everyday language:

bastante (bahs-táhn-teh)	*enough/rather*
casi (cáh-see)	*almost*
demasiado (deh-mah-see-áh-doh)	*too much*
más (mahs)	*more*
menos (méh-nohs)	*less, fewer*
mucho (móo-choh)	*much*
poco (póh-coh)	*little*
suficiente (soo-fee-see-éhn-teh)	*sufficient*

EXERCISE 15.8

Understand the meaning of the following sentences with adverbs of intensity and pronounce them in Spanish:

1. Hay bastante gente en el comedor hoy.
2. El cocinero puso casi dos onzas de mantequilla en el pastel.
3. La mesera usó demasiada agua para hacer la limonada.
4. Por favor, ponga más leche en el café.
5. Hoy hay menos gente en el restaurante.
6. Sé mucho español.
7. Lupita sabe poco inglés.
8. No tenemos suficientes sillas para el banquete.
9. Pepe sabe bastante italiano.
10. ¿Tiene usted queso? Sí, tengo un poco.

EXERCISE 15.9

In pairs, ask and answer the following phrases, making sure that you understand what you are asking or answering:

Estudiante uno: ¿Hay bastante jabón para lavar los platos?

Estudiante dos:	Sí, tenemos bastante.
Estudiante uno:	¿Cuántos clientes tenemos?
Estudiante dos:	Tenemos casi doscientos.
Estudiante uno:	¿Hizo el cocinero suficiente pan?
Estudiante dos:	Sí, hizo demasiado.
Estudiante uno:	¿Tiene usted calor?
Estudiante dos:	Sí, tengo mucho calor y mucha sed.
Estudiante uno:	¿Hay más o menos clientes que ayer?
Estudiante dos:	Hoy hay más.
Estudiante uno:	¿Trabaja Eugenio rápido?
Estudiante dos:	Sí, Eugenio trabaja bastante rápido.

CONVERSATIONAL PROFESSIONAL INTERACTION

In groups of two, translate, practice, and be ready to role-play the following dialogue between a human resource supervisor and a job applicant:

Estudiante uno (supervisor):   Buenas tardes. ¿Qué desea usted?

Estudiante dos (empleado por hora):   Buenas tardes. Busco trabajo como mesero.

Estudiante uno: ¿Tiene usted experiencia como mesero?

Estudiante dos: Sí señor. He trabajado en Chili's por tres años.

Estudiante uno: ¿Habla usted inglés?

Estudiante dos: Hablo bastante inglés. Lo aprendí en Puerto Rico.

Estudiante uno: Bien. Rellene esta solicitud de ingreso.

Estudiante dos: ¿Podría usted darme un bolígrafo?

Estudiante uno: Aquí lo tiene. ¿Le gustaría a usted trabajar en Reno?

Estudiante dos: No, señor. Preferiría trabajar an Las Vegas porque tengo familia allí.

Estudiante uno: Si tuviéramos una vacante en Las Vegas le contrataríamos. Solamente hay puestos de mesero en Reno.

Estudiante dos: De acuerdo. Trabajaré en Reno. ¿Ofrecen ustedes seguro médico y dental?

Estudiante uno: Sí. Además, le damos dos uniformes y una comida por turno gratis.

Estudiante dos: ¿Cuánto pagan por hora?

Estudiante uno: Pagamos el salario mínimo para empezar. Después de noventa días le pagaremos seis dólares y cincuenta centavos por hora. También hay horas extra los fines de semana.

Estudiante dos:	Trabajaría para ustedes si pagaran por lo menos seis dólares.
Estudiante uno:	Lo siento. Eso no es posible.
Estudiante dos:	Bien. Trabajaré por el salario mínimo los primeros noventa días. ¿Cuándo puedo empezar?
Estudiante uno:	Puede empezar el sábado por la mañana. Hasta el sábado.

📋 QUESTIONS TO THE CLASS 📋

Answer the following questions asked by your instructor (or by another student) without looking at your textbook or any class notes:

1. ¿Iría usted a Cayo Hueso si tuviera dinero?
2. ¿Conduciría usted a Oregón si tuviese un Rolls Royce?
3. ¿Vendría usted a la clase de español si estuviera enfermo(a)?
4. ¿Enviaría usted chocolates a su profesor(a) si tuviese dinero?
5. ¿Le gustaría ir a la playa conmigo?
6. ¿Hablaría usted español si viviese en Bolivia?
7. Y si viviese en Rusia, ¿hablaría usted ruso?
8. ¿Tiene usted bastante dinero para ir a un restaurante esta noche?
9. ¿Es el español un poco difícil o muy difícil?
10. ¿Le gusta mucho Mel Gibson, o le gusta solamente un poco?

CULTURAL VIGNETTE

Hispanic countries celebrate religious holidays nearly every month. An important religious time is Easter. Holy Week, or **Semana Santa** as it is called, is observed with processions through the streets of almost every city and town in the Hispanic world. In Mexico, people have a special devotion to the **Virgen de Guadalupe** whose sanctuary is visited by millions every year. Each community has a patron saint whose celebration occurs once a year, when people gather to hear mass, bring flowers, and ask for special personal favors. Many Hispanics emphasize the day of the patron saint they were named after more than they do their birthdays. If a hospitality manager hears the expression **Hoy es el día de mi santo,** he or she should assume that that day is of special significance for the worker in question.

CHAPTER 16

GRAMMATICAL EXPRESSIONS

NONPROFESSIONAL VOCABULARY

EXPRESSIONS OF EMOTION

OVERVIEW

The final chapter offers some grammatical expressions peculiar to the Spanish language, as well as a selection of expressions of emotion.

UNIT CONTENT

Technical Human Resources Vocabulary (III) • Grammatical Expressions (Selection) • Nonprofessional Vocabulary • Expressions of Emotion • Conversational Professional Interaction

Technical Human Resources Vocabulary (III)

rules and regulations	las ordenanzas (ohr-deh-náhn-sahs)
salary	el salario (sah-láh-ree-oh)
screening	la selección (seh-lehc-see-óhn)
seasonal work	el trabajo temporal (trah-báh-hoh tehm-poh-ráhl)
selection process	el proceso selectivo (proh-séh-soh seh-lehc-tée-voh)
sex	el sexo (séhc-soh)
sexual harassment	el acoso sexual (ah-cóh-soh sehc-soo-áhl)
sheriff	el alguacil (ahl-goo-ah-séel)

(to) sign	firmar (*v.*) (feer-máhr)
signature	la firma (féer-mah)
skill	la habilidad (ah-bee-lee-dáhd)
Social Security	la seguridad social (seh-goo-ree-dáhd soh-see-áhl)
Social Security number	el número de seguridad social (nóo-meh-roh deh seh-goo-ree-dáhd-soh-see-áhl)
state	el estado (ehs-táh-doh)
stationery	el papel de cartas (pah-péhl de cáhr-tahs)
(to) steal	robar (*v.*) (roh-báhr)
street	la calle (cáh-yeh)
suggestion box	el buzón de sugerencias (boo-sóhn deh soo-heh-réhn-see-ahs)
supervisor	el/la supervisor/a (soo-pehr-vee-sóhr/a)
tardiness	llegar tarde (*v.*) (yeh-gáhr táhr-deh)
(to) telephone	telefonear (*v.*) (teh-leh-foh-neh-áhr)
	llamar por teléfono (*v.*) (yah-máhr pohr teh-léh-foh-noh)
temporary job	el empleo temporal (ehm-pléh-oh tehm-poh-ráhl)
(to) terminate	despedir (*v.*) (dehs-peh-déer)
termination (dismissal)	el despido (dehs-pée-doh)
test	el test (tehst)
theft	el robo (róh-boh)
time card	la tarjeta registradora (tahr-héh-tah reh-gees-trah-dóh-rah)
time clock	el reloj registrador (reh-lóhh reh-gees-trah-dóhr)
(to) train	entrenar (*v.*) (ehn-treh-náhr)
trainer	el/la entrenador/a (ehn-treh-nah-dóhr/a)
training	el entrenamiento (ehn-treh-nah-mee-éhn-toh)
transportation	el medio de locomoción (méh-dee-oh deh loh-coh-moh-see-óhn)
truck	la camioneta (cah-mee-oh-néh-tah)
(to) type	escribir a máquina (*v.*) (ehs-cree-béer ah máh-kee-nah)
uniform	el uniforme (oo-nee-fóhr-meh)
vacations	las vacaciones (vah-cah-see-óh-nehs)
(to) verify	verificar (*v.*) (veh-ree-fee-cáhr)
wage	la paga por hora (páh-gah pohr óh-rah)
waiting list	la lista de espera (lées-tah deh ehs-péh-rah)
weapons	las armas (áhr-mahs)
work	el trabajo (trah-báh-hoh)
work contract	el contrato de trabajo (cohn-tráh-toh deh trah-báh-hoh)
workday	la jornada (hohr-náh-dah)
work hours	el horario de trabajo (oh-ráh-ree-oh deh trah-báh-hoh)
working days	los días laborables (dée-ahs lah-boh-ráh-blehs)
zip code	el código postal (cóh-dee-goh pohs-táhl)

EXERCISE 16.1

Match the following list of restaurant vocabulary words, practice their pronunciation, and be ready to speak them aloud:

1. *suggestion box*	_____ a. habilidad
2. *Social Security*	_____ b. días laborables
3. *theft*	_____ c. lista de espera
4. *zip code*	_____ d. robar
5. *sheriff*	_____ e. despido
6. *screening*	_____ f. jornada
7. *truck*	_____ g. medio de locomoción
8. *street*	_____ h. firmar
9. *weapons*	_____ i. tarjeta registradora
10. *working days*	_____ j. robo
11. *termination*	_____ k. seguridad social
12. *workday*	_____ l. calle
13. *skill*	_____ m. buzón de sugerencias
14. *transportation*	_____ n. armas
15. *waiting list*	_____ o. selección
16. *time card*	_____ p. camioneta
17. *(to) steal*	_____ q. alguacil
18. *(to) sign*	_____ r. código postal
19. *tardiness*	_____ s. trabajo temporal
20. *seasonal work*	_____ t. llegar tarde

Grammatical Expressions

Each language has its own idioms or special grammatical expressions. The selection that follows will help students understand some of the grammatical peculiarities of the Spanish language.

Negative Words and Their Affirmative Counterparts

Negative	Affirmative
nadie (*no one*)	alguien (*someone*)
nada (*nothing*)	algo (*something*)
ninguno/a/os/as (*none—not any*)	alguno/a/os/as (*some*)
ni . . . ni (*neither . . . nor*)	o . . . o (*either or*)

Negative words are not permitted after the verb unless a negative also precedes the verb. Example: **No veo a nadie** (*I see no one*).

EXERCISE 16.2

Translate the following sentences into English:

1. Juan está ayudando a alguien en el almacén. _____
_____

2. Ella no me dijo nada cuando me llamó por teléfono. _____
_____

3. El hotel no ofrece ni empleo temporal ni empleo de tiempo completo.
_____

Translate the following sentences into Spanish:

1. *The police officer didn't say anything.* _____
_____

2. *Either Lupita or Jorge will repair the time clock.* _____
_____

3. *He has none; I have some (speaking of time cards).* _____
_____

Shortened Forms of Adjectives

A limited number of words (mainly adjectives) are shortened when they are placed before masculine singular nouns. The most commonly used are:

bueno	becomes	buen	Example: Sirven buen café aquí.
malo	becomes	mal	Example: Ayer tuve un mal día.
primero	becomes	primer	Example: El primer piso está vacío.
tercero	becomes	tercer	Example: El tercer piso está listo.
uno	becomes	un	Example: Cómprese un uniforme.

EXERCISE 16.3

Translate the following sentences into English:

1. Mi jefe es un buen jefe. _____
2. Vaya al primer piso rápidamente. _____
_____

3. Sirven mal té en este restaurante. _____
_____

Translate the following sentences into Spanish:

1. *The third room on the right is not ready.* _____
_____

2. *I have a good supervisor (male).* _____
3. *It is a bad idea to be late to work.* _____

"Saber" and "Conocer"

The verbs **saber** and **conocer** translate as *to know*. As with **ser** and **estar,** students learning Spanish find it difficult to learn when to use one or the other. Generally, **saber** is used to indicate what you know or what you know how to do (something that you can act out) while **conocer** is used to indicate that you are acquainted or familiar with a person, place, or thing. For example, **José sabe hablar español bien** means that he is fluent in the language; **José no conoce Las Vegas** means that he has never been there.

The forms of the verbs are:

Present	Imperfect	Preterit	Future	Conditional	Subjunctive
sé	sabía	supe	sabré	sabría	sepa
sabe	sabía	supo	sabrá	sabría	sepa
sabemos	sabíamos	supimos	sabremos	sabríamos	sepamos
saben	sabían	supieron	sabrán	sabrían	sepan
conozco	conocía	conocí	conoceré	conocería	conozca
conoce	conocía	conoció	conocerá	conocería	conozca
conocemos	conocíamos	conocimos	conoceremos	conoceríamos	conozcamos
conocen	conocían	conocieron	conocerán	conocerían	conozcan

EXERCISE 16.4

With a partner, ask and answer the following sentences with **saber** and **conocer:**

1. ¿Sabe usted firmar? _____

2. ¿Sabe usted español? _____

3. ¿Conoce usted al jefe del departamento de alimentos y bebidas? _____
   _____

4. ¿Conoce Lupita a Jorge? _____

5. ¿Sabe usted trabajar de cocinero? _____

6. ¿Sabe usted cuál es el código postal de la Ciudad de México? _____
   _____

7. ¿Conocen ellos al gerente de este hotel? _____

8. Y usted, ¿conoce a la señora Rodríguez? _____

9. ¿Sabe usted algo de Pepe? _____

10. ¿Sabe usted dónde vive ella? _____

EXERCISE 16.5

With a partner, ask and answer the following phrases, making sure that you understand what you are asking or answering:

Estudiante uno:	¿Saben Leticia y Jaime inglés bien?
Estudiante dos:	Sí, ellos saben hablar inglés muy bien.
Estudiante uno:	¿Conoce usted San Clemente?
Estudiante dos:	Sí, estuve allí hace un año.
Estudiante uno:	¿Sabe usted si trabajo pasado mañana?
Estudiante dos:	Usted no trabaja el miércoles.
Estudiante uno:	¿Sabe usted la calle donde vive Lupita?
Estudiante dos:	No sé, pregunte a Jorge.
Estudiante uno:	¿Sabe usted donde está el buzón de sugerencias?
Estudiante dos:	Naturalmente, está en el vestidor de empleados.
Estudiante uno:	¿Le gustaría conocer a Michael Jackson?
Estudiante dos:	Sí, me gustaría conocerle.

Diminutives

To indicate smallness or cuteness, the suffixes **ito, ita, itos, itas** and, less commonly, **illo, illa, illos, illas** are attached to many words. A final vowel is often dropped before adding the ending. Examples: **una manzana pequeñita** (*a small apple*), **una amiguita de mi hijo** (*a little friend of my son's*). In some regions, the suffixes **ico, ica, icos, icas** are used.

EXERCISE 16.6

Understand the meaning of the following sentences and pronounce them in Spanish:

1. Por favor, traiga una sillita al comedor.
2. Juan tiene un hermanito en Acapulco.
3. Hay una ventanilla allí.
4. Juanita ha comprado un cochecito rojo.
5. Quiere un bistec con unas patatitas fritas.
6. Mi amiga Teresa es chiquita pero muy bonita.
7. Mi amigo Samuel tiene unos ojitos verdes que me gustan mucho.
8. ¿Podría usted servirme un vasito de vino tinto?
9. Rosario, hay unas manchitas sobre el cojín; quítelas con detergente y agua.
10. Paquito, le veré en un minutito.

EXERCISE 16.7

Provide the diminutives of the following words using the suffix **ito (ita, itos, itas):**

1. casa _____
2. Pedro _____
3. carro _____
4. hermanas _____
5. pequeñas _____
6. ahora _____
7. carta _____
8. chico _____
9. manzana _____
10. cuchillos _____

Nonprofessional Vocabulary

Clothing (sample)

la blusa (blóo-sah)	*blouse*
los calcetines (cahl-seh-tée-nehs)	*socks*
la camisa (cah-mée-sah)	*shirt*
la camiseta (cah-mee-séh-tah)	*T-shirt*
la chaqueta (chah-kéh-tah)	*jacket*
la falda (fáhl-dah)	*skirt*
la gorra (góh-rrah)	*cap*
las medias (méh-dee-ahs)	*stockings*
la ropa (róh-pah)	*clothes*
el traje (tráh-heh)	*suit*
el vestido (vehs-tée-doh)	*dress*

Human Body (sample)

la boca (bóh-cah)	*mouth*
el brazo (bráh-soh)	*arm*
la cabeza (cah-béh-sah)	*head*
el diente (dee-éhn-teh)	*tooth*
el estómago (ehs-tóh-mah-goh)	*stomach*
los labios (láh-bee-ohs)	*lips*
la mano (máh-noh)	*hand*
la nariz (nah-rées)	*nose*
el ojo (óh-hoh)	*eye*

la oreja (oh-réh-hah)	*ear*
el pie (pee-éh)	*foot*
la pierna (pee-éhr-nah)	*leg*

Travel (sample)

la aduana (ah-doo-áh-nah)	*customs*
el aeropuerto (ah-eh-roh-poo-éhr-toh)	*airport*
el avión (ah-vee-óhn)	*airplane*
el equipaje (eh-kee-páh-heh)	*baggage*
la estación (ehs-tah-see-óhn)	*station*
la estación de autobuses (ehs-tah-see-óhn deh ah-oo-toh-bóo-sehs)	*bus station*
la estación de ferrocarril (ehs-tah-see-óhn deh feh-rroh-cah-rréel)	*train station*
la maleta (mah-léh-tah)	*suitcase*
la migración (mee-grah-see-óhn)	*migration*
el tren (trehn)	*train*

Sports and Activities (sample)

el béisbol (béh-ees-bohl)	*baseball*
caminar (cah-mee-náhr)	*to walk*
cantar (cahn-táhr)	*to sing*
los deportes (deh-póhr-tehs)	*sports*
descansar (dehs-cahn-sáhr)	*to rest*
esquiar (ehs-kee-áhr)	*to ski*
el fútbol (fóot-bohl)	*soccer*
el fútbol americano (fóot-bohl ah-meh-ree-cáh-noh)	*football*
jugar (hoo-gáhr)	*to play (a sport)*
montar en bicicleta (mohn-tárh ehn bee-see-cléh-tah)	*to bike ride*
nadar (nah-dáhr)	*to swim*
el tenis (téh-nees)	*tennis*
tocar (toh-cáhr)	*to play (an instrument)*

EXERCISE 16.8

Write full sentences using nouns and verbs listed in the Nonprofessional Vocabulary section. Include the present, past, future, conditional, command, and subjunctive tenses.

Expressions of Emotion

Some interjections used in Hispanic countries are:

¡Caramba! (cah-ráhm-bah)	*Gee!*
¡Dios mío! (dee-óhs mée-oh)	*Oh my gosh!*

¡Estupendo (ehs-too-péhn-doh)	*Great!*
¡Madre mía! (máh-dreh mée-ah)	*Oh gee!*
¡Qué alegría! (keh ah-leh-grée-ah)	*What a joy!*
¡Qué bonita! (keh boh-née-tah)	*How pretty!*
¡Qué bueno! (keh boo-éh-noh)	*How good!*
¡Qué desastre! (keh deh-sáhs-treh)	*What a disaster!*
¡Qué guapo! (keh goo-áh-poh)	*How handsome!*
!Qué horror! (keh oh-rróhr)	*How horrible!*
!Qué lástima! (keh láhs-tee-mah)	*What a pity!*
¡Qué pena! (keh péh-nah)	*How sad!*
¡Qué sorpresa! (keh sohr-préh-sah)	*What a surprise!*
!Qué suerte! (keh soo-éhr-teh)	*How lucky!*
¡Qué triste! (keh trées-teh)	*How sad!*
¡Qué tontería! (keh tohn-teh-rée-ah)	*How silly!*

EXERCISE 16.9

Give an expression of emotion after each of the following situations:

1. *You have won the lottery.*
2. *Your favorite team (San Diego Padres) lost the game.*
3. *You meet Tom Cruise at a party.*
4. *You meet Michael Jackson at a party.*
5. *Your boyfriend's cat has died.*
6. *You find an old classmate on the street in San Francisco.*
7. *You look at a picture of your friend's sister and like her very much.*
8. *Your teacher cancels tomorrow's class.*
9. *You drop a tray full of glassware in the dining room.*
10. *You pass this class with an A.*

CONVERSATIONAL PROFESSIONAL INTERACTION

In groups of two, translate, practice, and be ready to role-play the following dialogue between a human resource supervisor and a job applicant:

Estudiante uno (supervisor):   ¿Puedo servirle en algo?

Estudiante dos (solicitud de empleado):   Quisiera trabajar en este hotel.

Estudiante uno: ¿En qué puesto quiere usted trabajar?

Estudiante dos: Me gustaría trabajar como electricista.

Estudiante uno: ¿Conoce usted alguien en este hotel?

Estudiante dos: Sí. Mi primo trabaja como electricista.

Estudiante uno:	¡Qué bueno! ¿Es Juanito su primo?
Estudiante dos:	Sí. Somos de Sonora. Me gustaría trabajar con él.
Estudiante uno:	Pero usted no sabe nada de electricidad.
Estudiante dos:	Sé algo. Trabajé tres meses como electricista.
Estudiante uno:	Lo siento no tenemos vacantes ahorita.
Estudiante dos:	¡Qué lástima! ¿Tienen puestos de jardinero?
Estudiante uno:	De jardinero sí. ¿Sabe usted plantar árboles?
Estudiante dos:	Naturalmente.
Estudiante uno:	¿Tiene usted medio de locomoción propio?
Estudiante dos:	Sí. Me compré un carrito el mes pasado.
Estudiante uno:	¿Puede usted trabajar los fines de semana?
Estudiante dos:	Puedo trabajar de lunes a domingo.
Estudiante uno:	¡Qué bueno! Venga el martes a las 8 de la mañana.
Estudiante dos:	¡Qué alegría! Estaré aquí a las 8 en punto.
Estudiante uno:	Muy bien. ¡Hasta el martes!

📋 QUESTIONS TO THE CLASS 📋

Answer the following questions asked by your instructor (or by another student) without looking at your textbook or any class notes:

1. ¿Conoce usted a alguien que trabaje en Marie Callender's?
2. ¿Es Pedro un buen estudiante?
3. ¿Sabe usted hacer camas?
4. ¿Conoce usted al director del Hotel Royal?
5. ¿Le gustan las naranjas grandes o pequeñitas?
6. ¿Tiene usted hermanitos o hermanitas?
7. ¿Viven sus abuelitos en Santa Fe?
8. ¿Sabe usted montar en bicicleta?
9. ¿Sabe usted tocar la guitarra?
10. ¿Conoce usted personalmente a Mel Gibson?

CULTURAL VIGNETTE

Women in Hispanic countries have traditionally been expected to be passive and sentimental, their influence limited to the family, while men tended to be active and outgoing influencing the greater world around them. These patterns, however, are changing very rapidly as women are becoming more educated and moving into the labor force. The kitchen, once an undisputed female domain, today might be shared with men who help out with dishwashing and who display their own culinary talents. While many Hispanic women may work as room attendants and dining room servers, their daughters are beginning to enter fields of business, education, and government. But, certain roles are still largely defined by gender. Although women work, men are still ultimately considered responsible for feeding, sheltering, and protecting the honor of their wives, sisters, mothers, and daughters. This attitude, called **machismo** in Spanish, indicates that men take great pride in having large, extended families. Men are also likely to endure illness or injury without seeking medical attention.

Women, though they may put in a long work day, are still the primary caregivers of children and older relatives. Considered to be the center of the family, Hispanic women willingly sacrifice their own needs for the good of their families. Hotel supervisors do well to be sensitive to these characteristics.

GLOSSARY

A

a (ah) *to/at*

a la derecha (ah lah deh-réh-chah) *to the right*

a la izquierda (ah lah ees-kee-éhr-dah) *to the left*

abajo (ah-báh-hoh) *down, downstairs*

la abeja (ah-béh-hah) *bee*

abonar (*v.*) (ah-boh-náhr) *(to) fertilize*

el abono (ah-bóh-noh) *fertilizer*

el abrelatas (ah-breh-láh-tahs) *can opener*

abril (ah-bréel) *April*

abrir (*v.*) (ah-bréer) *(to) open*

el/la abuelo/a (ah-boo-éh-loh/ah) *grandfather/grandmother*

la acción disciplinaria (ahc-see-óhn dees-see-plee-náh-ree-ah) *disciplinary action*

el aceite (ah-séh-ee-teh) *oil*

el aceite y vinagre (ah-seh-ée-teh ee vee-náh-greh) *oil and vinegar*

el acoso sexual (ah-cóh-soh sehc-soo-áhl) *sexual harassment*

acostarse (o→ue) (*v.reflex.*) (ah-cohs-táhr-seh) *(to) go to bed*

la actitud (ahc-tee-tóod) *attitude*

adentro (ah-déhn-troh) *inside*

el aderezo (ah-deh-réh-soh) *dressing*

el aderezo para ensaladas (ah-deh-réh-soh páh-rah ehn-sah-láh-dah) *salad dressing*

adiós (ah-dee-óhs) *good-bye*

la aduana (ah-doo-áh-nah) *customs*

el aeropuerto (ah-eh-roh-poo-éhr-toh) *airport*

afeitarse (*v. reflex.*) (ah-feh-ee-táhr-seh) *(to) shave*

afilado (*adj.*) (ah-fee-láh-doh) *sharp*

el aflojador de tierra (ah-floh-hah-dóhr deh tee-éh-rrah) *rototiller*

afuera (ah-foo-éh-rah) *outside*

la agencia de inmigración (ah-héhn-see-ah deh een-mee-grah-see-óhn) *immigration agency (INS)*

el/la agente de policía (ah-héhn-teh deh poh-lee-sée-ah) *police officer*

agosto (ah-góhs-toh) *August*

agua (áh-goo-ah) *water*

el agua caliente (áh-goo-ah cah-lee-éhn-teh) *hot water*

el agua jabonosa (áh-goo-ah hah-boh-nóh-sah) *soapy water*

el agua para riego (áh-goo-ah páh-rah ree-éh-goh) *irrigation water*

el agua potable (áh-goo-ah poh-táh-bleh) *potable/fresh water*

las aguas negras (áh-goo-ahs néh-grahs) *waste water*

el aguacate (ah-goo-ah-cáh-teh) *avocado*

la aguja (ah-góo-hah) *needle*

el agujero (ah-goo-héh-roh) *hole*

ahí (ah-ée) *there*

ahora (ah-óh-rah) *now*

ahorita (ah-oh-rée-tah) *right now*

el aire acondicionado (áh-ee-reh ah-cohn-dee-see-oh-náh-doh) *air-conditioned*

el ajo (áh-hoh) *garlic*

a la carta (*adj.*) (ah lah cáhr-tah) *a la carte*

el alambre (ah-láhm-breh) *wire*

la alberca (ahl-béhr-cah) *swimming pool*

la albóndiga (ahl-bóhn-dee-gah) *meatball*

la alfombra (ahl-fóhm-brah) *carpet/rug*

las algas (áhl-gahs) *algae*

algo (áhl-goh) *something*

el alguacil (ahl-goo-ah-séel) *sheriff*

el alguicida (ahl-guee-sée-dah) *algicide*

alguien (áhl-guee-ehn) *someone*

alguno (ahl-góo-noh) *some/any*

los alicates (ah-lee-cáh-tehs) *pliers*

los alimentos y bebidas (ah-lee-méhn-tohs ee beh-bée-dahs) *food and beverage*

allá (ah-yáh) *there*

allí (ah-yée) *there*

el almacén (ahl-mah-séhn) *storeroom*

la almeja (ahl-méh-hah) *clam*

el almidón (ahl-mee-dóhn) *starch*

almidonar (*v.*) (ahl-mee-doh-náhr) *(to) starch*

la almohada (ahl-moh-áh-dah) *pillow*

almorzar (o→ue) (*v.*) (ahl-mohr-sáhr) *(to) have lunch*

el almuerzo (ahl-moo-éhr-soh) *lunch*

alrededor (ahl-reh-deh-dóhr) *around*

alto (*adj.*) (áhl-toh)   *tall*
el/la ama de llaves (áh-mah deh yáh-vehs)   *executive housekeeper*
amable (*adj.*) (ah-máh-bleh)   *kind*
amarillo (ah-mah-rée-yoh)   *yellow*
el/la amigo/a (ah-mée-goh/gah)   *friend*
anaranjado (*adj.*) (ah-nah-rahn-háh-doh)   *orange (color)*
el andador (ahn-dah-dóhr)   *garden path*
anoche (ah-nóh-cheh)   *last night*
antes (áhn-tehs)   *before*
anunciar (*v.*) (ah-noon-see-áhr)   *(to) announce*
el año (áh-nyoh)   *year*
el apagador (ah-pah-gah-dóhr)   *light switch*
apagar (*v.*) (ah-pah-gáhr)   *(to) turn off*
el aparador (ah-pah-rah-dóhr)   *side stand*
el aparcamiento (ah-pahr-cah-mee-éhn-toh)   *parking*
aparcar (*v.*) (ah-pahr-cáhr)   *(to) park*
la apariencia personal (ah-pah-ree-éhn-see-ah pehr-soh-náhl)   *grooming*
el apellido (ah-peh-yée-doh)   *name (last)*
el aperitivo (ah-peh-ree-tée-voh)   *appetizer*
el apetito (ah-peh-tée-toh)   *appetite*
el apio (áh-pee-oh)   *celery*
el apodo (ah-póh-doh)   *nickname/alias*
aprender (*v.*) (ah-prehn-déhr)   *(to) learn*
el aprendizaje (ah-prehn-dee-sáh-heh)   *apprenticeship*
aquel (ah-kéhl)   *that*
aquí (ah-kée)   *here*
la araña (ah-ráh-nyah)   *spider*
el árbol (áhr-bohl)   *tree*
el arbusto (ahr-bóos-toh)   *bush*
el área de juegos (áh-reh-ah deh hoo-éh-gohs)   *playground*
las áreas públicas (áh-reh-ahs póo-blee-cahs)   *front of the house*
la arena (ah-réh-nah)   *sand*
Argentina (*f.*) (ahr-hehn-tée-nah)   *Argentina*
argentino (*adj.*) (ahr-hehn-tée-noh)   *Argentine*
las armas (áhr-mahs)   *weapons*
arreglar (*v.*) (ah-rreh-gláhr)   *(to) fix, repair*
arriba (ah-rrée-bah)   *upstairs*
el arroz (ah-rróhs)   *rice*
el asa (áh-sah)   *handle*
asado (*adj.*) (ah-sáh-doh)   *roasted*
asar (*v.*) (ah-sáhr)   *(to) roast, bake*
asar a la parrilla (*v.*) (ah-sáhr ah lah pah-rrée-yah)   *(to) grill/broil*
el ascensor (ahs-sehn-sóhr)   *elevator*
el aseo personal (ah-séh-oh pehr-soh-náhl)   *grooming*
así (ah-sée)   *thus/in this way/so*
el/la asistente (ah-sees-téhn-teh)   *assistant*
la aspiradora (ahs-pee-rah-dóh-rah)   *vacuum cleaner*

aspirar (*v.*) (ahs-pee-ráhr)   *(to) vacuum*
el atún (ah-tóon)   *tuna fish*
el aumento (ah-oo-méhn-toh)   *raise (wage)*
el aumento salarial (ah-oo-méhn-toh sah-lah-ree-áhl)   *pay raise*
la ausencia excesiva (ah-oo-séhn-see-ah ehc-seh-sée-vah)   *absenteeism*
el auto (áh-oo-toh)   *car*
el autobús (ah-oo-toh-bóos)   *autobús/bus*
el autoservicio (áh-oo-toh sehr-vée-see-oh)   *self-service*
la avería (ah-veh-rée-ah)   *breakdown (equipment)*
el avión (ah-vee-óhn)   *airplane*
la avispa (ah-vées-pah)   *wasp*
ayer (ah-yéhr)   *yesterday*
el/la ayudante de mesero (ah-yoo-dáhn-teh deh-meh-séh-roh)   *bus person*
ayudar (*v.*) (ah-yoo-dáhr)   *(to) help*
el azadón (ah-sah-dóhn)   *hoe*
la azotea (ah-soh-téh-ah)   *flat roof*
el/la azúcar (ah-sóo-cahr)   *sugar*
el azucarero (ah-soo-cah-réh-roh)   *sugar bowl*
azul (*adj.*) (ah-sóol)   *blue*
el azulejo (ah-soo-léh-hoh)   *tile*

B

la bacteria (bahc-téh-ree-ah)   *bacteria*
bailar (*v.*) (bah-ee-láhr)   *(to) dance*
bajo (*adj.*) (báh-hoh)   *short*
el balde (báhl-deh)   *bucket*
la baldosa (bahl-dóh-sah)   *tile*
la banana (bah-náh-nah)   *banana*
la bandeja (bahn-déh-hah)   *sheet pan/tray*
el banquete (bahn-kéh-teh)   *banquet*
la bañera (bah-nyéh-rah)   *bathtub*
el baño (báh-nyoh)   *bathroom*
el baño público (bah-nyoh póo-blee-coh)   *public bathroom*
el bar (bahr)   *bar*
barato (*adj.*) (bah-ráh-toh)   *inexpensive/cheap*
el barniz (bahr-nées)   *varnish*
barnizar (*v.*) (bahr-nee-sáhr)   *(to) varnish*
barrer (*v.*) (bah-rréhr)   *(to) sweep*
bastante (bahs-táhn-teh)   *enough*
la basura (bah-sóo-rah)   *trash/garbage*
la bata (báh-tah)   *frock, bathrobe*
el batido (bah-tée-doh)   *shake*
el batidor (bah-tée-dohr)   *wire whip*
batir (*v.*) (bah-téer)   *(to) whip*
beber (*v.*) (beh-béhr)   *(to) drink*
las bebidas (beh-bée-dahs)   *beverages*
las bebidas alcohólicas (beh-bée-dahs ahl-coh-óh-lee-cahs)   *alcoholic beverages*
el béisbol (béh-ees-bohl)   *baseball*
los beneficios (beh-neh-fée-see-ohs)   *benefits*

la bicicleta (bee-see-cléh-tah) *bicycle*
bien (bee-éhn) *well*
bien hecho (*adj.*) (bee-éhn éh-choh)
  well done
bienvenido (*adj.*) (bee-ehn-beh-née-doh)
  welcome
la bisagra (bee-sáh-grah) *hinge*
el bistec (bees-téhc) *beefsteak*
blanco (bláhn-coh) *white*
los blancos (bláhn-cohs) *bed/white linen*
el bloc de notas (blohc deh nóh-tahs)
  note pad
bloqueado (*adj.*) (bloh-keh-áh-doh) *blocked
  (room)*
la blusa (blóo-sah) *blouse*
la boca (bóh-cah) *mouth*
el bolígrafo (boh-lée-grah-foh) *ballpoint pen*
la bolsa (bóhl-sah) *bag*
la bolsa de basura (bóhl-sah deh bah-sóo-rah)
  trash bag
la bolsa de lavandería (bóhl-sah deh lah-
  vahn-deh-rée-ah) *laundry bag*
la bolsa sanitaria (bóhl-sah sah-nee-táh-ree-
  ah) *sanitary bag*
la bolsita de azúcar (bohl-sée-tah deh ah-sóo-
  cahr) *sugar packet*
la bolsita de té (bohl-sée-tah deh teh)
  tea bag
la bomba (bóhm-bah) *pump*
la bombilla (bohm-bée-yah) *light bulb*
bonito/a (*adj.*) (boh-née-toh/ah) *pretty*
la boquilla (boh-kée-yah) *nozzle*
el borde (bóhr-deh) *rim*
las botas de goma (bóh-tahs deh góh-mah)
  rubber boots
el bote (bóh-teh) *can*
el botón (boh-tóhn) *button*
el brazo (bráh-soh) *arm*
el brécol (bréh-cohl) *broccoli*
buenas noches (boo-énahs nóh-chehs) (after
  sunset) *good evening*
buenas tardes (boo-énahs táhr-dehs) (until
  sunset) *good afternoon*
bueno (*adj.*) (boo-éh-noh) *good*
buenos días (boo-éh-nohs dée-ahs) *good
  morning*
el buffet (boo-féh) *buffet*
buscar (*v.*) (boos-cáhr) *(to) look for*
el buzón de sugerencias (boo-sóhn deh soo-
  heh-réhn-see-ahs) *suggestion box*

C

la cabeza (cah-béh-sah) *head*
el cable (cáh-bleh) *cable*
café (*adj.*) (cah-féh) *coffee (color)*
el café (cah-féh) *coffee*
el café descafeinado (cah-féh dehs-cah-feh-
  ee-náh-doh) *decaffeinated coffee*
la cafetera (cah-feh-téh-rah) *coffee maker*

la cafetería (cah-feh-teh-rée-ah) *cafeteria*
la cafetería de empleados (cah-feh-teh-rée-ah
  deh ehm-pleh-áh-dohs) *employee cafeteria*
la caja (cáh-hah) *cash register/box*
la caja de herramientas (cáh-hah deh eh-rrah-
  mee-éhn-tahs) *tool box*
la caja de registro (cáh-hah deh reh-hées-troh)
  register box
la caja para llevar (cáh-hah pah-rah lleh-váhr)
  to-go box
el/la cajero/a (cah-héh-roh/ah) *cashier*
el cajón (cah-hóhn) *drawer*
la cal (cahl) *lime (not the fruit)*
los calamares (cah-lah-máh-rehs) *squid*
los calcetines (cahl-seh-tée-nehs) *socks*
la caldera (cahl-déh-rah) *boiler*
la calefacción (cah-leh-fahc-see-óhn)
  heating
el calentador de pan (cah-lehn-tah-dóhr deh
  pahn) *bread warmer*
caliente (*adj.*) (cah-lee-éhn-teh) *warm*
la calle (cáh-yeh) *street*
el calor (cah-lóhr) *heat*
la cama (cáh-mah) *bed*
la cama de matrimonio (cáh-mah deh mah-
  tree-móh-nee-oh) *double/queen bed*
la cama portátil (cáh-mah pohr-táh-teel) *cot*
la cámara congeladora (cáh-mah-rah cohn-
  heh-lah-dóh-rah) *walk-in freezer*
la cámara fría (cáh-mah-rah frée-ah) *walk-in
  refrigerator*
la camarera de pisos (cah-mah-réh-rah deh
  pée-sohs) *section housekeeper*
el/la camarero/a (cah-mah-réh-roh/ah)
  waiter/waitress
el/la camarista (cah-mah-rées-tah) *attendant (room)/section housekeeper*
los camarones (cah-mah-róh-nehs) *shrimp*
cambiar (*v.*) (cahm-bee-áhr) *(to) change*
el cambio de dirección (cáhm-bee-oh deh
  dee-rehc-see-óhn) *change of address*
caminar (*v.*) (cah-mee-náhr) *(to) walk*
la camioneta (cah-mee-oh-néh-tah) *truck*
la campana (cahm-páh-nah) *hood (kitchen)*
la camisa (cah-mée-sah) *shirt*
la camiseta (cah-mee-séh-tah) *T-shirt*
Canadá (*m.*) (cah-nah-dáh) *Canada*
el canapé (cah-nah-péh) *canapé*
la cancha de tenis (cáhn-chah deh téh-nees)
  tennis court
el cangrejo (cahn-gréh-hoh) *crab*
cansado/a (*adj.*) (cahn-sáh-doh/dah) *tired*
cantar (*v.*) (cahn-táhr) *(to) sing*
la carne (cáhr-neh) *meat*
la carne asada (cáhr-neh ah-sáh-dah)
  roasted/grilled meat
la carne de ave (cáhr-neh deh áh-veh)
  poultry
la carne de res (cáhr-neh deh rehs) *beef*

la carne molida (cáhr-neh moh-lée-dah)
ground meat
la carne picada (cáhr-neh pee-cáh-dah)
ground meat
caro *(adj.)* (cáh-roh) *expensive*
el carpintero (cahr-peen-téh-roh) *carpenter*
la carretilla (cah-rreh-tée-yah) *wheelbarrow*
el carro (cáh-rroh) *car*
el carro de postres (cáh-rroh deh póhs-trehs)
dessert cart
el carro de servicio (cáh-rroh deh sehr-vée-see-oh) *cart (maid)*
la carta (cáhr-tah) *menu/bill of fare/letter*
la carta de vinos (cáhr-tah deh vée-nohs)
wine list
casado/a *(adj.)* (cah-sáh-doh/dah) *married*
el cascajo (cahs-cáh-hoh) *gravel*
casi (cáh-see) *almost*
catorce (cah-tóhr-seh) *fourteen*
cavar *(v.)* (cah-váhr) *(to) dig*
el cazo (cáh-soh) *ladle*
la cazuela (cah-soo-éh-lah) *pan*
la cebolla (seh-bóh-yah) *onion*
el cemento (seh-méhn-toh) *cement*
la cena (séh-nah) *dinner*
cenar *(v.)* (seh-náhr) *dinner (to have)*
el cenicero (seh-nee-séh-roh) *ashtray*
las cenizas (seh-née-sahs) *ashes*
el centavo (sehn-táh-voh) *cent*
cepillar *(v.)* (seh-pee-yáhr) *(to) brush*
cepillarse *(v. reflex.)* (seh-pee-yáhr-seh)
(to) brush (one's hair/teeth)
el cepillo (seh-pée-yoh) *brush*
el cepillo de mano (seh-pée-yoh deh máh-noh) *hand brush*
la cera (séh-rah) *wax*
cerca (séhr-cah) *near*
la cerca (séhr-cah) *fence*
el cerdo (sehr-doh) *pork*
la cereza (seh-réh-sah) *cherry*
los/las cerillos/as (seh-rée-yohs/yahs)
matches
cero (séh-roh) *zero*
cerrado *(adj.)* (seh-rráh-doh) *closed*
la cerradura (seh-rrah-dóo-rah) *lock*
cerrar (e→ie) *(v.)* (seh-rráhr) *(to) close*
cerrar con llave *(v.)* (seh-rráhr cohn yáh-veh)
(to) lock
la cerveza (sehr-véh-sah) *beer*
el césped (séhs-pehd) *lawn*
la cesta (séhs-tah) *basket*
la cesta de frutas (céhs-tah deh fróo-tahs)
fruit basket
la cesta para pan (séhs-tah páh-rah pahn)
bread basket
el cesto de basura (séhs-toh deh bah-sóo-rah)
wastebasket
el champú (chahm-póo) *shampoo*
la chaqueta (chah-kéh-tah) *jacket*

la charola (chah-róh-lah) *tray*
el cheque salarial (chéh-keh sah-lah-ree-áhl)
pay check
el chicle (chée-cleh) *chewing gum*
chico *(adj.)* (chée-coh) *tiny*
el chile (chée-leh) *chili pepper*
el chile rojo (chée-leh róh-hoh) *pepper (red)*
el chile verde (chée-leh véhr-deh) *pepper (green)*
Chile *(m.)* (chée-leh) *Chile*
el chocolate (choh-coh-láh-teh) *chocolate*
la chuleta (choo-léh-tah) *chop (such as pork or lamb)*
la chuleta de cerdo (choo-léh-tah deh séhr-doh) *pork chop*
la chuleta de cordero (choo-léh-tah deh cohr-déh-roh) *lamb chop*
cien (see-éhn) *one hundred*
el cincel (seen-séhl) *chisel*
cinco (séen-coh) *five*
cincuenta (seen-coo-éhn-tah) *fifty*
la cita (sée-tah) *appointment*
la ciudad (see-oo-dáhd) *city*
la ciudadanía (see-oo-dah-dah-née-ah)
citizenship
el/la ciudadano/a (see-oo-dah-dáh-noh/ah)
citizen
clavar *(v.)* (clah-váhr) *(to) nail*
el clavo (cláh-voh) *nail*
el/la cliente (clee-éhn-teh) *customer*
el cloro (clóh-roh) *chlorine*
el closet (clóh-seht) *closet*
el cobertor (coh-béhr-tohr) *bed spread*
la cobija (coh-bée-hah) *blanket*
el coche (cóh-cheh) *car*
la cocina (coh-sée-nah) *kitchen*
cocinar *(v.)* (coh-see-náhr) *(to) cook*
el/la cocinero/a (coh-see-néh-roh/ah) *cook*
el código postal (cóh-dee-goh pohs-táhl)
zip code
el coffee break (cóh-fee bréh-eek) *coffee break*
el cojín (coh-héen) *cushion*
la coladera (coh-lah-déh-rah) *drain*
el colador (coh-lah-dóhr) *colander*
la colcha (cóhl-chah) *quilt*
el colchón (cohl-chóhn) *mattress*
colgar (o→ue) *(v.)* (cohl-gáhr) *(to) hang*
la coliflor (coh-lee-flóhr) *cauliflower*
la colilla (coh-lée-yah) *cigarette butt*
la comanda (coh-máhn-dah) *food order*
el comedor (coh-meh-dóhr) *dining room*
comenzar (e→ie) *(v.)* (coh-mehn-sáhr)
(to) begin
comer *(v.)* (coh-méhr) *(to) eat*
la comida (coh-mée-dah) *meal*
la comida gratis (coh-mée-dah gráh-tees)
free meal

como (cóh-moh)   *as, like*
¿cómo? (cóh-moh)   *how?*
¿cómo está usted? (cóh-moh ehs-táh oos-téhd)
   how are you?
¿cómo se llama usted? (cóh-moh seh yáh-mah
   oos-téhd?)   *what is your name?*
la compañía (cohm-pah-nyí-ah)   *company*
competente (*adj.*) (cohm-peh-téhn-teh)
   competent
comprar (*v.*) (cohm-práhr)   *(to) buy*
comprender (*v.*) (cohm-prehn-déhr)
   (to) understand
el compresor (cohm-preh-sóhr)   *compressor*
comprobar (o→ue) (*v.*) (cohm-proh-báhr)
   (to) check/inspect
con (cohn)   *with*
con leche (*adj.*) (cohn léh-cheh)   *with milk*
el condado (cohn-dáh-doh)   *county*
conducir (*v.*) (cohn-doo-séer)   *(to) drive*
el conducto (cohn-dóoc-toh)   *duct*
congelado (*adj.*) (cohn-heh-lah-doh)
   frozen
el congelador (cohn-heh-lah-dóhr)   *freezer*
congelar (*v.*) (cohn-heh-láhr)   *(to) freeze*
conocer (*v.*) (coh-noh-séhr)   *(to) know/be
   acquainted with*
contar (o→ue) (*v.*) (cohn-táhr)   *(to) count*
contento/a (*adj.*) (cohn-téhn-toh/ah)   *glad,
   pleased*
contestar (*v.*) (cohn-tehs-táhr)   *(to) answer*
contra (cóhn-trah)   *against*
contratar (*v.*) (cohn-trah-táhr)   *(to) hire*
el contrato (cohn-tráh-toh)   *contract*
el contrato de trabajo (cohn-tráh-toh deh trah-
   báh-hoh)   *work contract*
el control de plagas (cohn-tróhl deh pláh-
   gahs)   *pest control*
la copa (cóh-pah)   *goblet*
el corbatín (cohr-bah-téen)   *bow tie*
el cordero (cohr-déh-roh)   *lamb*
la correa (coh-rréh-ah)   *belt (motor)*
correr la cortina (*v.*) (coh-rréhr lah cohr-tée-
   nah)   *(to) draw the curtain*
la cortadora de césped (cohr-tah-dóh-rah deh
   séhs-pehd)   *lawn mower*
cortar (*v.*) (cohr-táhr)   *(to) cut*
cortar el césped (cohr-táhr ehl séhs-pehd)
   (to) mow the lawn
cortés (*adj.*) (cohr-téhs)   *courteous*
la cortina (cohr-tée-nah)   *curtain*
la cortina de ducha (cohr-tée-nah deh dóo-
   chah)   *shower curtain*
el cortocircuito (cohr-toh-seer-coo-ée-toh)
   short circuit
coser (*v.*) (coh-séhr)   *(to) sew*
costar (o→ue) (*v.*) (cohs-táhr)   *(to) cost*
Costa Rica (*f.*) (cóhs-tah rée-cah)   *Costa Rica*
creer (*v.*) (creh-éhr)   *(to) believe*
el cristal (crees-táhl)   *glass (pane)*

la cristalería (crees-tah-leh-rée-ah)
   glassware
el cuadro (coo-áh-droh)   *picture (hanging)*
¿cuál? (coo-áhl)   *which?*
¿cuándo? (coo-áhn-doh)   *when?*
¿cuánto? (coo-áhn-toh)   *how much?*
¿cuántos? (coo-áhn-tohs)   *how many?*
cuarenta (coo-ah-réhn-tah)   *forty*
cuarto (coo-áhr-toh)   *fourth*
el cuarto (coo-áhr-toh)   *room*
el cuarto listo (coo-áhr-toh lées-toh)   *ready-
   room*
el cuarto de salida (coo-áhr-toh deh sah-lée-
   dah)   *checkout room*
cuatro (coo-áh-troh)   *four*
Cuba (*f.*) (cóo-bah)   *Cuba*
la cubertería (coo-behr-teh-rée-ah)
   silverware
la cubeta (coo-béh-tah)   *bus tub*
los cubiertos (coo-bee-éhr-tohs)   *silverware*
los cubitos de hielo (coo-bée-tohs deh ee-éh-
   loh)   *ice cubes*
el cubo (cóo-boh)   *bucket*
el cubo de basura (cóo-boh deh bah-sóo-rah)
   garbage/trash can
cubrir (*v.*) (coo-bréer)   *(to) cover*
la cucaracha (coo-cah-ráh-chah)   *cockroach*
la cuchara (coo-cháh-rah)   *spoon*
la cuchara para sopa (coo-cháh-rah pah-rah
   sóh-pah)   *soup spoon*
la cucharilla (coo-chah-rée-yah)   *teaspoon*
el cucharón (coo-chah-róhn)   *serving spoon/
   ladle*
el cuchillo (coo-chée-yoh)   *knife*
el cuchillo para mantequilla (coo-chée-yoh
   páh-rah mahn-teh-kée-yah)   *butter knife*
la cuenta (coo-énh-tah)   *bill*
el cuidado (coo-ee-dáh-doh)   *care*
el cumpleaños (coom-pleh-áh-nyohs)
   birthday
la cuna (cóo-nah)   *crib*
la cuota de trabajo (coo-óh-tah deh trah-báh-
   hoh)   *workload*
el curriculum vitae (coo-rrée-coo-loom vée-
   tah)   *resumé*

D

dar (*v.*) (dahr)   *(to) give*
los datos personales (dáh-tohs pehr-soh-náh-
   lehs)   *personal information*
de (deh)   *of, from*
de acuerdo (deh ah-coo-éhr-doh)   *Okay*
décimo (déh-see-moh)   *tenth*
decir (*v.*) (deh-séer)   *(to) tell*
el dedo (déh-doh)   *finger*
el delantal (deh-lahn-táhl)   *apron*
delgado/a (*adj.*) (dehl-gáh-doh/dah)   *thin*
demasiado (deh-mah-see-áh-doh)   *too much*
el dentista (dehn-tées-tah)   *dentist*

el departamento (deh-pahr-tah-méhn-toh)
department

el departamento de alimentos y bebidas (deh-pahr-tah-méhn-toh deh ah-lee-méhn-tohs ee beh-bée-dahs) *food and beverage department*

el departamento de ama de llaves (deh-pahr-tah-méhn-toh deh áh-mah deh yáh-vehs) *housekeeping department*

el departamento de mantenimiento (deh-pahr-tah-méhn-toh deh mahn-teh-nee-mee-éhn-toh) *maintenance department*

el departamento de personal (deh-pahr-tah-méhn-toh deh pehr-soh-náhl) *personnel department*

el departamento de recursos humanos (deh-pahr-tah-méhn-toh deh reh-cóor-sohs oo-máh-nohs) *human resources department*

los deportes (deh-póhr-tehs) *sports*

derramar (*v.*) (deh-rrah-máhr) *(to) spill*

el desagüe (deh-sáh-goo-eh) *drain*

desayunar (*v.*) (deh-sah-yoo-náhr) *(to have) breakfast*

el desayuno (deh-sah-yóo-noh) *breakfast*

descafeinado (*adj.*) (dehs-cah-feh-ee-náh-doh) *decaffeinated*

descansar (*v.*) (dehs-cahn-sáhr) *(to) rest*

el descanso (dehs-cáhn-soh) *break (rest)*

el descanso para el almuerzo (dehs-cáhn-soh páh-rah ehl ahl-moo-éhr-soh) *lunch break*

descongelado (*adj.*) (dehs-cohn-he-láh-doh) *thawed*

descongelar (*v.*) (dehs-cohn-heh-láhr) *(to) thaw*

la descripción del puesto (dehs-creep-see-óhn dehl poo-éhs toh) *job description*

desde (déhs-deh) *from/since*

desear (*v.*) (deh-seh-áhr) *(to) wish*

desempolvar (*v.*) (deh-sehn-pohl-váhr) *(to) dust*

el desinfectante (deh-seen-fehc-táhn-teh) *disinfectant*

desmanchar (*v.*) (dehs-mahn-cháhr) *(to) de-stain*

desocupado (*adj.*) (dehs-oh-coo-páh-doh) *vacant*

el desodorante (deh-soh-doh-ráhn-teh) *deodorant*

despacio (dehs-páh-see-oh) *slowly*

despedir (*v.*) (dehs-peh-déer) *(to) terminate (an employee)*

la despensa (dehs-péhn-sah) *pantry*

el desperdicio (dehs-pehr-dée-see-oh) *waste*

los desperdicios (dehs-pehr-dée-see-ohs) *food scraps*

despertarse (e→ie) (*v. reflex.*) (dehs-pehr-táhr-seh) *(to) wake up*

el despido (dehs-pée-doh) *termination (dismissal)*

desportillado (*adj.*) (dehs-pohr-tee-yáh-doh) *chipped*

después (dehs-poo-éhs) *later/after*

el destapador (dehs-tah-pah-dóhr) *bottle opener*

el destornillador (dehs-tohr-nee-yah-dóhr) *screwdriver*

el detector de fuego (deh-tehc-tóhr deh foo-éh-goh) *fire detector*

el detector de humo (deh-tehc-tóhr deh óo-moh) *smoke detector*

el detergente (deh-tehr-héhn-teh) *detergent*

el día (dée-ah) *day*

el día de pago (dée-ah deh páh-goh) *payday*

el día festivo (dée-ah fehs-tée-voh) *holiday*

los días laborables (dée-ahs lah-boh-ráh-blehs) *working days*

el día libre (dée-ah lée-breh) *day off*

diciembre (dee-see-éhm-breh) *December*

el diente (dee-éhn-teh) *tooth*

diez (dee-éhs) *ten*

difícil (*adj.*) (dee-fée-seel) *difficult*

el dinero (dee-néh-roh) *money*

el diploma de estudios secundarios (dee-plóh-mah deh ehs-tóo-dee-ohs seh-coon-dáh-ree-ohs) *high school diploma*

la dirección (dee-rehc-see-óhn) *address*

la dirección postal (dee-rehc-see-óhn pohs-táhl) *mailing address*

el/la directora/a (dee-rehc-tóhr/ah) *manager*

el distribuidor de jabón (dees-tree-boo-ee-dóhr deh hah-bóhn) *soap dispenser*

divertirse (e→ie) (*v. reflex.*) (dee-vehr-téer-seh) *(to) have fun*

la división cuartos (dee-vee-see-óhn coo-áhr-tohs) *room division*

el doblador (doh-blah-dóhr) *linen folder*

el doblador de sábanas (doh-blah-dóhr deh sáh-bah-nahs) *sheet folder*

doblar (*v.*) (doh-bláhr) *(to) fold*

doce (dóh-seh) *twelve*

el doctor (dohc-tóhr) *doctor*

el dólar (dóh-lahr) *dollar*

el domingo (doh-méen-goh) *Sunday*

¿dónde? (dóhn-deh) *where?*

dorado (*adj.*) (doh-ráh-doh) *golden*

dormir (o→ue) (*v.*) (dorh-méer) *(to) sleep*

dormirse (o→ue) (*v. reflex.*) (dohr-méer-seh) *(to) fall sleep*

dos (dohs) *two*

dos veces (dohs véh-sehs) *twice*

el drenaje (dreh-náh-heh) *drainage*

las drogas (dróh-gahs) *drugs*

la ducha (dóo-chah) *shower*

ducharse (*v. reflex.*) (doo-cháhr-seh) *(to) take a shower*

dudar (*v.*) (doo-dáhr)   (to) doubt
dulce (*adj.*) (dóol-seh)   *sweet*

E

la educación (eh-doo-cah-see-óhn)
    education
el (ehl) (masc.)   *the*
él (ehl)   *he*
la electricidad (eh-lehc-tree-see-dáhd)
    electricity
el electricista (eh-lehc-tree-sées-tah)
    electrician
elegante (*adj.*) (eh-leh-gáhn-teh)   *elegant*
el elevador (eh-leh-vah-dóhr)   *elevator*
ella (éh-yah)   *she*
ellos/as (éh-yohs/ahs)   *they*
la emergencia (eh-mehr-héhn-see-ah)
    emergency
empanado (*adj.*) (ehm-pah-náh-doh)
    breaded
empanar (*v.*) (ehm-pah-náhr)   *(to) bread*
empezar (e→ie) (*v.*) (ehm-peh-sáhr)
    (to) begin
emplatar (*v*) (ehm-plah-táhr)   *(to) plate*
el/la empleado/a (ehm-pleh-áh-doh/ah)
    employee
el empleador (ehm-pleh-ah-dóhr)
    employer
el empleo (ehm-pléh-oh)   *job*
el empleo de tiempo completo (ehm-pléh-oh
    deh tee-éhm-poh cohm-pléh-toh)   *full-
    time job*
el empleo de tiempo parcial (ehm-pléh-oh
    deh tee-éhm-poh pahr-see-áhl)   *part-time
    job*
el empleo permanente (ehm-pléh-oh pehr-
    mah-néhn-teh)   *permanent work*
el empleo temporal (ehm-pléh-oh tehm-poh-
    ráhl)   *temporary job*
la empresa (ehm-préh-sah)   *company*
la empresa de igual oportunidad (ehm-préh-
    sah deh ee-goo-áhl oh-pohr-too-nee-dáhd)
    equal-opportunity employer
en (ehn)   *in/on/at*
en seguida (ehn seh-guée-dah)   *at once*
en su jugo (*adj.*) (ehn soo hóo-goh)   *au jus*
encantado(a) (ehn-cahn-táh-doh(ah))
    pleased to meet you
encender (e→ie) (*v.*) (ehn-sehn-déhr)
    (to) light/turn on
encerar (*v.*) (ehn-seh-ráhr)   *(to) wax*
encontrar (o→ue) (*v.*) (ehn-cohn-tráhr)
    (to) find
enero (eh-néh-roh)   *January*
enfadado/a (*adj.*) (ehn-fah-dáh-doh/dah)
    angry
enfermo/a (*adj.*) (ehn-féhr-moh-mah)   *sick,
    ill*
enfrente (ehn-fréhn-teh)   *in front*

enjuagar (*v.*)(ehn-hoo-ah-gáhr)   *(to) rinse*
la ensalada (ehn-sah-láh-dah)   *salad*
entender (e→ie) (*v.*) (ehn-tehn-déhr)
    (to) understand
la entrada (ehn-tráh-dah)   *entrance*
la entrada principal (ehn-tráh-dah preen-see-
    páhl)   *main entrance*
la entrada de empleados (ehn-tráh-dah deh
    ehm-pleh-áh-dohs) *employee entrance*
entre (éhn-treh)   *between*
el/la entrenador/a (ehn-treh-nah-dóhr-ah)
    coach
el entrenamiento (ehn-treh-nah-mee-éhn-toh)
    training
entrenar (*v.*) (ehn-treh-náhr)   *(to) coach*
la entrevista (ehn-treh-vées-tah)   *interview*
enviar (*v.*) (ehn-vee-áhr)   *(to) send*
envolver (o→ue) (*v.*) (ehn-vohl-véhr)
    (to) wrap
el equipaje (eh-kee-páh-heh)   *luggage*
el equipo (eh-kée-poh)   *team*
el equipo de relevo (eh-kée-poh deh reh-léh-
    voh)   *swing team*
la erosión (eh-roh-see-óhn)   *erosion*
la escalera (ehs-cah-léh-rah)   *stairs*
la escalera de servicio (ehs-cah-léh-rah deh
    sehr-vée-see-oh) *service stairs*
escardar (*v.*) (ehs-cahr-dáhr)   *(to) weed*
la escoba (ehs-cóh-bah)   *broom*
la escobilla (ehs-coh-bée-yah)   *toilet brush*
escribir (*v.*) (ehs-cree-béer)   *(to) write*
escribir a máquina (*v.*) (ehs-cree-béer ah
    máh-kee-nah)   *(to) type*
el escritorio (ehs-cree-tóh-ree-oh)   *desk*
el escurridor (ehs-coo-rree-dóhr)   *mop
    wringer*
ese (éh-seh)   *that*
el esmalte (ehs-máhl-teh)   *enamel*
España (*f.*) (ehs-páh-nyah)   *Spain*
español (*adj.*) (ehs-pah-nyóhl)   *Spanish*
el español (ehs-pah-nyóhl)   *Spanish (lan-
    guage)*
el espárrago (ehs-páh-rrah-goh)   *asparagus*
la espátula (ehs-páh-too-lah)   *spatula*
el espejo (ehs-péh-hoh)   *mirror*
esperar (*v.*) (ehs-peh-ráhr)   *(to) hope/wait*
las espinacas (ehs-pee-náh-cahs)   *spinach*
la esponja (ehs-póhn-hah)   *sponge*
el/la esposo/a (ehs-póh-soh/ah)
    husband/wife
la espumadera (ehs-poo-mah-déh-rah)
    skimmer
esquiar (*v.*) (ehs-kee-áhr)   *(to) ski*
la estación (ehs-tah-see-óhn)   *season/station*
la estación de autobuses (ehs-tah-see-óhn deh
    ah-oo-toh-bóo-sehs)   *bus station*
la estación de ferrocarril (ehs-tah-see-óhn deh
    feh-rroh-cah-rréel)   *train station*
la estación de servicio (ehs-tah-see-óhn deh

sehr-vée-see-oh) *floor closet (house-keeping)*
el estacionamiento (ehs-tah-see-oh-nah-mee-éhn-toh) *parking lot*
el estado (ehs-táh-doh) *state*
Los Estados Unidos (*m.*) (ehs-táh-dohs oo-née-dohs) *United States*
estar (*v.*) (ehs-táhr) *(to) be*
este (éhs-teh) *this*
la estera de goma (ehs-téh-rah deh góh-mah) *rubber mat*
el estiércol (ehs-tee-éhr-cohl) *manure*
el estofado (ehs-toh-fáh-doh) *stew*
el estómago (ehs-tóh-mah-goh) *stomach*
el estropajo (ehs-troh-páh-hoh) *scrub/scouring pad*
estropeado (*adj.*) (ehs-troh-peh-áh-doh) *not working/broken*
estudiar (*v.*) (ehs-too-dee-áhr) *(to) study*
la etiqueta (eh-tee-kéh-tah) *label*
la etiqueta con su nombre (eh-tee-kéh-tah cohn soo nóhm-breh) *name tag*
la evaluación (eh-vah-loo-ah-see-óhn) *appraisal*
la evaluación de empleados (eh-vah-loo-ah-see-óhn deh ehm-pleh-áh-dohs) *employee appraisal*
el examen (ehcs-sáh-mehn) *examination*
el examen médico (ehc-sáh-mehn méh-dee-coh) *physical examination*
la experiencia (ehcs-peh-ree-éhn-see-ah) *experience*
la experiencia de trabajo (ehs-peh-ree-éhn-see-ah deh trah-báh-hoh) *job experience*
el extinctor (es-teenc-tóhr) *fire extinguisher*
el extractor de aire (ehs-trahc-tóhr deh áh-ee-reh) *air exhaust*

F

fácil (*adj.*) (fáh-seel) *easy*
la falda (fáhl-dah) *skirt*
la familia (fah-mée-lee-ah) *family*
febrero (feh-bréh-roh) *February*
la fecha (féh-chah) *date*
la fecha de nacimiento (féh-chah deh nah-see-mee-éhn-toh) *date of birth*
fechar (*v.*) (feh-cháhr) *(to) date*
feliz (*adj.*) (feh-lées) *happy*
la felonía (feh-loh-née-ah) *felony*
la felpa (féhl-pah) *terry cloth*
la fiesta (fee-éhs-tah) *party*
fiesta de quinceañera (fee-éhs-tah deh keen-seh-ah-nyéh-rah) *fifteenth birthday celebration*
filtrar (*v.*) (feel-tráhr) *(to) filter/strain*
el filtro (féel-troh) *filter/strainer*
el fin de semana (feen deh seh-máh-nah) *weekend*
la firma (féer-mah) *signature*

firmar (*v.*) (feer-máhr) *(to) sign*
la flor (flohr) *flower*
el flotador (floh-tah-dóhr) *float*
el foco (fóh-coh) *light bulb*
los folletos (foh-yéh-tohs) *pamphlets*
el fontanero (fohn-tah-néh-roh) *plumber*
el fregadero (freh-gah-déh-roh) *sink (kitchen)*
fregar (e→ie) (*v.*) (freh-gáhr) *(to) scrub*
la fregona (freh-góh-nah) *mop*
la freidora (freh-ee-dóh-rah) *deep fryer*
freir (e→i) (*v.*) (freh-éer) *(to) fry*
las fresas (fréh-sahs) *strawberries*
fresco (*adj.*) (fréhs-coh) *fresh*
los frijoles (free-hóh-lehs) *dry beans*
frío (*adj.*) (frée-oh) *cold*
el frío (frée-oh) *cold*
frito (*adj.*) (frée-toh) *fried*
la fruta (fróo-tah) *fruit*
el fuego (foo-éh-goh) *fire*
la fuente (foo-éhn-teh) *fountain*
fuera de servicio (*adj.*) (foo-éh-rah deh sehr-vée-see-oh) *out of order*
la fuga de agua (fóo-gah deh áh-goo-ah) *water leak*
fumar (*v.*) (foo-máhr) *(to) smoke*
la funda de almohada (fóon-dah deh ahl-moh-áh-dah) *pillow case*
el fusible (foo-sée-bleh) *fuse*
el fútbol (fóot-bohl) *soccer*
el fútbol americano (fóot-bohl ah-meh-ree-cáh-noh) *football*

G

las galletas (gah-yéh-tahs) *crackers*
las galletas dulces (gah-yéh-tahs dóol-sehs) *cookies*
la gana (gáh-nah) *desire/eagerness*
el gancho (gáhn-choh) *hanger*
los garbanzos (gahr-báhn-sohs) *chick-peas*
el gas ciudad (gahs see-oo-dád) *natural gas*
la gasolina (gah-soh-lée-nah) *gas*
generalmente (heh-neh-ráhl-mehn-teh) *generally*
la gente (héhn-teh) *people*
el/la gerente (heh-réhn-teh) *manager*
el/la gerente general (heh-réhn-teh heh-neh-ráhl) *general manager*
el germicida (hehr-mee-sée-dah) *germicidal*
la gorra (góh-rrah) *cap*
el gorro (góh-rroh) *cap*
el gorro de baño (góh-rroh deh báh-nyoh) *shower cap*
los grados (gráh-dohs) *degrees*
grande (*adj.*) (gráhn-deh) *large*
la grasa (gráh-sah) *grease*
grasiento (*adj.*) (grah-see-éhn-toh) *greasy*
graso (*adj.*) (gráh-soh) *fat (foods)*
el grifo (grée-foh) *faucet*

gris (*adj.*) (grees) *gray*

el guajolote (goo-ah-hoh-lóh-teh) *turkey*

los guantes (goo-áhn-tehs) *gloves*

los guantes de goma (goo-áhn-tehs deh góh-mah) *rubber gloves*

guapo/a (*adj.*) (goo-áh-poh) *handsome/pretty*

la guarnición (goo-ahr-nee-see-óhn) *garnish (food)*

Guatemala (*f.*) (goo-ah-teh-máh-lah) *Guatemala*

la guía de servicios (guée-ah deh sehr-vée-see-ohs) *service directory*

la guía de teléfonos (guée-ah deh teh-léh-foh-nohs) *telephone book*

la guía de televisión (guée-ah deh teh-leh-vee-see-óhn) *television-program guide*

gustar (*v.*) (goos-táhr) *(to) like*

H

la habilidad (ah-bee-lee-dáhd) *skill*

la habitación (ah-bee-tah-see-óhn) *room/ guest room*

hablar (*v.*) (ah-bláhr) *(to) speak*

hacer (*v.*) (ah-séhr) *(to) do/make*

hacer la cama (*v.*) (ah-séhr lah cáh-mah) *(to) make the bed*

hacer ingletes (*v.*) (ah-séhr een-gléh-tehs) *(to) miter*

el hambre (áhm-breh) *hunger*

la hamburguesa (ahm-boor-guéh-sah) *hamburger*

la harina (ah-rée-nah) *flour*

hasta (áhs-tah) *until, to, up to*

hasta la vista (áhs-tah lah vées-tah) *see you again*

hasta luego (áhs-tah loo-éh-goh) *see you later*

hasta mañana (áhs-tah mah-nyáh-nah) *see you tomorrow*

hay (áh-ee) *there is, there are*

hay que (áh-ee keh) *it is necessary to*

hecho (*adj.*) (éh-choh) *done/made*

el helado (eh-láh-doh) *ice cream*

el herbicida (ehr-bee-sée-dah) *herbicide*

el/la hermano/a (ehr-máh-noh/ah) *brother/sister*

la herramienta (eh-rrah-mee-éhn-tah) *tool*

hervir (e→ie) (*v.*) (ehr-véer) *(to) boil*

hervir a fuego lento (*v*) (her-véer ah foo-éh-goh léhn-toh) *(to) poach*

la hielera (ee-eh-léh-rah) *ice bucket*

el hielo (ee-éh-loh) *ice*

la hierba (ee-éhr-bah) *grass*

la higiene (ee-hee-éh-neh) *hygiene*

la higiene personal (ee-hee-éh-neh pehr-soh-náhl) *personal hygiene*

el/la hijo/a (ée-hoh/ah) *son/daughter*

la hoja (óh-hah) *blade (tool)/leaf (tree)*

¡hóla! (óh-lah) *hi*

los hongos (óhn-gohs) *fungi*

la honradez (ohn-rah-déhs) *honesty*

la hora (óh-rah) *hour*

el horario de trabajo (oh-ráh-ree-oh deh trah-báh-hoh) *work hours*

la hormiga (ohr-mée-gah) *ant*

el hormigón (ohr-mee-góhn) *concrete*

el horno (óhr-noh) *oven*

los hors d'oeuvres (ohrs déhvrs) *hors d'oeuvres*

hoy (óh-ee) *today*

el hoyo (óh-yoh) *hole (in the ground)*

el hueso (oo-éh-soh) *bone*

el/la huésped (oo-éhs-pehd) *guest*

la huevera (oo-eh-véh-rah) *egg cup*

el huevo (oo-éh-voh) *egg*

el huevo duro (oo-éh-voh dóo-roh) *hard-boiled egg*

el huevo pasado por agua (oo-éh-voh pah-sáh-doh pohr áh-goo-ah) *soft-boiled egg*

los huevos revueltos (oo-éh-vohs reh-voo-éhl-tohs) *scrambled eggs*

el humo (óo-moh) *smoke*

I

la idea (ee-déh-ah) *idea*

igualmente (ee-goo-áhl-mehn-teh) *same to you*

importante (*adj.*) (eem-pohr-táhn-teh) *important*

imposible (*adj.*) (eem-poh-sée-bleh) *impossible*

la ingeniería (een-heh-nee-eh-rée-ah) *engineering*

injertar (*v.*) (een-hehr-táhr) *(to) graft*

el injerto (een-héhr-toh) *graft*

el/la inmigrante (een-mee-gráhn-teh) *immigrant*

el/la inmigrante legal (een-mee-gráhn-teh leh-gáhl) *legal immigrant*

el inodoro (ee-noh-dóh-roh) *toilet bowl*

el insecticida (een-sehc-tee-sée-dah) *insecticide*

el insecto (een-séhc-toh) *insect*

insistir (*v.*) (een-sees-téer) *(to) insist*

la insubordinación (een-soo-bohr-dee-nah-see-óhn) *insubordination*

inteligente (*adj.*) (een-teh-lee-héhn-teh) *intelligent*

interesante (*adj.*) (een-teh-reh-sáhn-teh) *interesting*

el internado (een-tehr-náh-doh) *internship*

el interruptor (een-teh-rroop-tóhr) *light switch*

el inventario (een-vehn-táh-ree-oh) *inventory*

el invierno (een-vee-éhr-noh) *winter*

invitar (*v.*) (een-vee-táhr) *(to) invite*

ir (*v.*) (eer) *(to) go*
irse (*v. reflex.*) (éer-seh) *(to) go away*

J

el jabón (hah-bóhn) *soap*
el jabón de baño (hah-bóhn deh báh-nyoh) *bath soap*
el jabón líquido (hah-bóhn lée-kee-doh) *liquid soap*
el jabón de tocador (hah-bóhn deh toh-cah-dóhr) *hand soap*
la jabonera (hah-boh-néh-rah) *soap dish*
la jalea (hah-léh-ah) *jelly*
el jamón (hah-móhn) *ham*
el jarabe (ha-ráh-beh) *syrup*
el jardín (hahr-déen) *garden*
el/la jardinero/a (hahr-dee-néh-roh/ah) *gardener*
la jarra (háh-rrah) *pitcher/jar/jug*
la jarra para agua (háh-rrah pah-rah áh-goo-ah) *water pitcher*
la jarra para café (háh-rrah páh-rah cah-féh) *coffeepot*
la jarrita para leche (hah-rrée-tah páh-rah léh-cheh) *creamer*
el/la jefe/a (héh-feh/ah) *boss*
el/la jefe/a de departamento (héh-feh/ah deh deh-pahr-tah-méhn-toh) *department head*
el/la jefe/a de cocina (héh-feh/ah deh coh-sée-nah) *chef*
la jornada (hohr-náh-dah) *workday*
el jueves (hoo-éh-vehs) *Thursday*
jugar (*v.*) (hoo-gáhr) *(to) play (a sport)*
el jugo (hóo-goh) *juice*
julio (hóo-lee-oh) *July*
junio (hóo-nee-oh) *June*
la junta (hóon-tah) *meeting*
la junta de departamento (hóon-tah deh deh-pahr-tah-méhn-toh) *department meeting*

K

el ketchup (kéht-choop) *ketchup*

L

la/s (lah/s) *the*
los labios (láh-bee-ohs) *lips*
el ladrillo (lah-drée-yoh) *brick*
la lámpara de pie (láhm-pah-rah deh pee-éh) *floor lamp*
la lana (láh-nah) *wool*
la langosta (lahn-góhs-tah) *lobster*
el lápiz (láh-pees) *pencil*
la lata (láh-tah) *can*
el lavabo (lah-váh-boh) *sink (guestroom)*
la lavadora (lah-vah-dóh-rah) *washer*

la lavandería (lah-vahn-deh-rée-ah) *laundry room*
el/la lavaplatos (lah-vah-pláh-tohs) *dishwasher (person)*
el lavaplatos (lah-vah-pláh-tohs) *dishwasher (machine)*
lavar (*v.*) (lah-váhr) *(to) wash*
lavarse (*v. reflex.*) (lah-váhr-seh) *(to) wash oneself*
la leche (léh-cheh) *milk*
la lechuga (leh-chóo-gah) *lettuce*
las legumbres (leh-góom-brehs) *vegetables*
la lejía (leh-hée-ah) *bleach*
lejos (*adj.*) (léh-hohs) *far*
la lencería (lehn-seh-rée-ah) *linen*
las lentejas (lehn-téh-hahs) *lentils*
levantar (*v.*) (leh-vahn-táhr) *(to) raise/lift*
levantarse (*v. reflex.*) (leh-vahn-táhr-seh) *(to) get up/rise*
la libra (lée-brah) *pound (weight)*
la libreta de apuntes (lee-bréh-tah deh ah-póon-tehs) *writing pad*
la licencia para manejar (lee-séhn-see-ah páh-rah mah-neh-háhr) *driver's license*
la lima (lée-mah) *lime*
el limón (lee-móhn) *lemon*
la limonada (lee-moh-náh-dah) *lemonade*
el/la limpiador(a) (leem-pee-ah-dóhr) *janitor*
el limpiador de cristales (leem-pee-ah-dór deh crees-táh-lehs) *window cleaner*
limpiar (*v.*) (leem-pee-áhr) *(to) clean*
limpiar a fondo (*v.*) (leem-pee-áhr ah fóhn-doh) *(to) deep clean*
limpiar a seco (*v.*) (leem-pee-áhr ah séh-coh) *(to) dry clean*
limpiar la mesa (*v.*) (leem-pee-áhr lah méh-sah) *(to) clear the table*
la limpieza a seco (leem-pee-éh-sah ah séh-coh) *dry cleaning*
limpio (*adj.*) (léem-pee-oh) *clean*
la lista de espera (lées-tah deh ehs-péh-rah) *waiting list*
la lista de lavandería (lées-tah deh lah-vahn-deh-rée-ah) *laundry list*
listo (*adj.*) (lées-toh) *ready*
listo para alquilar (*adj.*) (lees-toh páh-rah ahl-kee-láhr *ready to rent (room)*
el litro (lée-troh) *liter*
los (lohs) *the*
la loza (lóh-sah) *china*
lubricar (*v.*) (loo-bree-cáhr) *(to) lubricate/oil*
las luces de emergencia (lóo-sehs deh eh-mehr-héhn-see-ah) *emergency lighting*
el lunes (lóo-nehs) *Monday*
la luz (loos) *light*
la luz de salida (loos deh sah-lée-dah) *exit light*

LL

la llamada (yah-máh-dah)   *call*

llamar (*v.*) (yah-máhr)   *(to) call*

llamar a la puerta (*v.*) (yah-máhr ah lah poo-éhr-tah)   *(to) knock on the door*

llamar por teléfono (*v.*) (yah-máhr pohr teh-léh-foh-noh)   *(to) telephone*

llamarse (*v. reflex.*) (yah-máhr-seh)   *(to) be called*

la llave (yáh-veh)   *key*

la llave de paso (yáh-veh deh páh-soh)   *pass key/shutoff valve*

la llave maestra (yáh-veh máh-ehs-trah)   *master key*

llegar (*v.*) (yeh-gáhr)   *(to) arrive*

llegar tarde (*v.*) (yeh-gáhr táhr-deh)   *(to) arrive late*

llevar (*v.*) (yéh-vahr)   *(to) carry, bring*

llevar puesto (*v.*) (yeh-váhr poo-éhs-toh)   *(to) wear*

M

la maceta (mah-séh-tah)   *flower pot*

la madera (mah-déh-rah)   *wood*

la madre (máh-dreh)   *mother*

la madrugada (mah-droo-gáh-dah)   *dawn/early morning*

maduro (*adj.*) (mah-dóo-roh)   *ripe*

el maíz (mah-ées)   *corn*

mal (mahl)   *bad/badly*

la maleta (mah-léh-tah)   *suitcase*

malo (*adj.*) (máh-loh)   *bad*

la mamá (mah-máh)   *mommy*

la mancha (máhn-chah)   *stain*

el/la manejador/a (mah-neh-hah-dóhr/ah)   *manager*

la manguera (mahn-guéh-rah)   *hose*

la mano (máh-noh)   *hand*

el manómetro (mah-nóh-meh-troh)   *pressure gage*

la manta (máhn-tah)   *blanket*

el mantel (mahn-téhl)   *tablecloth*

la mantelería (mahn-teh-leh-rée-ah)   *napery/table linen*

el mantenimiento (mahn-teh-nee-mee-éhn-toh)   *maintenance*

el mantenimiento preventivo (mahn-teh-nee-mee-éhn-toh preh-vehn-tée-voh)   *preventive maintenance*

la mantequilla (mahn-teh-kée-yah)   *butter*

el manual de empleados (mah-noo-áhl deh ehm-pleh-áh-dohs)   *employee handbook*

la manzana (mahn-sáh-nah)   *apple*

mañana (mah-nyáh-nah)   *tomorrow*

la mañana (mah-nyáh-nah)   *morning*

la máquina (máh-kee-nah)   *machine*

la máquina de hielo (máh-kee-nah deh ee-éh-loh)   *ice machine*

la máquina de refrescos (máh-kee-nah deh reh-fréhs-cohs)   *soda dispenser*

la máquina lavaplatos (máh-kee-nah lah-vah-pláh-tohs)   *diswashing machine*

la máquina para limpiar alfombras (máh-kee-nah páh-rah leem-pee-áhr ahl-fóhm-brahs)   *rug shampooer*

marcar (*v.*) (mahr-cáhr)   *(to) clock (in and out)*

los mariscos (mah-rées-kohs)   *shellfish*

la marmita (mahr-mée-tah)   *kettle*

la marmita al vapor (mahr-mée-tah ahl vah-póhr)   *steamer*

marrón (*adj.*) (mah-rróhn)   *brown*

el martes (máhr-tehs)   *Tuesday*

el martillo (mahr-tée-yoh)   *hammer*

marzo (máhr-soh)   *March*

más (mahs)   *more*

la masa (máh-sah)   *dough*

el material (mah-teh-ree-áhl)   *material*

mayo (máh-yoh)   *May*

la mayonesa (mah-yoh-néh-sah)   *mayonnaise*

me (meh)   *me, to me*

me llamo . . . (meh yáh-mo)   *my name is . . .*

las medias (méh-dee-ahs)   *stockings*

el médico (méh-dee-coh)   *doctor/physician*

el medio de locomoción (méh-dee-oh deh loh-coh-moh-see-óhn)   *transportation*

medio hecho (*adj.*) (méh-dee-oh éh-choh)   *medium done*

mejor (meh-hóhr)   *better*

el melón (meh-lóhn)   *melon*

menos (méh-nohs)   *less*

el mensaje (mehn-sáh-heh)   *message*

el menú (meh-nóo)   *menu*

la mermelada (mehr-meh-láh-dah)   *jam*

la mermelada de durazno (mehr-meh-láh-dah deh doo-ráhs-noh)   *peach jam*

la mermelada de fresa (mehr-meh-láh-dah deh fréh-sah)   *strawberry jam*

la mermelada de naranja (mehr-meh-láh-dah deh nah-ráhn-hah)   *orange marmalade*

la mermeladera (mehr-meh-lah-déh-rah)   *jam holder*

el mes (mehs)   *month*

la mesa (méh-sah)   *table*

la mesa de servicio (méh-sah deh sehr-vée-see-oh)   *service table*

el/la mesero/a (meh-séh-roh/ah)   *waiter/waitress*

la mesilla de noche (meh-sée-yah deh nóh-cheh)   *night stand/bed-side table*

mexicano (*adj.*) (meh-hee-cáh-noh)   *Mexican*

México (*m.*) (méh-hee-coh)   *Mexico*

el mezclador (mehs-clah-dóhr)   *mixer*

mezclar (*v.*) (mehs-cláhr)   *(to) mix*
mi (mee)   *my*
mí (mee) (after preposition)   *me/myself*
el microondas (mee-croh-óhn-dahs)   *micro-wave oven*
el miedo (mee-éh-doh)   *fear*
la miel (mee-éhl)   *honey*
el miércoles (mee-éhr-coh-lehs)   *Wednesday*
las migajas (mee-gáh-hahs)   *crumbs*
la migración (mee-grah-see-óhn)   *migration*
mil (meel)   *one thousand*
el minuto (mee-nóo-toh)   *minute*
mío (mée-oh)   *mine*
moler (*v.*) (moh-léhr)   *(to) grind*
molestar (*v.*) (moh-lehs-táhr)   *(to) bother*
el molino de café (moh-lée-noh deh cah-féh)   *coffee grinder*
montar en bicicleta (*v.*) (mohn-tárh ehn bee-see-cléh-tah)   *(to) bikeride*
morado (*adj.*) (moh-ráh-doh)   *purple*
moreno (*adj.*) (moh-réh-noh)   *brown (hair)*
la mostaza (mohs-táh-sah)   *mustard*
el mostrador (mohs-trah-dóhr)   *counter*
el motor (moh-tóhr)   *motor*
la motosierra (móh-toh-see-éh-rrah)   *chain saw*
mover (o→ue) (*v.*) (moh-véhr)   *(to) move*
el/la mozo/a (móh-soh/ah)   *waiter/waitress*
el/la mozo/a de pisos (móh-soh/ah deh pée-sohs)   *houseperson*
mucho/s (móo-choh/s)   *much/many*
mucho gusto (móo-choh góos-toh)   *nice to meet you*
los muebles (moo-éh-blehs)   *furniture*
la mugre (móo-greh)   *dirt*
muy (móo-ee)   *very*

N

nada (náh-dah)   *nothing*
nadar (*v.*) (nah-dáhr)   *(to) swim*
nadie (náh-dee-eh)   *no one*
naranja (*adj.*) (nah-ráhn-hah)   *orange (color)*
la naranja (nah-ráhn-hah)   *orange*
la nariz (nah-rées)   *nose*
necesario (*adj.*) (neh-seh-sáh-ree-oh)   *necessary*
necesitar (*v.*) (neh-seh-see-táhr)   *need*
negro (*adj.*) (néh-groh)   *black*
ni (nee)   *neither/nor*
ninguno (neen-góo-noh)   *none*
la niñera (nee-nyéh-rah)   *babysitter*
no (noh)   *no, not*
la noche (nóh-cheh)   *night*
no fumar (noh foo-máhr)   *no smoking*
el nombre (nóhm-breh)   *first name*
norteamericano/a (*adj.*) (nohr-teh-ah-meh-ree-cáh-noh/ah)   *North American*
nos (nohs)   *us, to us*

nos vemos (nohs véh-mohs) (informal)   *see you*
nosotros/as (noh-sóh-trohs/ahs)   *we*
notificar (*v.*) (noh-tee-fee-cáhr)   *(to) notify*
novecientos (noh-veh-see-éhn-tohs)   *nine hundred*
noveno (noh-véh-noh)   *ninth*
noventa (noh-véhn-tah)   *ninety*
noviembre (noh-vee-éhm-breh)   *November*
nuestro (noo-éhs-troh)   *our*
nueve (noo-éh-veh)   *nine*
nuevo (*adj.*) (noo-éh-voh)   *new*
el número (nóo-meh-roh)   *number*
el número de habitación (nóo-meh-roh deh ah-bee-tah-see-óhn)   *room number*
el número de seguridad social (nóo-meh-roh deh seh-goo-ree-dáhd-soh-see-áhl)   *Social Security number*
nunca (nóon-cah)   *never*

O

o (oh)   *or*
los objetos extraviados (ohb-héh-tohs ehs-trah-vee-áh-dohs)   *lost and found*
ochenta (oh-chéhn-tah)   *eighty*
ocho (óh-choh)   *eight*
ochocientos (oh-choh-see-éhn-tohs)   *eight hundred*
octavo (ohc-táh-voh)   *eighth*
octubre (ohk-tóo-breh)   *October*
ocupado (*adj.*) (oh-coo-páh-doh)   *occupied*
la oficina (oh-fee-sée-nah)   *office*
ofrecer (*v.*) (oh-freh-séhr)   *(to) offer*
ojalá (oh-hah-láh)   *God grant*
el ojo (óh-hoh)   *eye*
la olla (óh-yah)   *pot*
once (óhn-seh)   *eleven*
la onza (óhn-sah)   *ounce*
la orden (óhr-dehn)   *order (food)*
el ordenador (ohr-deh-nah-dóhr)   *computer*
las ordenanzas (ohr-deh-náhn-sahs)   *rules and regulations*
la orden de trabajo (óhr-dehn deh trah-báh-hoh)   *work order*
la oreja (oh-réh-hah)   *ear*
la ostra (óhs-trah)   *oyster*
el otoño (oh-tóh-nyoh)   *autumn*

P

el padre (páh-dreh)   *father*
los padres (páh-drehs)   *parents*
la paga por hora (páh-gah pohr óh-rah)   *wage*
pagar (*v.*) (pah-gáhr)   *(to) pay*
la pala (páh-lah)   *shovel*
la palmera (pahl-méh-rah)   *palm tree*
la palomita (pah-loh-mée-tah)   *bow tie*
el pan (pahn)   *bread*

el pan dulce (pahn dóol-seh) *pastry*
el panecillo (pah-neh-sée-yoh) *roll (bread)*
Panamá (*m.*) (pah-nah-máh) *Panama*
el panqueque (pahn-kéh-keh) *pancake*
los pantalones (pahn-tah-lóh-nehs) *pants*
la pantalla (pahn-táh-yah) *screen*
los pañuelos de papel (pah-nyoo-éh-lohs deh
pah-péhl) *facial tissue*
el papá (pah-páh) *daddy*
la papa (páh-pah) *potato*
las papas fritas (páh-pahs frée-tahs) *French
fries*
el papel (pah-péhl) *paper*
el papel de cartas (pah-péhl deh cáhr-tahs)
letterheads/stationery
el papel higiénico (pah-péhl ee-hee-éh-nee-
coh) *toilet paper*
el papel tapiz (pah-péhl tah-pées) *wallpaper*
la papelera (pah-peh-léh-rah) *paper basket*
la papelería (pah-peh-leh-rée-ah) *paper
work*
para (páh-rah) *for/to/by/in order to*
la pared (pah-réhd) *wall*
la parrilla (pah-rrée-yah) *broiler/grill*
el patrón (pah-tróhn) *employer*
pasado mañana (pah-sáh-doh mah-nyáh-nah)
the day after tomorrow
el pasillo (pah-sée-yoh) *hallway*
el pastel (pahs-téhl) *pie*
la pastelería (pahs-teh-leh-rée-ah) *pastry
shop*
la patata (pah-táh-tah) *potato*
el patio (páh-tee-oh) *courtyard*
el pavo (páh-voh) *turkey*
el pedido (peh-dée-doh) *requisition*
pedir (e→i) (*v.*) (peh-déer) *(to) ask*
peinarse (*v. reflex.*) (peh-ee-náhr-seh)
(to) comb/brush
pelado (*adj.*) (peh-láh-doh) *peeled*
pelar (*v.*) (peh-láhr) *(to) peel*
peor (peh-óhr) *worse*
el pepino (peh-pée-noh) *cucumber*
pequeño (*adj.*) (peh-kéh-nyoh) *small*
la pera (péh-rah) *pear*
perder (e→ie) (*v.*) (pehr-déhr) *(to) lose*
el perejil (peh-reh-héel) *parsley*
el periódico (peh-ree-óh-dee-coh) *newspaper*
el período de prueba (peh-rée-oh-doh deh
proo-éh-bah) *probationary period*
el permiso para conducir (pehr-mée-soh páh-
rah cohn-doo-séer) *driver's licence*
permitir (*v.*) (pehr-mee-téer) *(to) permit*
pero (péh-roh) *but*
la persiana (pehr-see-áh-nah) *venetian
blind*
la persona (pehr-sóh-nah) *person*
el pesticida (pehs-tee-sée-dah) *pesticide*

picar (*v.*) (pee-cáhr) *(to) mince*
el pie (pee-éh) *foot*
la piedra (pee-éh-drah) *rock/stone*
la pierna (pee-éhr-nah) *leg*
la pieza (pee-éh-sah) *part*
el pimentero (pee-mehn-téh-roh) *pepper
shaker*
la pimienta (pee-mee-éhn-tah) *pepper
(seasoning)*
el pimiento (pee-mee-éhn-toh) *pepper (veg)*
pintar (*v.*) (peen-táhr) *(to) paint*
la pintura (peen-tóo-rah) *paint*
las pinzas (péen-sahs) *tongs*
la piña (pée-nyah) *pineapple*
la piscina (pees-sée-nah) *swimming pool*
el piso (pée-soh) *floor/storey*
la pista de tenis (pées-tah deh téh-nees)
tennis court
el pizarrón (pee-sah-rróhn) *blackboard*
la placa (pláh-cah) *electricity plate (on wall)*
la placa con su nombre (pláh-cah cohn soo
nóhm-breh) *name tag*
el plan de retiro (plahn deh reh-tée-roh)
retirement plan
la plancha (plán-chah) *iron*
planchado (*adj.*) (plahn-cháh-doh) *ironed*
la planchadora (plahn-chah-dóh-rah)
ironer/mangle
planchar (*v.*) (plahn-cháhr) *(to) iron*
la planta (pláhn-tah) *plant*
plantar (*v.*) (plahn-táhr) *(to) plant*
el plaqué (plah-kéh) *place setting*
el plátano (pláh-tah-noh) *banana*
el platillo (plah-tée-yoh) *meal course, menu
item*
el plato (pláh-toh) *dish, meal course, plate*
el plato base (pláh-toh báh-seh) *base plate*
el plato caliente (pláh-toh cah-lee-éhn-teh)
hot plate
el plato de café (pláh-toh deh cah-féh)
saucer
el plato de ensalada (pláh-toh deh ehn-sah-
láh-dah) *salad plate*
el plato de postre (pláh-toh deh póhs-treh)
dessert plate
el plato para pan (pláh-toh páh-rah pahn)
bread plate
el plato para sopa (pláh-toh pah-rah sóh-pah)
soup plate
el plato sopero (pláh-toh soh-péh-roh) *soup
plate*
la playa (pláh-yah) *beach*
el plomero (ploh-méh-roh) *plumber*
la pluma (plóo-mah) *pen*
poco (póh-coh) *little*
poco hecho (*adj.*) (póh-coh éh-choh)
medium rare
podar (*v.*) (poh-dáhr) *(to) prune*

poder (o→ue) (*v.*) (poh-déhr) *(to) be able/can*
la polea (poh-léh-ah) *pulley*
la policía (poh-lee-sée-ah) *police*
el pollo (póh-yoh) *chicken*
el polvo (póhl-voh) *dust*
el polvo limpiador (póhl-voh leem-pee-ah-dóhr) *cleaning powder*
el pomelo (poh-méh-loh) *grapefruit*
poner (*v.*) (poh-néhr) *(to) put*
poner la mesa (*v.*) (poh-néhr lah méh-sah) *(to) set the table*
ponerse (*v. reflex.*) (poh-néhr-seh) *(to) put on/start doing something*
por (pohr) *for/during/per/by*
por ahora (pohr ah-óh-rah) *for now*
por ciento (pohr see-éhn-toh) *percent*
por ejemplo (pohr eh-héhm-ploh) *for example*
por favor (pohr fah-vóhr) *please*
por la mañana (pohr lah mah-nyáh-nah) *in the morning*
por la noche (pohr lah nóh-cheh) *in the evening/at night*
por la tarde (pohr lah táhr-deh) *in the afternoon/evening*
¿por qué? (pohr keh) *why?*
porque (póhr-keh) *because*
el portamaletas (pohr-tah-mah-léh-tahs) *luggage rack*
posible (*adj.*) (poh-sée-bleh) *possible*
el postre (póhs-treh) *dessert*
probable (*adj.*) (proh-báh-bleh) *probable*
el protector de colchón (proh-tehc-tóhr deh cohl-chóhn) *mattress pad*
preferir (e→ie) (*v.*) (preh-feh-réer) *(to) prefer*
preguntar (*v.*) (preh-goon-táhr) *(to) ask for*
la preparación del salón (preh-pah-rah-see-óhn dehl sah-lóhn) *room set-up*
preparado (*adj.*) (preh-pah-ráh-doh) *prepared/ready*
preparar (*v.*) (preh-pah-ráhr) *(to) prepare*
la presión (preh-see-óhn) *pressure*
la primavera (pree-mah-véh-rah) *spring*
primero (pree-méh-roh) *first*
el primer plato (pree-méhr pláh-toh) *first course*
la prisa (prée-sah) *hurry*
probar (o→ue) (*v.*) (proh-báhr) *(to) taste*
el proceso selectivo (proh-séh-soh seh-lehc-tée-voh) *selection process*
los productos químicos (proh-dóoc-tohs kée-mee-cohs) *chemicals*
prohibir (*v.*) (proh-ee-béer) *(to) prohibit/forbid*
la propina (proh-pée-nah) *tip/gratuity*
la prueba (proo-éh-bah) *quiz*
el puerco (poo-éhr-coh) *pork*

la puerta (poo-éhr-tah) *door*
Puerto Rico (*m.*) (poo-érh-toh rée-coh) *Puerto Rico*
el puesto (poo-éhs-toh) *position (work)*
pulir (*v.*) (poo-léer) *(to) polish*
el pulpo (póol-poh) *octopus*
puntual (*adj.*) (poon-too-áhl) *punctual*
la puntualidad (poon-too-ah-lee-dáhd) *punctuality*

Q

que (keh) *what, that, than*
¿qué? (keh) *what?*
que lo pase bien (keh loh páh-seh bee-éhn) *have a good time*
¿qué pasa? (keh páh-sah) (informal) *what is going on?*
¿qué tal? (keh tahl) *how is it going?*
querer (e→ie) (*v.*) (keh-réhr) *(to) want*
el queso (kéh-soh) *cheese*
¿quién? (kee-éhn) *who?*
¿de quién? (deh kee-éhn) *whose?*
quince (kéen-seh) *fifteen*
quinientos (kee-nee-éhn-tohs) *five hundred*
quinto (kéen-toh) *fifth*
quitar (*v.*) (kee-táhr) *(to) remove/take away*
quitarse (*v. reflex.*) (kee-táhr-seh) *(to) take off (one's clothes/shoes/hat)*
quizás (kee-sáhs) *perhaps*

R

la radio (ráh-dee-oh) *radio*
la raíz (rah-ées) *root*
la rama (ráh-mah) *branch (tree)*
rápidamente (ráh-pee-dah-mehn-tch) *quickly*
rápido (*adj.*) (ráh-pee-doh) *fast*
rascar (*v.*) (rahs-cáhr) *(to) scrape*
el rastrillo (rahs-trée-yoh) *rake*
la rata (ráh-tah) *rat*
el ratón (rah-tóhn) *mouse (rodent)*
la ratonera (rah-toh-néh-rah) *mousetrap*
la razón (rah-sóhn) *reason*
la rebanada (reh-bah-náh-dah) *slice*
rebanar (*v.*) (reh-bah-náhr) *(to) slice*
la recepción (reh-sehp-see-óhn) *front desk*
el/la recepcionista (reh-sehp-see-oh-nées-tah) *front desk clerk/host*
el reclutamiento (reh-cloo-tah-mee-éhn-toh) *recruiting*
el recogedor (reh-coh-héh-dohr) *dustpan*
la recomendación (reh-coh-mehn-dah-see-óhn) *reference/recommendation*
recomendar (*v.*) (reh-coh-mehn-dáhr) *(to) recommend*
recordar (o→ue) (*v.*) (reh-corh-dáhr) *(to) remember*

los recursos humanos (reh-cóor-sohs oo-máh-nohs) *human resources*
la redecilla (reh-deh-sée-yah) *hair net*
el refresco (reh-fréhs-coh) *soft drink*
el refrigerador (reh-free-heh-rah-dóhr) *refrigerator*
la regadera (reh-gah-déh-rah) *shower*
regar (e→ie) (*v.*) (reh-gáhr) *(to) water*
la rejilla (reh-hée-yah) *air vent*
el reloj (reh-lóhh) *watch*
el reloj despertador (reh-lóhh dehs-pehr-tah-dóhr) *alarm clock*
el reloj registrador (reh-lóhh reh-gees-trah-dóhr) *time clock*
rellenar (*v.*) (reh-yeh-náhr) *(to) refill/fill out*
remojar (*v.*) (reh-moh-háhr) *(to) soak*
reparar (*v.*) (reh-pah-ráhr) *(to) repair*
la repisa (reh-pée-sah) *shelf*
el reporte (reh-póhr-teh) *report*
el reporte de camarista (reh-póhr-teh deh cah-mah-rées-tah) *housekeeper report*
el reporte de mañana (reh-póhr-teh deh mah-nyáh-nah) *A.M. report (housekeeping)*
el reporte de ocupación (reh-póhr-teh deh oh-coo-pah-see-óhn) *occupancy report*
el reporte de tarde (reh-póhr-teh deh táhr-deh) *P.M. report*
residente legal (*adj.*) (reh-see-déhn-teh leh-gáhl) *legal resident*
la responsabilidad (rehs-pohn-sah-bee-lee-dáhd) *responsibility*
el restaurante (rehs-tah-oo-ráhn-teh) *restaurant*
restregar (e→ie) (*v.*) (rehs-treh-gáhr) *(to) scrub*
reunirse (*v. reflex.*) (reh-oo-néer-seh) *(to) meet/get together*
rico/a (*adj.*) (rée-coh/ah) *rich (moneywise)/tasty (foods)*
los riñones (ree-nyóh-nehs) *kidneys*
robar (*v.*) (roh-báhr) *(to) steal*
el robo (róh-boh) *theft*
el rociador (roh-see-ah-dóhr) *sprayer/sprinkler*
rociar (*v.*) (roh-see-áhr) *(to) spray*
el rodillo (roh-dée-yoh) *rolling pin*
el roedor (roh-eh-dóhr) *rodent*
rojo (*adj.*) (róh-hoh) *red*
la ropa (róh-pah) *linen/clothes*
la ropa limpia (róh-pah léem-pee-ah) *clean linen*
la ropa sucia (róh-pah sóo-see-ah) *dirty linen*
rosa (*adj.*) (róh-sah) *pink (color)*
la rosa (róh-sah) *rose*
rosado (*adj.*) (roh-sáh-doh) *pink*
rotar (*v.*) (roh-tár) *(to) rotate*
roto (*adj.*) (róh-toh) *broken*
rubio (*adj.*) (róo-bee-oh) *blond*

S

el sábado (sáh-bah-doh) *Saturday*
la sábana (sáh-bah-nah) *sheet*
la sábana bajera (sáh-bah-nah bah-héh-rah) *bottom sheet*
saber (*v.*) (sah-béhr) *(to) know*
el sacacorchos (sah-cah-cóhr-chohs) *corkscrew*
el sacatapón (sah-cah-tah-póhn) *corkscrew*
sacudir (*v.*) (sah-coo-déer) *(to) dust*
la sal (sahl) *salt*
salado (*adj.*) (sah-láh-doh) *salty*
el salario (sah-láh-ree-oh) *salary/pay*
el salario mínimo (sah-láh-ree-oh mée-nee-moh) *minimum wage*
la salchicha (sahl-chée-chah) *sausage*
el salero (sah-léh-roh) *salt shaker*
la salida (sah-lée-dah) *checkout (room)/exit*
la salida de empleados (sah-lée-dah deh ehm-pleh-áh-dohs) *employee exit*
salir (*v.*) (sah-léer) *(to) leave*
el salmón (sahl-móhn) *salmon*
el salón (sah-lóhn) *living room/hall*
el salón de descanso (sah-lóhn deh dehs-cáhn-soh) *employee lounge*
el salón de juegos (sah-lóhn deh hoo-éh-gohs) *game room*
la salsa (sáhl-sah) *sauce*
la salsa de tomate (sáhl-sah deh toh-máh-teh) *tomato sauce*
salteado (*adj.*) (sahl-teh-áh-do) *sautéed*
saltear (*v.*) (sahl-teh-áhr) *(to) sauté*
saludar (*v.*) (sah-loo-dáhr) *(to) greet*
la sandía (sahn-dée-ah) *watermelon*
el sandwich (sahn-oo-eech) *sandwich*
el saneamiento (sah-neh-ah-mee-éhn-toh) *sanitation*
sanear (*v.*) (sah-neh-áhr) *(to) sanitize*
sangrante (*adj.*) (sahn-gráhn-teh) *rare (meats)*
la sartén (sahr-téhn) *frying pan*
la secadora (seh-cah-dóh-rah) *dryer*
secar (*v.*) (seh-cáhr) *(to) dry*
secarse (*v. reflex.*) (seh-cáhr-seh) *(to) dry off*
la sección de cuartos (sehc-see-óhn deh coo-áhr-tohs) *room section*
seco (*adj.*) (séh-koh) *dry*
la sed (sehd) *thirst*
segundo (seh-góon-doh) *second*
el segundo plato (seh-góon-doh pláh-toh) *second course*
la seguridad (seh-goo-ree-dáhd) *security*
la seguridad social (seh-goo-ree-dáhd soh-see-áhl) *Social Security*
seguro (*adj.*) (seh-góo-roh) *sure/ reliable*
el seguro (seh-góo-roh) *insurance*
el seguro de enfermedad (seh-góo-roh deh ehn-fehr-meh-dahd) *medical insurance*

el seguro dental (seh-góo-roh dehn-táhl)
    dental insurance
el seguro de vida (seh-góo-roh deh vée-dah)
    life insurance
el seguro médico (seh-góo-roh méh-dee-coh)
    medical insurance
seis (séh-ees) *six*
seiscientos (seh-ees-see-éhn-tohs) *six hundred*
la selección (seh-lehc-see-óhn) *screening*
la semana (seh-máh-nah) *week*
la semana que viene (seh-máh-nah keh vee-éh-neh) *next week*
sembrar (v.) (sehm-bráhr) *(to) seed*
sentar (e→ie) (v.) (sehn-táhr) *(to) sentar*
sentarse (e→ie) (v. reflex.) (sehn-táhr-seh)
    (to) sit down
sentir (e→ie) (v.) (sehn-téer) *(to) feel/be sorry*
el señor (seh-nyóhr) *mister (Mr.)*
la señora (seh-nyóh-rah) *mistress (Mrs.)*
la señorita (seh-nyoh-rée-tah) *miss*
separar (v.) (seh-pah-ráhr) *(to) sort/separate*
septiembre (sehp-tee-éhm-breh) *September*
séptimo (séhp-tee-moh) *seventh*
ser (v.) (sehr) *(to) be*
el serpentín (sehr-pehn-téen) *coil*
el servicio (sehr-vée-see-oh) *service*
el servicio a cuartos (sehr-vée-see-oh ah coo-áhr-tohs) *room service*
el servicio de cortesía (sehr-vée-see-oh deh cohr-teh-sée-ah) *turndown service*
la servilleta (sehr-vee-yéh-tah) *napkin*
la servilleta de papel (sehr-vee-yéh-tah deh pah-péhl) *paper napkin*
la servilleta de servicio (sehr-vee-yéh-tah deh sehr-vée-see-oh) *service napkin*
el servilletero (sehr-vee-yeh-téh-roh) *napkin holder*
servir (e→i) (v.) (sehr-véer) *(to) serve*
sesenta (seh-séhn-tah) *sixty*
la seta (séh-tah) *mushroom*
setecientos (seh-teh-see-éhn-tohs) *seven hundred*
setenta (seh-téhn-tah) *seventy*
el seto (séh-toh) *hedge*
el sexo (séhc-soh) *sex*
sexto (séhks-toh) *sixth*
sí (see) *yes*
siempre (see-éhm-preh) *always*
la sierra (see-éh-rrah) *saw*
siete (see-éh-teh) *seven*
la silla (sée-yah) *chair*
la silla de niños (sée-yah deh née-nyohs) *high chair*
el sillón (see-yóhn) *armchair*
sin (seen) *without*
sin equipaje (seen eh-kee-páh-heh) *no baggage (room with)*

sobre (sóh-breh) *on/upon*
el sobre (sóh-breh) *envelope (letter)*
el sofá (soh-fáh) *couch/sofa*
el sofá cama (soh-fáh cáh-mah) *bed couch*
el sol (sohl) *sun*
la solicitud de empleo (soh-lee-see-tóod deh ehm-pléh-oh) *job application*
la solicitud de ingreso (soh-lee-see-tóod deh een-gréh-soh) *application form*
la sopa (sóh-pah) *soup*
el sótano (sóh-tah-noh) *basement*
su (soo) *his/her/its/your/their*
subir (v.) (soo-béer) *(to) go up, bring up*
la suciedad (soo-see-eh-dáhd) *dirt*
sucio (adj.) (sóo-see-oh) *dirty*
el suelo (soo-éh-loh) *floor*
el sueño (soo-éh-nyoh) *sleep*
la suerte (soo-éhr-teh) *luck*
suficiente (soo-fee-see-éhn-teh) *sufficient/enough*
sugerir (v.) (soo-heh-réer) *(to) suggest*
los suministros (soo-mee-nées-trohs) *supplies*
los suministros de clientes (soo-mee-nées-trohs deh clee-éhn-tehs) *guest supplies*
los suministros de limpieza (soo-mee-nées-trohs deh leem-pee-éh-sah) *cleaning supplies*
el/la supervisor/a (soo-pehr-vee-sóhr/ah) *supervisor*
el/la supervisor/a de cuartos (soo-pehr-vee-sóhr deh coo-áhr-tohs) *housekeeping supervisor*
el surtidor de leche (soor-tee-dóhr deh léh-cheh) *milk dispenser*
surtir (v.) (soor-téer) *(to) stock*
suyo (sóo-yoh) *his/hers/yours/theirs*

T

la tabla (táh-blah) *board (wood)*
la tabla de cortar (táh-blah deh cohr-táhr) *cutting board*
la tabla de planchar (táh-blah deh plahn-chár) *ironing board*
el taller (tah-yéhr) *maintenance shop*
también (tahm-bee-éhn) *also*
el tanque (táhn-keh) *tank*
tanto (táhn-toh) *as much*
tanto gusto (táhn-toh góos-toh) *glad to meet you*
la tapadera (tah-pah-déh-rah) *lid*
tapar (v.) (tah-páhr) *(to) cover*
el tapete de baño (tah-péh-teh deh báh-nyoh) *bath mat*
la tapicería (tah-pee-seh-rée-ah) *upholstery*
el tapón (tah-póhn) *cork*
tarde (táhr-deh) *late*
la tarde (táhr-deh) *afternoon/evening*

la tarjeta de comentarios (tahr-héh-tah deh coh-mehn-táh-ree-ohs)   *comment card*

la tarjeta de identificación (tahr-héh-tah deh ee-dehn-tee-fee-cah-see-óhn)   *identification card*

la tarjeta de no molestar (tahr-héh-tah deh noh moh-lehs-táhr)   *do not disturb sign*

la tarjeta de presentación (tahr-héh-tah deh preh-sehn-tah-see-óhn)   *room table-tent*

la tarjeta postal (tahr-héh-tah pohs-táhl)   *postcard*

la tarjeta registradora (tahr-héh-tah reh-gees-trah-dóh-rah)   *time card*

la tarjeta verde (tahr-héh-tah véhr-deh)   *green card*

la tarta (táhr-tah)   *pie*

la taza (táh-sah)   *cup*

la taza de café (táh-sah deh cah-féh)   *cup of coffee*

la taza para café (táh-sah pah-rah cah-féh)   *coffee cup*

el tazón (tah-sóhn)   *bowl*

el té (teh)   *tea*

el té frío (teh frée-oh)   *iced tea*

el techo (téh-choh)   *ceiling*

la tela de alambre (téh-lah deh ah-láhm-breh)   *screen (wire)*

telefonear (v.) (teh-leh-foh-neh-áhr)   *(to) telephone*

el teléfono (teh-léh-foh-noh)   *telephone/phone*

la televisión (teh-leh-vee-see-óhn)   *television*

el televisor (teh-leh-vee-sóhr)   *TV set*

temer (v.) (teh-méhr)   *(to) fear/dread*

la temperatura (tehm-peh-rah-tóo-rah)   *temperature*

temprano (tehm-práh-noh)   *early*

tender la cama (v.) (tehn-déhr lah cáh-mah)   *(to) make the bed*

el tenedor (teh-neh-dóhr)   *fork*

el tenedor de ensalada (teh-neh-dóhr deh ehn-sah-láh-dah)   *salad fork*

tener (v.) (teh-néhr)   *(to) have*

tener . . . años (teh-néhr áh-nyohs)   *to be . . . years old*

tener calor (teh-néhr cah-lóhr)   *to be warm*

tener ganas de (teh-néhr gáh-nahs deh)   *to be desirous of*

tener miedo (teh-néhr mee-éh-doh)   *to be afraid*

tener prisa (teh-néhr prée-sah)   *to be in a hurry*

tener que (teh-néhr keh)   *to have to*

tener razón (teh-néhr rah-sóhn)   *to be right*

el tenis (téh-nees)   *tennis*

tercero (tehr-séh-roh)   *third*

terminar (v.) (tehr-mee-náhr)   *(to) finish, end*

el termostato (tehr-mohs-táh-toh)   *thermostat*

la ternera (tehr-néh-rah)   *veal*

la terraza (teh-rráh-sah)   *balcony*

el test (tehst)   *test/exam*

el test de aptitud (tehst deh ahp-tee-tóod)   *aptitude test*

el test profesional (tehst proh-feh-see-oh-náhl)   *professional test*

la tetera (teh-téh-rah)   *tea pot*

el tiempo (tee-éhm-poh)   *time/weather*

el tiempo extra (tee-éhm-poh éhs-trah)   *overtime*

la tierra (tee-éh-rrah)   *soil*

las tijeras (tee-héh-rahs)   *scissors*

la tina (tée-nah)   *bathtub*

tinto (teen-toh)   *red (for wines)*

el/la tío/a (tée-oh/ah)   *uncle/aunt*

la toalla (toh-áh-yah)   *towel*

la toalla de baño (toh-áh-yah deh báh-nyoh)   *bath towel*

la toalla de mano (toh-áh-yah deh máh-noh)   *hand towel*

la toalla de papel (toh-áh-yah deh pah-péhl)   *paper towel*

la toalla facial (toh-áh-yah fah-see-áhl)   *washcloth*

el toallero (toh-ah-yéh-roh)   *towel rack*

el tocador (toh-cah-dóhr)   *dresser*

tocar (v.) (toh-cáhr)   *(to) touch/play an instrument*

tocar en la puerta (v.) (toh-cáhr ehn lah poo-éhr-tah)   *(to) knock at the door*

el tocino (toh-sée-noh)   *bacon*

todavía (toh-dah-vée-ah)   *still/yet*

todavía no (toh-dah-vée-ah noh)   *not yet*

todo (tóh-doh)   *all/everything*

tomar (v.) (toh-máhr)   *(to) take, drink*

tomar la comanda (toh-máhr lah coh-máhn-dah)   *(to) take the order*

el tomate (toh-máh-teh)   *tomato*

el tornillo (tohr-née-yoh)   *screw*

el tope de puerta (tóh-peh deh poo-éhr-tah)   *door stopper*

la toronja (toh-róhn-hah)   *grapefruit*

la tortilla (tohr-tée-yah)   *tortilla*

la tortilla de huevos (tohr-tée-yah deh oo-éh-vohs)   *omelet*

la tostada (tohs-táh-dah)   *toast*

tostado (*adj.*) (tohs-táh-doh)   *toasted*

la tostadora (tohs-tah-dóh-rah)   *toaster*

tostar (o→ue) (v.) (tohs-táhr)   *(to) toast*

trabajar (v.) (trah-bah-háhr)   *(to) work*

el trabajo (trah-báh-hoh)   *job/work*

el trabajo temporal (trah-báh-hoh tehm-poh-ráhl)   *seasonal work*

traer (v.) (trah-éhr)   *(to) bring*

el traje (tráh-heh)   *suit*

la trampa de grasa (tráhm-pah deh gráh-sah)   *grease trap*

transplantar (*v.*) (trahns-plahn-táhr)
  (to) transplant
el trapeador (trah-peh-ah-dóhr)   *mop (floor)*
trapear (*v.*) (trah-peh-áhr)   *(to) mop*
el trapo (tráh-poh)   *rag*
trece (tréh-seh)   *thirteen*
treinta (treh-éen-tah)   *thirty*
el tren (trehn)   *train*
tres (trehs)   *three*
el triturador (tree-too-rah-dohr)   *garbage disposal*
la tubería (too-beh-rée-ah)   *piping*
el tubo (tóo-boh)   *pipe/tube*
el tubo fluorescente (tóo-boh floo-oh-rehs-séhn-teh)   *fluorescent tube*
la tuerca (too-éhr-cah)   *screw nut*
el turno (tóor-noh)   *shift*

U

un/a (oon/ah)   *a*
una vez (óo-nah vehs)   *once*
el uniforme (oo-nee-fóhr-meh)   *uniform*
uno/a (óo-noh/ah)   *one*
la uña (óo-nyah)   *fingernail*
usar (*v.*) (oo-sáhr)   *(to) use*
usted (oos-téhd)   *you (sing.)*
ustedes (oos-téh-dehs)   *you (pl.)*
las uvas (óo-vahs)   *grapes*

V

las vacaciones (vah-cah-see-óh-nehs)   *vacation*
la vacante (vah-cáhn-teh)   *job opening*
vaciar (*v.*) (vah-see-áhr)   *(to) empty*
vacío (*adj.*) (vah-sée-oh)   *empty*
vacío y limpio (*adj.*) (vah-sée-oh ee léem-pee-oh)   *vacant and clean (room)*
vacío y sucio (*adj.*) (vah-sée-oh ee sóo-see-oh)   *vacant and dirty (room)*
valer (*v.*) (vah-léhr)   *(to) be worth/cost*
el valet (vah-léh)   *valet*
la válvula (váhl-voo-lah)   *valve*
la válvula de cierre (váhl-voo-lah deh see-éh-rreh)   *screw valve*
el vaso (váh-soh)   *glass*
el vaso de plástico (váh-soh deh pláhs-tee-coh)   *plastic glass*
el vaso para agua (váh-soh pah-rah áh-goo-ah)   *water glass*
el vaso para llevar (váh-soh pah-rah yeh-váhr)   *to-go cup*
el vaso para vino (váh-soh pah-rah vée-noh)   *wine glass*

veinte (veh-éen-teh)   *twenty*
la vela (véh-lah)   *candle*
el veneno (veh-néh-noh)   *poison*
venir (*v.*) (veh-néer)   *(to) come*
la ventana (vehn-táh-nah)   *window*
el ventilador (vehn-tee-lah-dóhr)   *fan*
ver (*v.*) (vehr)   *(to) see*
el verano (veh-ráh-noh)   *summer*
verde (*adj.*) (véhr-deh)   *green*
las verduras (vehr-dóo-rahs)   *vegetables*
verificar (*v.*) (veh-ree-fee-cáhr)   *(to) verify*
el vertedero (vehr-teh-déh-roh)   *dumpster*
el vestíbulo (vehs-tée-boo-loh)   *lobby*
el vestido (vehs-tée-doh)   *dress*
el vestidor de empleados (vehs-tee-dóhr deh ehm-ple-áh-dohs) *locker room (employee)*
vestir (e→i) (*v.*) (vehs-téer)   *(to) dress*
vestirse (e→i) (*v. reflex.*) (vehs-téer-seh)   *(to) get dressed*
la vez (vehs)   *turn/time*
viejo (*adj.*) (vee-éh-hoh)   *old*
el viento (vee-éhn-toh)   *wind*
el viernes (vee-éhr-nehs)   *Friday*
el vinagre (vee-náh-greh)   *vinegar*
el vino (vée-noh)   *wine*
el vino blanco (vée-noh bláhn-coh)   *white wine*
el vino rosado (vée-noh roh-sáh-doh)   *rosé wine*
el vino tinto (vée-noh téen-toh)   *red wine*
los visillos (vee-sée-yohs)   *sheers*
vivir (*v.*) (vee-véer)   *(to) live*
el voltaje (vohl-táh-heh)   *voltage*
el volteo de colchón (vohl-téh-oh deh cohl-chóhn)   *mattress rotation*
volver (o→ue) (*v.*) (vohl-véhr)   *(to) come back/return*
vuelto poco hecho (*adj.*) (voo-éhl-toh póh-coh éh-choh)   *over-easy*

Y

y (ee)   *and*
ya (yah)   *already*
la yema no hecha (yéh-mah noh éh-chah)   *sunny side up (eggs)*
el yeso (yéh-soh)   *plaster*
yo (yoh)   *I*

Z

la zanahoria (sah-nah-óh-ree-ah)   *carrot*
la zanja (sáhn-hah)   *ditch/trench*
los zapatos (sah-páh-tohs)   *shoes*
el zumo (sóo-moh)   *juice*

INDEX

CPSIA information can be obtained at www.ICGtesting.com
Printed in the USA
BVOW030806030812

296950BV00002B/1/P